Tourism and Embodiment

The role of the body and the concept of embodiment have largely been ne-glected in anthropological studies of tourism. This book explores the notion of the tourist body and develops understanding of how touristic practice is embodied practice, not only for tourists but also for those who work in tourism.

This book provides a more holistic understanding of the role of the body in making and re-making self and world by engaging with tourism. This collection brings together scholars whose work intersects with the anthro-pology of tourism who each draw upon ethnographically informed research based on international case studies that include India, Turkey, Australia and Tasmania, Denmark, the United States, Nepal, France, Italy, South Africa and Spain. The case studies focus on a variety of themes including human and nonhuman 'bodies'.

The range of case studies gives the book an international appeal that makes it valuable to academic researchers and students in the disciplines of social anthropology, cultural geography, sociology, philosophy and the field of tourism studies itself.

Catherine Palmer, PhD, is an anthropologist, Centre for Memory, Narra-tive and Histories, University of Brighton, UK, and a Fellow of the Royal Anthropological Institute.

Hazel Andrews, PhD, is a social anthropologist and Reader in Tourism, Culture and Society at Liverpool John Moores University, UK.

Routledge Advances in Tourism and Anthropology

Series Editors: Dr Catherine Palmer (University of Brighton, UK)
Dr Jo-Anne Lester (University of Brighton, UK)

To discuss any ideas for the series please contact Faye Leerink, Commissioning Editor: faye.leerink@tandf.co.uk or the Series Editors.

This series draws inspiration from anthropology's overarching aim to explore and better understand the human condition in all its fascinating diversity. It seeks to expand the intellectual landscape of anthropology and tourism in relation to how we understand the experience of being human, providing critical inquiry into the spaces, places and lives in which tourism unfolds. Contributions to the series will consider how such spaces are embodied, imagined, constructed, experienced, memorialised and contested. The series provides a forum for cutting-edge research and innovative thinking from tourism, anthropology and related disciplines such as philosophy, history, sociology, geography, cultural studies, architecture, the arts and feminist studies.

Tourism and Ethnodevelopment
Inclusion, Empowerment and Self Determination
Edited by Ismar Borges de Lima and Victor King

Everyday Practices of Tourism Mobilities
Packing a Bag
Kaya Barry

Tourism and Indigenous Heritage in Latin America
As Observed through Mexico's Magical Village Cuetzalan
Casper Jacobsen

Tourism and Embodiment
Edited by Catherine Palmer and Hazel Andrews

For more information about this series please visit: www.routledge.com/Routledge-Advances-in-Tourism-and-Anthropology/book-series/RATA

Tourism and Embodiment

Edited by
Catherine Palmer and Hazel Andrews

Routledge
Taylor & Francis Group

LONDON AND NEW YORK

First published 2020 by Routledge

2 Park Square, Milton Park, Abingdon, Oxon, OX14 4RN
605 Third Avenue, New York, NY 10017

Routledge is an imprint of the Taylor & Francis Group, an informa business

First issued in paperback 2020

British Library Cataloguing-in-Publication Data
A catalogue record for this book is available from the British
Library

Library of Congress Cataloging-in-Publication Data
Names: Palmer, Catherine (Catherine A.), editor. |
Andrews, Hazel, editor.
Title: Tourism and embodiment / edited by Catherine Palmer and
Hazel Andrews.
Description: Abingdon, Oxon ; New York : Routledge, 2019. |
Series: Routledge advances in tourism and anthropology |
Includes bibliographical references and index.
Identifiers: LCCN 2019017659
Subjects: LCSH: Tourism—Anthropological aspects. |
Tourism—Social aspects. | Holistic tourism.
Classification: LCC G156.5.A58 T64 2019 | DDC 306.4/819—dc23
LC record available at https://lccn.loc.gov/2019017659

ISBN: 978-1-138-57355-0 (hbk)
ISBN: 978-0-367-78525-3 (pbk)

Typeset in Times New Roman
by codeMantra

Contents

List of figures and tables

Figures

Table

Notes on contributors

Hazel Andrews (Editor), PhD, is a social anthropologist and Reader in Tourism, Culture and Society at Liverpool John Moores University, UK. With a particular focus on practices of embodiment, consumption, habitus and place, Hazel's research and publications have examined social and symbolic constructions of national, regional and gendered identities in the context of British tourists to Mallorca. Her current research involves the application of theories of existential anthropology to understandings of tourists' experiences and an examination of discourses of nationalism in tourism imagery. Hazel is the author of numerous texts on her work in Mallorca including *The British on Holiday. Charter Tourism, Identity and Consumption* (2011), *Liminal Landscapes: Travel, Experience and Spaces Inbetween* (2012) and *Tourism and Violence* (2014). She is also a founding editor of the *Journal of Tourism Consumption and Practice*.

Kaya Barry, PhD, is a Postdoctoral Research Fellow with the Griffith Centre for Social and Cultural Research at Griffith University. Her research in tourism and cultural geography explores the intersections of mobilities, migration, creativity and material practices. She has exhibited creative artworks in Australia, UK, Iceland, Finland and online, and recently published the monograph *Everyday Practices of Tourism Mobilities* (2018, Routledge).

Geoffrey R. Bird, PhD, is an Associate Professor and chair of the School of Tourism and Hospitality Management at Royal Roads University, Victoria, Canada. Geoff is the lead for the War Heritage Research Initiative (warheritage.royalroads.ca), directing and producing over 30 documentary vignettes. He has had a long fascination with the interplay between remembrance, landscapes of war and tourism from various perspectives: researcher, guide, former naval officer, tourist and educator. He has over 30 years of experience in the field of tourism in a variety of areas, including poverty alleviation, war heritage, and education policy and programme design.

Rafael Cruces Portales, PhD, is a Lecturer in Sustainable Tourism, specialising in accessible tourism, at Ostelea, School of Tourism and Hospitality, Madrid, Spain. He is a member of the Culturdes Research Group at Universitas Miguel Hernandez, Spain. In 2015, he published a paper related to the future of accessible tourism titled: 'Removing "invisible" barriers: opening paths towards the future of accessible tourism' *Journal of Tourism Futures*. His main research interest is related to the performance of the body image in the touristic scenario.

Anna de Jong, PhD, is a Lecturer with the School of Hospitality and Tourism Management, University of Surrey, UK. As a cultural geographer, Anna's research focuses on gender, sexuality, belonging, place-making and planning within tourism and events contexts.

Michael Haldrup, PhD, is Professor (wsr) in Visual Culture and Performance Design, Roskilde University, Denmark with a special interest in relations between everyday life, culture and heritage. He has published extensively on performance, embodiment and tourism including the books *Performing Tourist Places* (with Bærenholdt, Larsen and Urry, Ashgate) and *Tourism, Performance and the Everyday* (with Larsen, Routledge). More broadly publications focus on such as the production of affect in relation to space, performance and materiality and on heritage performances. He is currently co-managing a national project on experimental museum design and experiences *Our Museum* (http://ourmuseum.dk/).

Christopher A. Howard, PhD, is a Lecturer in Cultural Anthropology at Chaminade University of Honolulu. He was previously Visiting Lecturer at Boston University, and has worked at academic institutions in Japan and New Zealand. His research is concerned with the changing relations between society, technology and environment, which he interprets mainly through a mobilities perspective, social theory, phenomenology and philosophical anthropology. He has published on various aspects of tourism, pilgrimage and lifestyle mobilities, including the imagination, narrative and the embodied, affective dimensions of travel experience. These and other topics are covered in a number of articles, book chapters and the monograph, *Mobile Lifeworlds: an ethnography of pilgrimage and tourism in the Himalayas* (Routledge).

Jenny Huberman, PhD, is an Associate Professor of Anthropology at the University of Missouri-Kansas City. While her early research focused on tourism in India, currently she is working on a book manuscript entitled, *Ancestors and Avatars: Anthropological Approaches to the Study of Transhumanism.*

Anna Elisabeth Kuijpers is a Dutch Anthropologist and graduate from the University of Amsterdam (2010) after which she worked for three years as a junior lecture in the University's Anthropology Department. She currently works at the KU Leuven as a teaching assistant in the department of Social and Cultural Anthropology. She is also a PhD researcher affiliated with the department of Social and Cultural studies at the University of Zurich, Switzerland. Her PhD thesis is concerned with the way images of a village in the southeast of Turkey are created for touristic purposes and the way people in the village interact with these images in everyday life.

Professor Wendelin M. Küpers is a Professor of Leadership and Organisation Studies at Karlshochschule International University in Karlsruhe, Germany. Combining a phenomenological and cross-disciplinary orientation, his research focuses on embodied, emotional and creative, respectively, transformational dimensions in relation to more responsible, and wise forms of organising and managing. Furthermore, his research focuses on integrating artful and aesthetic dimensions of practical wisdom into leadership and organisation theory and practice.

Hilary Leighton, PhD, a lifelong apprentice to nature and psyche, is an Assistant Professor at Royal Roads University, an eco-psychotherapist and Registered Clinical Counsellor in private practice. Leighton draws upon the wisdom of ecopsychology, depth psychology, systems thinking, mythology, embodied, nature- and arts-based practices, and poetry. Her research and teaching reflect the ethical dilemma, suffering and loss of our relationships with what is wild and contemplates learning as an initiatory journey towards maturation and a more soulful way of belonging to the world. She sees guiding others towards their true natures and genius as a blessing.

Patrick McCartney, PhD, is a Research Fellow at Kyoto University, Japan and a Visiting Fellow at the Australian National University. He is a sociolinguistic anthropologist working at the intersection of the economics of religion, the sociology of spirituality, the economics of desire, and the politics of memory and imagination. Employing a broad range of qualitative and quantitative analytical methods his research focuses on the imaginative consumption of wellness tourism; and, more specifically, on the transglobal yoga industry, including spiritual tourism.

Ann-Kathrin McLean is a Doctor of Social Sciences candidate at Royal Roads University, Victoria, Canada. Her research evaluates the interplay between heritage tourism, war remembrance and place-based pedagogy. Of specific focus is how young Germans interpret sites of Nazi war heritage and construct individual meaning. She is also interested in understanding how the increase in fascist populism in Germany can tint young minds and their reflections of the Holocaust. To help mitigate the memory loss across generations, McLean investigates how new media can assist in bridging the gap between memory, remembrance and education for future generations.

Sally Ann Ness is a Professor of Anthropology, at University of California, Riverside. She has written on tourism and festival life, dance and sport, as well as on tourism development in Southeast Asia and in Yosemite National Park, California. Her books include *Choreographies of Landscape; Signs of Performance in Yosemite National Park* (2016, Berghahn) and *Where Asia Smiles; an Ethnography of Philippine Tourism* (2002, University of Pennsylvania). She is a co-editor, with Patrick Alcedo and Hendrik Maier, of *Religious Festivals in Contemporary Southeast Asia* (2016, Ateneo de Manila) and, with Carrie Noland, of *Migrations of Gesture* (2008, University of Minnesota).

Antonio Miguel Nogués-Pedregal, PhD, is an Associate Professor of social anthropology at the Universitas Miguel Hernández, Spain. His research focuses on the relationship between tourism, cultural heritage, power and development. He delivers seminars and undertakes research in Johannes Gutenberg-Universität, University of Oxford, Univerza v Ljubljani and KU Leuven. He edited *Cultura y turismo* (Signatura ediciones 2003) and *Culture and society in tourism contexts* (Emerald 2012). Several of his scientific articles have been translated into English, German and Italian and he was acknowledged as one 'of the [two] most important scholars of the anthropology of tourism in Spain since the 1990s' *Anthropology News* 55 (2014).

Catherine Palmer (Editor), PhD, is an anthropologist, University of Brighton, UK and a Fellow of the Royal Anthropological Institute of Great Britain and Ireland. Her research focuses on identity, heritage and materiality; post-conflict/memorial landscapes; embodiment, tourism; the coast/seaside. She is the joint book series editor for *Routledge Advances in Tourism Anthropology* (with Jo-Anne Lester), and the author of the Routledge monograph *Being and Dwelling through Tourism: An anthropological perspective*. She is the co-editor of *Creating Heritage for Tourism* (with Jacqueline Tivers), *Tourism Research Methods: Integrating Theory and Practice* (with Peter Burns and Brent Ritchie) and *Tourism and Visual Culture: Volume 1 Theories and Concepts* (with Peter Burns and Jo-Anne Lester).

Solène Prince, PhD, is a researcher at Mid-Sweden University, Östersund where she obtained her PhD in tourism studies in 2017. She is affiliated with the European Tourism Research Institute (ETOUR). Her work touches upon subjects related to volunteer tourism, rural tourism and non-representational landscape theory and has taken her to Iceland, Denmark and rural Sweden. She has a Master's of science in sustainable development from Uppsala University.

Bradley Rink, PhD, is a human geographer and Senior Lecturer in the Department of Geography, Environmental Studies and Tourism at the University of the Western Cape (UWC) in Cape Town, South Africa. His research and teaching focuses on mobilities, tourism and urban place-making. His recent tourism research focuses on Cape Town's De Waterkant enclave. Emerging from the broader project on De Waterkant is a critical analysis of the *Pink Map*, and the role of the body in the material and discursive shaping of urban leisure space. His recent outputs have been published in *Mobilities, Transfers, and Tourism Geographies.*

Amy Speier, PhD, is a medical anthropologist and Assistant Professor, Sociology and Anthropology at the University of Texas at Arlington, USA where she specialises in reproductive health, globalisation and medical tourism. She is interested in how the analysis of tourism can be refined through ethnographically based research in medical anthropology, specifically the motivations of people travelling for the sake of their health. She is currently researching couples travelling to North America seeking fertility treatment. She is the author of the book *Fertility Holidays: IVF Tourism and the Reproduction of Whiteness*, New York University Press.

Professor Soile Veijola is the Professor of Cultural Studies of Tourism at the Multidimensional Tourism Institute, University of Lapland, Finland. With a background in sociology, her research focuses on the social production of knowledge, social relations, gender and embodiment; tourism work; future tourist communities, and silence and slowness in tourism. She is widely published, most frequently with Eeva Jokinen, encompassing book chapters and articles that examine tourism and hospitality from a critical and feminist perspective.

1 Tourism and embodiment

Animating the field

Catherine Palmer and Hazel Andrews

Introduction

Within anthropology, the body is studied from a variety of perspectives. For example, the body as culture and as text reveals a range of other bodies such as the gendered body, the medical body, the social and the performed body. However, the tourist body remains a neglected area of anthropology generally and particularly so in terms of the concept of embodiment. This is despite the fact that the relationship between tourism, the body and embodiment has moved increasingly centre stage since Veijola and Jokinen's seminal article (1994) highlighting the absence of the body in tourism. Since the mid-1990s, studies focusing on the tourism-body relationship have adopted a variety of perspectives to focus on such as the senses (Dann and Jacobsen 2002, Waitt and Duffy 2010, Merchant 2011), interrogating the relationship between tourism, gender and embodiment (Pritchard et al. 2007) or that between the body and the nation (Palmer 1998, Andrews 2005). There is also an increasing focus on embodiment in relation to the experiences of differently abled tourists (Richards et al. 2010, Small and Darcy 2011, Small et al. 2012).

As insightful as these studies are there is as yet no sustained analysis of the concept of embodiment in relation to tourism. This is surprising as the body of the tourist is a social body, it engages with other bodies, things and activities, with other places and ways of living. The body is also affected by the experience of and engagement with nature and the natural world. It shapes and is shaped by technology and may be subject to out of body experiences. In addition, there is not one tourist body but a range of bodies, male, female, transgender, transsexual and as noted above bodies that are physically and/or sensory impaired. Given the complexities inherent in the body-tourism relationship, our intention here is to explore the connection between tourism and embodiment generally rather than focus on a singular sense-based approach to the concept of embodiment within tourism. Such an approach is holistic, acknowledging the inseparable and interrelated relationship between the body, the senses and the lifeworld, what Palmer (2018) refers to as sensuous dwelling.

Anthropology and embodiment

Our focus on embodiment highlights the phenomenological context of and purpose behind our thinking. The intention of this chapter is to lay the foundations for the embodied perspective adopted by this book, foundations grounded in the overarching aim of anthropology namely to uncover what being human means and how we make ourselves human through the coming together of body, mind and world (Csordas 1994). Indeed, Andrews (2011, 2017) argues a phenomenological approach derived from anthropology moves us away from the world as object towards the world as it is experienced. This is important because the pursuit of experience(s) lies at the heart of tourism, and it is through experience that a body learns how to be a tourist and how to do tourism. The concept of embodiment is useful here because it not only focuses attention on the holistic nature of experience but also highlights the role of the body in making and re-making the world as experience. As Csordas argues, embodiment is '.... about culture and experience insofar as these can be understood from the standpoint of bodily being-in-the-world' (1999:143).

Although the body and the concept of embodiment are significant themes within anthropology, this has not always been the case. Prior to the identification of an absent body within tourism studies by Veijola and Jokinen (1994), Lock expressed a similar concern about anthropology arguing that '... a perusal of the canon of social and cultural anthropology indicates that the body's explicit appearance has been sporadic throughout the history of the discipline' (1993:133). An exception to the lack of attention paid to the body is the 1977 Association of Social Anthropology's Conference on *The Anthropology of the Body*, which resulted in an edited book of the same name (Blacking 1977). Contributors to the edited collection highlighted the physical, social and symbolic significance of the body, whereby virtually all parts of the body convey meaning to the individual and to others from within the same society. At the same time, bodies inform outsiders of the beliefs, rituals and cultural practices of that particular society.

Anthropologically, embodiment as the coming together of body, mind and the senses is about culture in its broadest sense because culture is a constitutive element of lived experience. Indeed, Jackson argues that culture should be re-constituted as embodied experience because 'human experience is grounded in bodily movement within a social and material environment...' (1983:330), and individuals actively body forth the world through patterns of body use as they interact with this environment. The significance of this argument for tourism is clear. Tourism gathers together the social, cultural, material and physical components of particular environments and turns them into destinations, attractions and activities for tourists. How this gathering *works* to body forth the experience of being a tourist can tell us much about the ways in which the social processes that instruct individuals how to behave as a tourist, come into being.

The bodily being of a tourist shapes and is shaped by the coming together of culture and experience as specific types of tourism, for example, heritage tourism, adventure tourism, culinary tourism and so on. Knowing what is expected, knowing how to behave in particular tourism environments is learned through the body. An embodied approach to tourism means that the body is not something to be studied in relation to culture as if it were an object, it is the very subject of culture. In this respect, Mauss' (1979) concept of *habitus*, or embodied knowledge, illustrates how the body learns the techniques and repertoires of bodily practice that distinguish individuals and groups. Such that ways of digging, swimming and running are reflections of particular cultures, particular ways of being, and in Ghana *seselelame* is the Anlo-Ewe expression to describe feeling or hearing skin sensations linked to intuition and premonition (Geurts 2002). Likewise, the Cashinahua of Peru speak of heart knowledge, ear knowledge, eye knowledge, hand knowledge, skin knowledge and so on (Kensinger 1995).

Bourdieu's (1977) focus on habitus highlights the everyday structures, processes and practices that coalesce to create and internalise particular body behaviours, producing a collective history of how to behave in any given context. According to Bourdieu, bodies learn and remember how to behave '...by the hidden persuasion of an implicit pedagogy which can instil a whole cosmology, through injunctions as insignificant as 'sit up straight' or 'don't hold your knife in your left hand'...' (1990:69).

The notion of habitus as embodied knowledge is useful for tourism because embodiment is a way of understanding culture and the self in relation to practices of movement, thinking and sensing. All of which are deeply embedded within the activities, attractions and destinations that inscribe the culture of the tourist habitus on the body/ies of tourists. Explorations of culture are therefore explorations of how bodies shape and are shaped by their experience in the world, as Kissel argues '...an embodied being is necessarily a being embedded in a social context ...' (2001:2). This is interesting because tourism is a particular type of social context in which bodies engage with and through culturally determined codes of conduct that shape how the body of a tourist is expected to behave. This is most clearly evident in the differences between western and non-western patterns of body use that prescribe which parts of the body may or may not be open to public scrutiny and in what circumstances. A bikini might be acceptable on a beach in Spain but not in a shopping mall. A woman wearing a burkini in Turkey might go largely unnoticed, but in 2009, the mayor of Cannes banned a burkini body in the South of France.

As such, the relationship between body, mind and culture defines the experience of tourism, which is predicated on the coming together of human and nonhuman 'bodies' in what are in effect tightly choreographed encounters in and with the spaces, places and activities associated with tourism. For example, hotels, national parks and attractions: beaches, airports and cruise ships: walking, sightseeing and diving: backpacking, cycling and volunteering. All of which require and encourage different types of bodily reactions and different ways in which the body is to be used. Indeed, tourism-related body use can be at odds with that of everyday life and may subject the body to pressures, exertions, emotional and psychological responses that cause temporary or permanent change, such as skin damage resulting from sunburn. The patterns of body use experienced through tourism remind individuals of the holiday, the trip or the day out. They are memories that serve to perpetuate how the body becomes a tourist. To adapt a phrase from Connerton (1989), bodily experiences of being a tourist gather together over time to become a history of travel sedimented in the body.

The above arguments serve as a guiding framework for this book, a framework supporting our overall purpose, which is to start a conversation about the relationship between tourism and embodiment. The contributions included here are an important part of what we hope will become an ongoing dialogue with, through and about the body, embodiment and tourism. The conversation begins with a brief overview of each chapter.

Overview of chapters

Following on from this first chapter, Jenny Huberman focuses on re-encountering bodies: tourists and children on the riverfront of Banaras. Here, she argues that western tourists' experiences in India are profoundly mediated through the body. Smells, sounds, heat, dust, crowds, colours and tastes are the key means through which tourists come to know and enjoy the country. But this sensory overload also leaves many tourists feeling disoriented and overwhelmed. How might an emphasis on embodiment enhance analyses of touristic experience in India and beyond? Huberman explores this question by returning to earlier research on encounters between western tourists and the children who worked as peddlers and guides along the riverfront in the city of Banaras, India. She revisits these encounters with two goals in mind. First, to illuminate how the embodied nature of touristic experience influenced encounters between western tourists and children on the riverfront. And second, to demonstrate how 'the paradigm of embodiment' (Csordas 1993) might be used to supplement semiotic and textually driven analyses of tourism.

Chapter 3, Never just an any body: tourist encounters with wild bears in Yosemite National Park by Sally Ann Ness, explores the relationship between tourism studies and animal studies. In this chapter, Ness argues that the anthropology of tourism has generally reinforced an anthropocentric view of tourism and one way to counteract this is by asking the question what might a zoocentric theory of tourism look like? Her response to this question is to approach the study of live tourist/animal interaction *choreographically*. By way of illustration, she analyses an unplanned and unwanted trans-species encounter between tourists and California Black Bears in Yosemite National Park in California. An encounter that demonstrates how human and bear bodies observed choreographically can serve as emergent, morally charged sites of touristic meaning making and interpretation.

Queer bodies and the construction of tourism destination space (Chapter 4) by Bradley Rink utilises Cape Town's *Pink Map* to demonstrate the role of the body in the production and consumption of the tourist/leisure enclave of De Waterkant in Cape Town, South Africa. Rink argues that the *Pink Map* offers tourists a cartographic rendering of the city that highlights lesbian, gay, bisexual and transgender (LGBT) leisure spaces. His discursive analysis of the *Map's* embodied cartography not only demonstrates the limited range of bodily representations of queerness but also demonstrates how sexually Othered bodies are used to depict the landscape for tourist consumption. In so doing, he highlights the need to take seriously the role of the body in the socio-cultural construction of tourism destination space.

Rafael Cruces Portales and Antonio Miguel Nogués-Pedregal's focus in Chapter 5 is Rethinking the body in the touristic scenario: the elusiveness of embodying disability into tourism. The chapter describes the process by which the body of the disabled tourist disrupts taken-for-granted assumptions about the representation of tourism spaces and places. The tourism industry is continually trying to create the image of a desirable and idyllic earthly paradise. However, they question the extent to which the disabled body has been invited to represent this 'paradise'. Drawing on ethnographic fieldwork, they describe the emergence of and the practices that sustain what they refer to as aesthetic prejudice. This concept encompasses the function of filtering; classifying and shaping images that are eventually accepted or rejected according to a pre-established social code of disability. They argue that aesthetic prejudice acts as a powerful yet silent agent working to prevent the integration of the embodiment of disability in the touristic setting.

In Chapter 6, Yoga as an embodied journey towards flexibility, openness and balance, Amy Speier combines medical anthropology's understandings of embodiment with tourism studies to examine the concept of embodiment through the lens of yoga holidays. Yoga retreats are heavily marketed through images of celebrities striking yoga poses on beaches, and popularised by movies like *Eat, Pray, Love*. Such depictions of yoga evoke particular notions of health in terms of what constitutes a healthy body generally and in relation to travelling as contributing to bodily health. Based on participant observation and interviews with British and North American women in Northern Italy, the chapter examines the overlapping motivations for practising yoga and for travelling arguing that such holidays are a platform for empowering the female body.

Patrick McCartney develops the relationship between the body, yoga and tourism in Chapter 7 through a focus on yoga-scapes, embodiment and imagined spiritual tourism. Here, he argues that the binary distinction between tourist/pilgrim and religious/secular loses its analytical potency when examined through the experience of a yoga practitioner. McCartney explores how the subjective, embodied experience of the practitioner challenges us to reflect on the different ways in which the individual can be both a tourist and a pilgrim and how through pilgrimage the body is potentially transformed.

Following on from McCartney, Anna de Jong's chapter entitled Embodying dyke on bike: motorcycling, travel and the politics of belonging on-the-move focuses on the Queensland Dykes on Bikes during their 1800 kilometres return journey from Brisbane to the Sydney Gay and Lesbian Mardi Gras Parade. Here, the concept of belonging is mobilised through an examination of the lived experiences of six women claiming non-normative sexualities, who rode their bikes to Mardi Gras, as part of a larger group of 20 riders. The demands of preparing the riding body, knowing the rules and the gendered characterisations of both the bike and embodied riding performances illustrate how belonging emerges on-the-move, to identify clearly the Dyke on Bike identity.

In Chapter 9, A matter of life and death: tourism as sensual remembrance, Geoffrey Bird, Hilary Leighton and Ann-Kathrin McLean unpack battle-field or remembrance tourism from the perspective of a more embodied and sensual way of knowing. Drawing on the findings of research into the visitor experience of the D-Day landscape of war in Normandy, France, they demonstrate how the lived experience of the relationship between death, the body and tourism is inextricably linked through the senses. What they refer to as the embodiment of remembrance is illustrated via four interrelated themes, attirement, movement, touch and sound. Through these themes, they argue that a more embodied approach to the role of the senses in tourism demonstrates how mind, body and landscape work together to connect person to place and past.

Bodies at sea: 'water' as interface in Viking heritage communication by Michael Haldrup provides the focus for Chapter 10. Despite the fact that there are numerous signs and markers at museums and heritage sites instructing bodies how to move around the site or signs warning bodies to pay attention to their environment, to 'stop, look and listen' (Ingold 2011), the embodied choreography of the museum/heritage encounter remains relatively underexplored. Haldrup addresses this gap by focusing on the visitor experience at the Viking Ship Museum, Roskilde, Denmark. Here, Viking culture is enacted and experienced through the corporeal and ludic performances of bodies at/on the sea as the visitors learn to sail and to row a Viking Ship, resulting in a profoundly embodied experience of 'becoming Vikings'.

Chapter 11, by Anna Elisabeth Kuijpers, focuses on the embodied experience of making slow food for touristic purposes by women in Halfeti, southeast Turkey. One of the ways the town is marketed for tourism is as a *slow city* (Cittaslow), in which slow food plays an important role. This chapter uncovers the daily-embodied experiences behind the making of slow food, experiences that are not as romantic as the images suggest. The heavy workload causes strain and stress on the body and in the mind but it also creates ties between the women who make the food as female bodies join together to help each other. The daily-embodied experiences of the women involved in making slow food in Halfeti reveal the influence of tourism on the female body.

In the next chapter, Chapter 12, entitled Clay, glass and everyday life: craft-artists' embodiment in the tourist landscape, Solène Prince argues that tourism scholars have yet to seriously examine tourism as a part of the everyday life of those who dwell within toured landscapes. She draws on her study of craft-artists from Bornholm, a popular summer resort in Denmark to illustrate how the tourism landscape is transformed through the embodied movements of the artists. The material properties and techniques used to turn clay and glass into artistic creations are essential for defining the type of interactions the different craft-artists have with tourists. Her chapter illustrates the central role of materials in shaping the tourist landscape.

Chapter 13, Material-bodily assemblages on a multi-day wilderness walk by Kaya Barry, explores how tourist bodies merge with nonhuman technologies such as backpacks, boots, clothing, light-weight food, and walking-sticks during a multi-day wilderness walk in Tasmania, Australia. Using extracts from her fieldwork journal, she reveals how the hiking bag mediates movements between the tourist body, the materials and equipment carried, and the surrounding environment, fusing material and bodily sensations together in an assemblage. These material-bodily assemblages play a significant role in how tourists come to feel entangled with the more-than-human world. This entanglement of body, materiality and world operates to reconfigure the tourist body, and in so doing to reshape and co-produce tourist experiences.

Christopher Howard and Wendelin Küpers (Chapter 14) explore the convergence of embodiment, tourism and mobile technologies in a globally networked context in a chapter entitled Phenomenological anthropology of interactive travel: mediated responsivity and inter-placed mobilities. Drawing on ethnographic research in the Himalayan region of Nepal and India undertaken by Howard, they highlight the role the internet and mobile technologies play in mediating embodied perceptions and performances of place. In doing so, they reveal how the dynamics of technological mobility in relation to places are transforming the embodied involvement and responsiveness of emplaced travellers.

Soile Veijola's Afterword to the book, Chapter 15, inspired by the previous chapters, is a reflective piece on the embodied relationship between tourism teaching, research and scholarship.

References

Andrews, H. (2005) Feeling at home: Embodying Britishness in a Spanish charter tourism resort. *Tourist Studies*, 5(3): 247–266.

Andrews, H. (2011) *The British on Holiday. Charter Tourism, Identity and Consumption*. Bristol: Channel View Publications.

Andrews, H. (2017) Becoming through tourism: Imagination in practice. *Suomen Antropologi*, 42(1): 31–44.

Blacking, J. Ed. (1977) *The Anthropology of the Body*. London: Academic Press.

Bourdieu, P. (1977) *Outline of a Theory of Practice*. Cambridge: Cambridge University Press.

Connerton, P. (1989) *How Societies Remember.* Cambridge: Cambridge University Press.

Csordas, T. J. (1993) Somatic modes of attention. *Cultural Anthropology,* 8(2): 135–156.

Csordas, T. J. Ed. (1994) *Embodiment and Experience. The Existential Ground of Culture and Self.* Cambridge: Cambridge University Press.

Csordas, T. J. (1999) Embodiment and cultural phenomenology, in G. Weiss and H. Haber (eds.) *Perspectives on Embodiment. The Intersections of Nature and Culture.* New York: Routledge, pp. 143–162.

Dann, G. M. S. and Jacobsen, J. K. S. (2002) Leading the tourist by the nose, in G. M. S. Dann (ed.) *The Tourist as a Metaphor of the Social World.* Wallingford: CAB International, pp. 209–235.

Geurts, K. L. (2002) *Culture and the Senses. Bodily Ways of Knowing in an African Community.* Berkeley: University of California Press.

Ingold, T. (2011) The Perception of the Environment. Essays on Livelihood, Dwelling and Skill, new preface edition. London: Routledge.

Kensinger, K. (1995) *How Real People Ought to Live: The Cashinahua of Eastern Peru.* Prospect Heights, IL: Waveland Press.

Lock, M. (1993) Cultivating the body: Anthropology and epistemologies of bodily practice and knowledge. *Annual Review of Anthropology,* 22: 133–144.

Mauss, M. (1979) *Sociology and Psychology. Essays by Marcel Mauss.* London: Routledge.

Merchant, S. (2011) Negotiating underwater space: The sensorium, the body and the practice of scuba-diving. *Tourist Studies,* 11(3): 215–234.

Palmer, C. (1998) From theory to practice. Experiencing the nation in everyday life. *Journal of Material Culture,* 3(2): 175–199.

Palmer, C. (2018) *Being and Dwelling through Tourism: An Anthropological Perspective.* Abingdon: Routledge.

Pritchard, A., Morgan, N., Ateljevic, I. and Harris, C. (2007) *Tourism and Gender: Embodiment, Sensuality and Experience.* Wallingford: CABI.

Richards, V., Pritchard, A. and Morgan, N. (2010) (Re)envisioning Tourism and Visual Impairment. Annals of Tourism Research, 37(4): 1097–1116.

Small, J. and Darcy, S. (2011). Understanding tourist experience through embodiment: The contribution of critical tourism and disability studies, in D. Buhalis and S. Darcy (eds.) *Accessible Tourism: Concepts and Issues.* Bristol: Channel View Publications, pp. 72–96.

Small, J., Packer, T. and Darcy, S. (2012) The embodied tourist experiences of people with vision impairment: Management implications beyond the visual gaze. Tourism Management, 33: 941–950.

Veijola, S. and Jokinen, E. (1994) The body in tourism. *Theory, Culture & Society,* 11: 125–151.

Waitt, G. and Duffy, M. (2010) Listening and Tourism Studies. *Annals of Tourism Research,* 37(2): 457–477.

2 Re-encountering bodies

Tourists and children on the riverfront of Banaras

Jenny Huberman

Introduction

In this chapter, I explore the relationship between embodiment and tourism by returning to my earlier research on encounters between western tourists, and the lower class and lower caste children who worked as unlicensed peddlers and guides along the riverfront in the city of Banaras, India (Huberman 2012). Western tourists' experiences in India are profoundly mediated through the body. Smells, sounds, heat, dust, crowds, colours and tastes provide key means through which tourists come to know and enjoy the country. And yet, this 'sensory overload', as tourists often call it, also leaves many visitors feeling disoriented and overwhelmed.[1] How might an emphasis on embodiment enhance analyses of touristic experience in India and beyond? And, how might paying attention to the embodied dimensions of touristic experience contribute more generally to anthropological debates about interpretation and meaning?

I will explore these questions by drawing upon two years of fieldwork, which sought to explain why western tourists had such powerful and often polarised reactions to the children on the riverfront, ranging from expressions of utter adoration to absolute disgust. Some tourists praised these young workers as self-sacrificing, innocent children who required (and in some cases, even provided) support and protection. Other tourists castigated them for their apparent corruption asserting that they were 'the worst kids' they had encountered in India and 'totally ruined'.

In *Ambivalent Encounters*, I argued that tourists' reactions to the children were shaped by multiple determinations. They were mediated by tourists' cultural conceptions of childhood, by the tropes and themes through which tourists came to know India, by the ways tourists actively read and interpreted the space of the riverfront, and of course, by the children themselves. Drawing upon concepts from psychoanalytic theory, I also proposed that tourists' reactions were reflective of unconscious defence mechanisms (Klein 1975 [1948], 1987 [1946]) that enabled tourists to better cope with the anxiety and guilt that the children and surrounding environment so often evoked in them. I showed how processes of splitting, idealisation and denial variously lead tourists to embrace these youngsters as 'innocent children' or, alternatively, castigate them as 'little adults masquerading in kids' bodies'. As Klein explained, splitting is a psychological defence mechanism that enables people to cope with feelings of guilt and anxiety by treating others as either all good or all bad, rather than 'whole objects' with both positive and negative attributes. Employing Klein's work led me to conclude that the classification of children should not be reduced to an exclusively social or cultural phenomenon. Psychodynamics also animate the ways children come to be affirmed or denied in different contexts. For instance, when tourists cast these children as virtuous innocents or alternatively, denied them the status of children altogether, tourists were less plagued with feelings of guilt and anxiety and they did not second-guess their interactions with the children as much.

And yet, while my analysis focused on the cultural and psychological motivations that influenced tourists' reactions to the children on the riverfront, it did not pay particularly close attention to the embodied nature of tourists' experiences. Looking back now, I realise that the tourists' bodies were largely silent in my initial analysis, or rather, downplayed by my more pointed interest in the way symbols, signs and feelings mediated these encounters. In this chapter, therefore, I revisit some of these data with two goals in mind. First, I want to more precisely show how the embodied nature of touristic experience influenced encounters between western tourists and children on the riverfront of Banaras. And second, I want to use this re-encounter with my earlier research to demonstrate how 'the paradigm of embodiment' (Csordas 1993) might be used to supplement psychoanalytic, as well as semiotic and textually driven analyses of tourism.

Embodiment and somatic attention

What does it mean to revisit ethnographic data from the 'paradigm of embodiment'?[2] As Thomas Csordas explains, 'By paradigm I mean simply a consistent methodological perspective that encourages reanalyses of existing data and suggests new questions for empirical research' (1990:5). Instead of treating the body solely as an object or text upon which cultural meanings, signs, power relations and forms of discipline are inscribed, and then 'read' by the ethnographer, the paradigm of embodiment takes 'the "lived body" as a methodological starting point' (Csordas 1993:136). It treats the body not just as an object, but as a subject of lived experience, proposing that 'embodied experience is the starting point for analyzing human participation in a cultural world' (Csordas 1993:135). As Csordas emphasises, 'the point of elaborating a paradigm of embodiment is then not to supplant' semiotic or textual approaches, but rather 'to complement' them with a 'dialectical partner' that takes the phenomenological experience of being-in-the world seriously (1994:12).

More specifically, Csordas suggests that the paradigm of embodiment involves focusing on the various modes of 'somatic attention' through which human actors engage the world and others around them. 'Somatic modes of attention', he writes, 'are culturally elaborated ways of attending to and with one's body in surroundings that include the embodied presence of others' (Csordas 1993:139) Csordas provides the example of Catholic Charismatic faith healers who learn to attend to bodily sensations of heaviness, tingling and heat as signs of 'anointing' by God. As he observes, 'attention *to* a bodily sensation can thus become a mode of attending to the intersubjective milieu that give rise to that sensation. Thus, one is paying attention *with* one's body' (ibid: 138 original italics).

Indeed, although I did not formulate it in these terms at the time, one of the central arguments I made in *Ambivalent Encounters* was that there has been a notable shift in the somatic modes of attention that are valued and cultivated by western tourists in India. For instance, during the colonial period, western travellers in Banaras prioritised vision as the central mode of attending *with* their bodies and *to* their travel environments.[3] They preferred to 'consume' the city through the carefully orchestrated 'tourist gaze' (Urry 1990), peering out on the city from boat and carriage rides, scenic hotel balconies, or through carefully managed guided tours that kept locals and other kinds of sensory stimuli and intrusions safely at bay. The primacy of the gaze as a mode of somatic attention can be vividly gleaned in the 1896 travel memoirs of Frenchman, Andre Chevrillion. Recounting his boat ride along the riverfront of Banaras, he wrote,

> We have gone over two miles, and the spectacle is the same. The crowd, the architecture, the sunlight, seem to be visions of some opium-dream, where time, space, and all they contain, appear enormously magnified and multiplied...from all this moving, praying singing multitude rises a great noise, a confused rustle of human life. Everywhere on the edge of the great careless river there is the same swarming life, the same vast wave of humanity heaping itself up.
>
> (Chevrillion 1896:79)

While Chevrillion may have enjoyed the vista from the boat, like most colonial travellers, he was not eager to immerse himself in the 'swarming' and 'confused rustle of human life' that Banaras offered. For him, the return to the hotel marked a welcome return to 'European tranquility and reasonableness, fine, calm order, and correct costume' (ibid: 81).

By contrast, many of the backpacking tourists who were travelling in Banaras in the early 2000s, and who were at the centre of my study, did not want to just gaze at the city and its inhabitants from a 'safe' and removed distance. They were looking for more authentic and intimate experiences.[4] In order to achieve this, they actively sought to immerse themselves in the sights, sounds and lives of people in the city and this frequently put them in touch, both physically and emotionally, with the children who worked along the riverfront. For instance, during her stay in Banaras, Carla, a twenty-six-year-old traveller from Canada remarked:

> These days so many people are traveling in these countries and I think everyone is looking for a unique experience. If you meet a child and spend time with them, it glorifies your experience because you're seeing what every other traveller is but you know, you're making a personal connection and that feels really good, especially when you think the connection is genuine. It just makes it a hundred percent more the experience really.

In the remainder of this chapter, I revisit a few of these encounters in order to highlight how tourists' embodied experiences attuned them to their travel environment and shaped the ways they evaluated the children on the riverfront.

Embodying power and privilege

Among the tourists I interviewed, it was not just the case that their visits to India were profoundly mediated *through* the body and experiences of 'sensory overload', it was also the case that being in India frequently made tourists *aware* of their body and senses in new ways. Bodily attributes often taken for granted at home, such as size, skin, hair or eye colour, came to be foregrounded and in some cases, *experienced* as new sources of power, privilege and pleasure. This could play a significant role in how tourists responded to the children on the riverfront. For instance, several tourists commented on how 'fat and rich' they felt compared to people in India. Their bodily heft became a very immediate reminder of their economic status. As Mark a thirty-two-year-old tourist from the United States remarked rather sheepishly, 'When these kids on the riverfront come up to sell me postcards, I feel guilty. I'm fat, I'm carrying around my expensive camera, and they've got nothing'. Alternatively, several of the male travellers I interviewed gleefully remarked that being in India made them feel like 'rock stars'. As Charles, a forty-year-old traveller from the United States exclaimed,

> I love it! I am like a rock star here! I feel famous! I really stand out here. First of all, I'm like three heads taller than most of the people around me, and I'm white, and people are just curious, they want to take pictures with me, touch me. The kids here on the riverfront, they always want to play with me, hang on me, and I don't mind because I know they are curious.

For Charles, therefore, it wasn't just that his body was being interpreted in new ways. Charles also clearly came to *experience* his body in new ways. The attention it garnered became a visceral source of pleasure for him and it enabled him to tolerate, if not enjoy it, when the children began to 'hang' on him.

Moreover, this embodied sense of security and privilege also influenced the ways tourists physically interacted with the children on the riverfront. Jorgen was a thirty-one-year-old Dutch tourist who had originally come to Banaras with the intention of staying only three days. After meeting a young boy named Mohan, who offered to be his guide, he decided to extend his visit to over a week. Throughout his stay in the city, Mohan accompanied Jorgen virtually everywhere he went. I spent a considerable amount of time observing interactions between them and even mediated an encounter between Jorgen and Mohan's mother, when at the end of his stay, Jorgen decided he was going to open up a bank account for Mohan so he could continue to wire him money from home. One of the things, that continually struck (and admittedly disturbed) me about Jorgen, was the way he so readily expressed and exerted his bodily dominance over Mohan. He very quickly assumed tactile liberties with Mohan that would have been nearly unthinkable had he been dealing with a young boy he had just met at home. He was continually holding Mohan's hand, ushering him away from the traffic, pulling him closer to him, as though he had a paternal right and obligation to make sure that no harm came to Mohan on his watch.

Moreover, it was not just that Jorgen enjoyed embodying the role of the benevolent protector, it was also that Mohan's comparatively smaller stature and presumably less cunning mind, made Jorgen feel more in control. When Jorgen spoke about why he liked having Mohan as a guide he explained,

> I much rather be taken around by a young boy like Mohan. I think it makes a big difference…it is much more easy for me to control him in doing what I want than it would be for me to control an adult Indian to do what I want.

The security that came with being able to physically dominate the children on the riverfront was also expressed by Alexandra, a twenty-six-year-old female tourist from Switzerland. When I asked her about her experiences in Banaras, she remarked,

A: I like to have more contact with the kids because you can see them from here, you can look down [on them]. But most men you have to treat them also as kids but they are taller than you, so it's a bit difficult.

JH: Why do you have to treat most men as kids?

A: Well, they act like kids, I mean, I have the feeling sometimes I am either a one rupee bank note, or it's written here, 'Fuckable and enjoy me', yeah that's it. But with kids, no, they prefer to play with you, and they are more pure in a way.

Indeed, for female tourists like Alexandra, the sense of physical comfort and security they experienced with the children on the riverfront, stood in stark contrast to the sense of bodily vulnerability they experienced when confronted with the ubiquitous presence of lecherous men. Western female tourists continually complained about how difficult it was to safeguard their bodies in India, and in some cases, this made women travellers quite eager to engage in interactions with the children on the riverfront. For instance, in recounting his experience at the evening puja ceremony Charles, who I introduced above, exclaimed:

> Oh God! I saw a woman sitting right next to the Pepsi stand with like a baby at the breast, and another one just hanging on her knee and she was feeding them and very just, having a great time, everybody was loving it! I mean come on, I've seen so many like her. They come to India thinking they're going to [making quote gestures with his fingers] 'Save the Children', become Mother Theresa or Patrick Swazye from *The City of Joy*. Give me a break!

Charles' remarks were clearly intended as a snarky form of ridicule; however, they nonetheless contain some apt insights into the way women's embodied experiences in India could influence their reactions to the children on the riverfront. It wasn't just that holding children on their laps, or as Charles put it, 'at their breasts', provided them with an opportunity to indulge their 'Mother Theresa' fantasies. It was also the case that having children by their sides, or clinging to their bodies could serve as a useful shield against aggressive and intruding men, and it could provide these women with an enhanced sense of bodily comfort and security which, in many cases, enabled them to negotiate the riverfront with greater ease, joy and confidence.[5]

There were many occasions when I, like Charles, witnessed western female tourists cuddling the children close to them, or holding them in their laps. Sara, for example, was a twenty-nine-year-old nurse from Canada who had been working as a volunteer in Nepal and had come to Banaras for a two-week vacation to celebrate the holiday of Holi. During her stay, she befriended several of the children who worked along the riverfront and it seemed as though everywhere she went, she had a child on her arm or in her lap. When I ran into Sara near the end of her stay, I commented on this and she said, 'Well, I've found that in India, if I've got kids around me, the men don't bother me as much' and then with a chuckle she added, 'It's been great, I've spent two weeks here, four hundred dollars, and now I've got about twenty foster kids!'

Embodying vulnerability

If some tourists were able to find comfort and security in the bodies and presence of the children on the riverfront, many others came to feel persecuted and preyed upon by them. The children's 'relentless pestering', as tourists frequently put it, exacerbated their sense of bodily vulnerability making them feel like they had 'targets on their backs', or were nothing more than 'walking dollar signs' or 'cash cows'. Indeed, in contrast to travellers like Charles, many tourists explicitly complained about the ways these children violated their sense of personal space and 'hung on their bodies'. Priya, for instance, was an eight-year-old girl from a lower caste family and was known as one of the most successful, but from the tourists' standpoint, most 'aggravating' postcard sellers on the riverfront. Unlike some of the other children, who tried to win over customers with small chat and smiles, Priya's success derived in large part from her persistence and her ability to wear customers down by following after them, and tugging on their arms and clothing until they agreed to buy a postcard from her. For some tourists, encountering children like Priya generated so much discomfort and anxiety that they literally hid their bodies away from the riverfront, and rarely left their guesthouses.

Such was the case with Erin, a thirty-eight-year-old carpenter from the United States, who was travelling through India with Charles. Far from feeling like a rock star, Erin felt like a 'freak', and found it very difficult to be a tourist in Banaras. While initially I had observed him spending time on the riverfront with Charles, after a few days in the city, Erin's presence became less frequent. When I inquired about his absence, Charles told me that Erin had been 'done in' by an encounter with some kids selling postcards and had decided 'to hole up' in the guesthouse where he could enjoy a scenic view of the riverfront without being 'hassled'. When I went to pay Erin a visit at his guesthouse, he agreed to let me interview him over lunch. Erin ordered a self-proclaimed 'bevy of comfort food' which included tomato soup, cheese toast and fries. About twenty minutes into our interview, I asked him about his experiences with the children on the riverfront.[6] Erin responded quickly and excitedly:

> These kids, they're very good at one thing that has been taught to them by probably someone who beats them if they don't do it. I don't know, I mean I don't know how it is enforced, and I've seen enough kids fighting amongst themselves, and there's a certain base level of aggression that uh, it's not beyond their character to get a little rise out of getting a little rise out of you. It's a little bit like kind of fun to see what this tourist freak is going to do.

While tourists like Erin holed up and hid away due to the aggravating presence of these kids, other tourists responded by becoming more aggressive themselves, and purposively assumed a more hostile demeanour. As Nicholas, a twenty-two-year-old tourist from Seattle, remarked when commenting on his interactions with the children on the riverfront,

> At first I was very polite, and I said no thank you I don't want your candles- but after being *bombarded* by these kids again and again, I've become much nastier, I even give them mean looks to try and scare them away.

This was also the case with Usha, a twenty-three-year-old traveller from Germany who had come to India in search of 'spiritual enlightenment'.

After becoming enchanted with one of the *sadhus* or religious holy men who lived along the riverfront, Usha decided to spend several weeks in Banaras, and ended up living across the hall in the same guesthouse as me. In *Ambivalent Encounters*, I discussed my interview with Usha at length as it was certainly one of the more memorable interviews I conducted during my fieldwork. During our conversation, Usha provided a dramatic, and at times explosive, re-enactment of her encounters with the children on the riverfront, which involved her excitedly waving her arms and mimicking their voices, thereby creating the sense that there were several interlocutors in the room with us. Moreover, throughout our conversation, it appeared that Usha was on an emotional rollercoaster where feelings of frustration, guilt or sympathy for the children could quickly give way to expressions of anger and resentment. When I asked Usha to reflect upon her experiences, she began her account by taking a deep breath and exhaling purposively:

> The first time I came to the ghats, I thought, 'Oh no what can I do? There are so many children around me, oohh they are taking away my peace. Oh this is not nice', and then I walk straight and I don't look anywhere, and sometimes I put on my Walkman, then I cannot listen and people see 'Oh she cannot hear', and then they do not come to you. They come and then they go...At first you think, oh, this is a small boy, I cannot say so harshly, 'Hey go away', oh this is a sweet small boy and he asks you [making her voice soft and cute], 'Oh would you like to buy postcards?' And in one way its sweet, it's nice and you cannot say like this, [in a deep stern voice] 'Hey go!' But then when it's getting too much because it's not only one, then you learn to be, to...and sometimes I take their neck like here [making the sweeping and grabbing gesture with her hand] and push them away, and say, 'GO!' Not hard, but like if you're swimming and you make some rubbish...rubbish... [making clearing away movements with her arms] very gentle go.

For Usha, the tourist's body was clearly a besieged body. Her reaction to the children on the riverfront was absolutely linked to her embodied experience of feeling attacked. When 'tuning the children out' with her Walkman and headphones did not work, she too resorted to more aggressive physical measures. Moreover, like Mark, Usha also equated tourists' 'fat' bodies with economic power; however, in her experience, this generated profound feelings of dehumanisation rather than privilege. For instance, when I asked Usha, 'What do you think it is like for these kids who work on the riverfront? What do you think they think of tourists?' She exploded with the following reply, again mimicking the voices of the children:

> I think they are very...[in an explosive voice] I think they *hate* tourists! I think that they hate tourists and need them and they hate...and they think also that tourists are very stupid people, very stupid, and fat, and

big money, and tourists are only good for making money because they are stupid and you can get on their nerves and no problem, they are not the same human being as Indians, they are more polite also and so you can step on them, you can go one more step with them. You cannot go to an Indian and say, 'Ooohhh' and pull their clothes and say, 'Please buy colours', and 'Buy me a chocolate and this and this and this', it's not possible but with the tourists they think, 'Oh, yeah, they have enough, they are fat with big cameras and they are only good to give money, and only good to buy my stuff and they'll take it, why not? They have enough, so I have the full right to go there and get on their nerves and they are all stupid!'

Usha's response provides a classic example of projection. Projection, as Klein and others have explained, is an unconscious psychological defence mechanism in which unwanted or angry feelings that are experienced as potentially threatening are displaced onto another person. By displacing these bad feelings onto the other, they then appear as a threat from the external world, rather than something that comes from within (Klein 1975 [1948], 1987 [1946]). I suggested that the hateful feelings Usha attributed to the children on the riverfront were in large part expressions of her own sense of guilt and self-hatred. As the semiotician Jonathan Culler has noted, and as I myself frequently observed, tourists are often afflicted by powerful feelings of 'self-loathing' (Culler 1981) and this is particularly pronounced in places like India, where the economic disparity between the hosts and guests can be extreme.

And yet, while I still support this interpretation, my initial analysis did not adequately appreciate the way Usha's *embodied experiences* on the riverfront contributed to her sense of persecutory anxiety, and even influenced the ways she came to classify the children. In revisiting Usha's interview, it is clear to me that Usha was 'attending to' these children and her environment as much 'with' her body, as she was with her mind and feelings. Her tendencies to idealise these children as sweet and innocent, or alternatively deny them the status altogether, were intimately linked to her own sense of *bodily* security and vulnerability. This final excerpt from my interview with Usha illustrates this vividly. As Usha went on to explain,

U: I think, I think after some time you forget that children are.....children are trying to sell you something. It's like uh....for me they are often like flies and because if there are only a few, maybe one or two or three, you can try and be very honest and very kind to them, because it is not too much, but when they are all hanging around you then you want to take, take your body and go away, you want only that they go away, you don't think about their personality, about their family or their money, you only think, 'I'm coming here, I want to walk this way and I don't ask for your postcards, I don't ask for your colours so please don't hang on my body'.

JH: It bothers you if they touch you?

U: Yeah. Yeah, and then also when they don't touch me they come so close that you have the feeling that they are hanging on you. But you come with this idea, 'I'm coming for a walk', but when there are ten people around you then you cannot enjoy your walk anymore, then you try to push them away, 'Go, let me...' and this mixed feeling of being afraid and angriness, then you, then you forget, 'Oh they're children, or maybe they have poor families'. You think this when the first one is coming, but not when there are so many around. You only want to have your peace. These ghat kids bother you so much with their postcards and candles and make you so mad that you forget they are children and you don't speak kindly to them, you just want them to go away [her voice softening] and then after you yell at them and shoo them off you feel bad and think 'Oh, this is just a poor child I shouldn't be like this'.

Again, the point here is not to discount the usefulness of psychoanalytic concepts in understanding tourists' reactions to the children on the riverfront. Usha's response did evidence mechanisms of projection, splitting, idealisation and denial, which, in turn, helped her defend against feelings of guilt and anxiety. By casting these children as 'flies', by denying them the status of childhood altogether, Usha found a way to defend against her guilty feelings, and when the situation called for it, this enabled her to treat the children harshly and even 'shoo' them away. Only in her more reflective, or 'depressive' moments, when Usha was able to step back and view these children as 'whole objects' with both good and bad attributes, did she openly express remorse.[7] Thus, the point in revisiting this material is, as Csordas has proposed, to 'complement' rather than supplant my initial analysis. Looking back now I am able to see how Usha's body *also* became a generative site for the production of meaning and understanding; her very tendencies to engage in acts of idealisation and denial were in part, motivated by 'the lived experiences' of her body.

Conclusion

This chapter began by asking, how might an emphasis on embodiment enhance analyses of tourism in India and beyond? And, how might paying attention to tourists' embodied experiences contribute more generally to anthropological debates about interpretation and meaning? While the foregoing discussion has tried to address these questions by revisiting data from my earlier research, in concluding I want to provide some more explicit responses.

As regards the first question, the paradigm of embodiment strikes me as particularly promising for studies of tourism precisely because the tourist's body is so frequently a de-routinised, and therefore, a hyper-conscious body. Whether it be a product of sensory overload, swarming kids or contexts that make one feel like a 'freak' or a 'rock star', the taken-for-granted relationships that tourists have to their bodies are often profoundly disrupted when they leave home and arrive in unfamiliar places and this, in turn, can make tourists aware of their bodies in new ways. Moreover, since tourists frequently find themselves in situations where verbal forms of communication with locals are limited, the body often becomes charged with extra communicative responsibilities; it becomes even more relied upon as a tool for 'attending to' one's environment and the others who move within it. As such, the injunction to take 'embodied experience' as 'the methodological starting point' for analysing 'participation in a cultural world' (Csordas 1993:135) seems especially apt when it comes to studying tourists' experiences.

Second, an emphasis on embodiment encourages scholars to more carefully consider how different forms of tourism imply or prioritise different modes of somatic attention. More studies could ask, how are tourists implicitly and explicitly taught to attend to their surroundings with their bodies? And, how does this influence the kinds of experiences they have? For instance as I noted earlier, whereas western colonial travellers relied upon the gaze as the primary mode of appropriating and experiencing Banaras, present-day backpackers often want a 'full-on sensory immersion' that puts them in touch physically and emotionally with inhabitants of the city. To attend to such differences is to highlight the fact that the tourist's body is an imminently social and historical body. Treating the body as a lived subject should not, as Csordas reminds us, be conflated with treating the body as an utterly individual entity.

Third, an emphasis on embodiment presents an opportunity for anthropologists of tourism, and otherwise, to think more creatively about data and research methods. While re-analysing my data from the paradigm of embodiment enabled me to look upon old material with fresh eyes, and while it did generate some new insights, I am also aware of the limitations of this exercise. Trying to infer tourists' embodied experiences from the way they talk about them in interviews is not nearly as productive as paying detailed attention to tourists' embodied reactions as they unfold in real time and in actual touristic settings. And even then, careful observation may fall short of capturing the phenomenological subtleties that shape people's experiences. If the goal is to go beyond treating the tourist's body as a text and discern how the 'lived experience' of the body influences participation in a social world, anthropologists might benefit from a more robust discussion of research methods. What are the most fruitful ways to attend to such experiences, and what are the best ways to inscribe them without falling into the trap of reifying the body as an object?

Throughout this chapter, I have also sought to demonstrate how paying attention to the embodied dimensions of touristic experience contributes more generally to anthropological debates about interpretation and meaning. In *Ambivalent Encounters*, for instance, I argued that tourists' reactions to the children on the riverfront, and their tendencies to variously affirm them as innocent children, or deny them the status of children altogether, were shaped by their cultural conceptions of childhood, as well as by the psychological conflicts they experienced as tourists in India. My goal was to show how these children took on meaning as *both* cultural and 'personal symbols' (Obeyesekere 1981).[8] In elaborating my position, I wrote,

> tourists' reactions [to the children on the riverfront] were in large part motivated by the powerful fantasies and persecutory anxieties that came with being a foreign tourist in India. In Ganaanath Obeyesekere's terms, we might say that tourists related to the children not just as social or cultural symbols but as 'personal' ones (Obeyesekere 1981). Their reactions were as much determined by 'intrapsychic' conflicts and defense mechanisms as they were by the social and cultural significance these children took on.
>
> (Huberman 2012:115)

In this chapter, I have tried to supplement my initial psycho-social interpretation by taking tourists' embodied experiences more seriously. I have sought to show how the tourist's body itself became a generative site for the production of meaning and understanding; the physical sensation of being swarmed upon or attacked, as opposed to cuddled and comforted did influence how tourists ultimately interpreted and classified these children. Thus, if this chapter has something to contribute to broader debates about interpretation and meaning it is to suggest that other anthropological analyses might also benefit from triangulating between these three perspectives. By attending simultaneously to the social, psychological and embodied dimensions of human interactions, we might be able to expand our interpretive tool kit and generate a fuller understanding of how and why human encounters take on different forms of significance for the people involved.

Notes

1 For instance, upon her return from a twenty-four-day excursion through India, Jules visited the Fodor's travel site and posted, 'as any of you who have visited India would I think agree, India is total sensory overload. The sights, the sounds, the smells, absolutely everything. It is what helps make a trip to India so unique'. Available at: www.fodors.com/community/asia/24-days-of-total-sensory-overload-in-indiafantastic.cfm [accessed August 21, 2017].
2 As Csordas himself notes, anthropologists writing from an embodiment perspective 'do not adhere strictly to any one paradigmatic position. The reader will note variations in the use of the term embodiment itself: most authors regard it as an existential condition, others as a process in which meaning is taken into or upon the body' (Csordas 1994:2).
3 In elaborating the concept of somatic modes of attention, Csordas includes the gaze as one such example. He proposes, however, that we often think of attending to the world with the eyes as more of a cognitive function rather than a bodily engagement. He writes, 'attending with one's eyes is really part

of this same phenomenon, but we less often conceptualize visual attention as a "turning toward" than as a disembodied, beam-like "gaze". We tend to think of it as a cognitive function rather than as a bodily engagement' (Csordas 1993:138).

4 Within the past few decades, there have been numerous studies of backpackers. Surveying this literature, Darya Maoz writes,

> The studies generally define backpackers as self-organised pleasure tourists on a prolonged multiple-destination journey with a flexible itinerary. They are often keen to experience the local lifestyles, attempt to "look local", and cite "meeting other people" as a key motivation. Their recreational activities are likely to focus around nature, culture, or adventure. This pattern is consonant with the tendency of backpackers to travel more widely than other tourists, seeking unusual routes. Many travel under a strictly controlled budget, often due to the relatively long duration of their journey. They are described as people who search for authentic experiences, a search based on exclusion of other tourists.
>
> (Maoz 2007:123)

5 This strategy, of course, was not always successful. There were numerous occasions where I observed men tell the children to get lost so that they could talk with the tourist. Typically, this just made the women tourists angrier.

6 Indeed, one of the key ways tourists tried to recalibrate their bodily sense of disequilibrium in India was precisely by seeking out familiar comfort foods. This should also be considered a touristic mode of somatic attention.

7 Klein derived her ideas about the paranoid schizoid and depressive positions from her studies of early infancy. For Klein, the paranoid schizoid position marks an earlier phase in the psychological development of the infant. During this period, the infant's relationship to the mother is animated by the defence mechanism of splitting. The infant tends to relate to the mother as either an idealised, all good object who makes the infant feel safe and secure, or as an all bad object who generates profound feelings of persecutory anxiety and towards whom aggression is projected and experienced. As such, Klein observed that infants tend to oscillate between experiences of feeling safe and secure and experiences of falling to pieces. With the onset of the depressive position, the infant is able to treat the mother, and increasingly the self, as a whole object with both good and bad attributes. As this integration occurs, however, it can make the child feel guilty or remorseful for any negative feelings he or she has towards the mother. While Klein initially derived these two positions, and their respective anxieties and defence mechanisms, from the study of infancy and childhood development, she ultimately concluded that human beings move in and out of these positions throughout the course of their lives. As such, she proposed that these two positions could be viewed as ideal types that would provide analysts with a useful way of 'understanding and unravelling emotional situations' (Klein 1975:37).

8 Obeyesekere urges anthropologists to not only consider the way symbols take on collective, cultural meanings but to also explore how such symbols take on personal meanings. He asks us to consider the psychological as well as cultural motivations that animate people's behaviours and understandings of the world. As he notes, anthropologists must 'articulate the symbol to the cultural, social and psychological dimensions' of our informants, and explore 'the interdigitation of deep motivation and public culture' (Obeyesekere 1981:1). While I followed this lead in my initial analysis, in this chapter I have argued that such an approach could be further enriched by also considering the embodied dimensions of our informants' experiences.

References

Chevrillon, A. (1896) *In India*. New York: Holt, trans. W. Marchant.

Csordas, T. (1990) Embodiment as a paradigm for anthropology. *Ethos*, 18(1): 5–47.

Csordas, T. (1993) Somatic modes of attention. *Cultural Anthropology*, 8(2): 135–156.

Csordas, T. (1994) Introduction, in T. Csordas (ed.) *Embodiment and Experience: The Existential Ground of Culture and Self.* Cambridge: Cambridge University Press, pp. 1–24.

Culler, J. (1981) Semiotics of tourism. *American Journal of Semiotics*, 1: 127–140.

Huberman, J. (2012) *Ambivalent Encounters: Childhood, Tourism, and Social Change in Banaras, India*. New Brunswick, NJ: Rutgers University Press.

Klein, M. (1975 [1948]) On the theory of anxiety and guilt, in M. Klein (ed.) *Envy and Gratitude and Other Works 1946–1963*. New York: Delacorte, pp. 25–40.

Klein, M. (1987 [1946]) Notes on some schizoid mechanisms, in J. Mitchell (ed.) *The Selected Melanie Klein*. New York: Free Press, pp. 175–200.

Klein, M. (1987 [1955]) The psychoanalytic play technique, in J. Mitchell (ed.) *The Selected Melanie Klein*. New York: Free Press, pp. 35–54.

Maoz, D (2007) Backpackers' motivations: The role of culture and nationality. *Annals of Tourism Research*, 34(1): 122–140.

Obeyesekere, G. (1981) *Medusa's Hair: An Essay on Personal Symbols and Religious Experience*. Chicago, IL: University of Chicago Press.

Urry, J (1990) *The Tourist Gaze: Leisure and Travel in Contemporary Societies*. London: Sage.

3 Never just an any body
Tourist encounters with wild bears in Yosemite National Park

Sally Ann Ness

Chapter epigraphs

Almost every week ethologists discover more and more semiotic cognition among nonhuman animals ... Humans need, thus, to become much more aware than we have generally been, in the modern period, of our confraternity with, as well as existential dependence upon, the lives of nonhumans on this planet.
(Wendy Wheeler 2016:130–131)

We can no longer regard animals as mere machines, but as subjects whose essential activity consists in perceiving and acting ....
(Jakob von Uexküll 1957:6)

... we human animals have the same basic bodily possibilities—to move toward and away from, to effect, manipulate, gesture, posture, and the like ... In fact, the notion that difference and inaccessibility across species lines constitutes a more radical cleavage than that across culture, history, or even developmental period is often an unexamined and speciesist prejudice.
(Kenneth Shapiro 1990:192)

Introduction[1]

Tourism is typically construed as uniquely human in character, never encountered in other species – a perspective that may be seen to preserve 'speciesist prejudices' coming increasingly under fire by animal studies scholars such as Kenneth Shapiro, and specialists in biosemiotics such as Wendy Wheeler and Jakob von Uexküll cited above, as well as scholars in various other fields now challenging what has come to be called *human exceptionalism*. Established views on humans and tourism, nonetheless, would seem to carry the full weight of common sense. Worker ants may be observed to put in many hours at the anthill over the course of their relatively short lives, but they are never seen to go on holiday. Butterflies, birds, fish and various other species are often observed to travel regularly to visit various places around the world throughout the year, but these journeys are never understood as recreational in character. Animals have on occasion been described as 'playful', sometimes controversially so (Bateson 1972), but never in the ways that tourists are. For better and for worse, only humans appear capable of embodying the character of the tourist. To suggest otherwise would be to invite accusations of extreme anthropomorphism.

The anthropology of tourism, until very recently, has generally accepted and reinforced this anthropocentric view of tourism.[2] It has approached tourism largely through the study of discourses and cultural performances that have been assumed to be exceptionally human in symbolic design even when they involve nonhumans (Graburn 1977; Bruner 1984, 1986, 2005; Pernecky 2012; Gmelch 2018).[3] The choice to work on the interface between animal studies and tourism studies, however, and to move towards producing a 'natureculture multispecies ethnography' or 'anthrozoography/ zooethnography' of tourism (Fuentes 2010, Haraway 2010, Kirksey and Helmreich 2010, Madden 2014), compels a closer critical examination of anthropocentric approaches. The interface allows us to ask: what might a zoocentric theory of tourism look like? What might its benefits be?

Such a theory, ideally, would move beyond a view of tourists as 'standing on the outside of animals looking in' (Madden 2014:286 referencing Fine 2004:642), and instead place human tourists and other animals on a more level interpretive 'humanatural' or 'ecocultural' playing field (Milstein and Krolokke 2012). It would take animals more seriously (DeGrazia 1996), developing a perspective on tourism that could recognise more wisely and inclusively the presence, life experience, history and significance of individual nonhuman animals as they factor into touristic relationships. In Raymond Madden's terms, it would, 'attempt, if possible, to "see through the eyes" of humans and animals' (2014:280). Such an assignment, however, seems fraught with the perils of unintended anthropomorphising of the most blatantly romanticising kind.

Taking my cue, nonetheless, from Jane Desmond's seminal work on bodies, animals, dance and tourism (1999, 2016), and from the work of the philosopher/psychologist, Vinciane Despret (2004, 2008, 2013), whose thinking about human and animal bodies permeates this chapter, I will argue that one way to successfully advance such a zoocentric theory of tourism is to approach the study of live tourist/animal interaction *choreographically*. The term itself may at first seem anthropomorphising, and, perhaps, unscientific as well. Curiously, however, researchers from varied disciplines, who have studied trans- and multispecies interactions in touristic contexts and elsewhere, have repeatedly arrived at the idea of choreography, as well as dance, in their attempts to characterise the encounters and relationships they seek to understand (Shapiro 1990, Smuts 2008, Parreñas 2012, Despret 2013, Keul 2013, Marchesini 2017, Overend and Lorimer 2018). Joining Desmond, who has taken dance as seriously as she has taken animals and tourism, I attempt in what follows to work with the concept of choreography less impressionistically, using it to develop what Vinciane Despret (2004:122, 130) has characterised as an 'anthropo-zoo-genetic' approach to live tourist/animal interactions. I hope to demonstrate that studying tourists and animals choreographically does not necessarily entail romantic anthropomorphising, nor is it inherently lacking in rigor. On the contrary, a choreographic approach can actually compel researchers to attend more carefully, and more '*care*-fully', to the actual graphic details of tourist/animal encounters, providing fresh insights and raising new questions about how these interactions might best be investigated and managed.

The idea of 'the choreographic' is itself not simple (Ness 1992, 1996, 1997, 2016, Noland and Ness 2008, Noland 2009). Its advantages are multiple, but three stand out for the purposes at hand. First, the concept orchestrates and provides analytical clarity to virtually all of the kinds of embodied interactive processes on which multispecies scholars have tended to focus: 'reciprocal interfacing', 'intra-acting', 'transcorporeal interconnecting', 'co-becoming', 'entangling', 'engaging', 'living with', 'encountering' and 'niche co-producing', to mention a few (Kirksey and Helmreich 2010). Among these, a choreographic perspective grants central significance to one mode of embodying interaction in particular, what Ray Acampora has identified as 'intersomaticity' (2006). In multispecies inquiry, this concept has been used to identify those aspects of embodied relationality that are neither exclusively human nor nonhuman in experiential character but which are shared transcorporeally.

Intersomaticity testifies to the fact that the bodies human beings themselves embody are more than simply human in form and function. They are also bodies that provide, as Kenneth Shapiro noted some time ago, the most basic common ground on which humans and nonhumans may gain access to one another, however imperfectly (1990:184). Intersomaticity, moreover, is also a phenomenon that choreographers and dancers cultivate in human-to-human creative work, relying on it to adapt, attune and anticipate the conduct of their fellow performers, teachers and directors – treating each other as animals, as it were (which, of course, they are). In this regard, a choreographic perspective compels attention be given to aspects of embodiment that are most helpful in developing a zoocentric awareness of tourist/animal interaction.

Second, a choreographic perspective views all animal bodies, human bodies included – and not excepting the researcher's own – as fundamentally interesting *instruments* of worldly discovery. Bodies, employed choreographically, disclose movingly what (and who) it is that matters to them in the spaces, places, environments and landscapes that are made available through them. In this instrumental, exploratory regard, a choreographic approach necessarily foregrounds aspects of embodied conduct that are intersomatically, co-performatively *semiotic* and communicative. It rejects the assumption that the embodied aspects of meaning-making are only the mute, 'nonverbal' partners or somatic accompaniments to verbally scripted performances. In a zoocentric orientation, it espouses a semiotic realism that understands nonhuman animals, like human ones, as intentionally and purposefully inhabiting meaningful worlds of signs – *umwelts*, in Jakob von Uexküll's term (1957) – meaning here defined in Gregory Bateson's biosemiotics terms as the relational patterning of 'differences that make a difference' (1972:453). As Desmond has noted, such orientations tend uncover 'deeply embedded nodes of meaning making' as they can be observed to signify in shared tourist/animal lifeworlds (2016:13, 237, 242).

Finally, and, perhaps, most beneficial for the study of tourist/animal encounters is that the bodies involved in any given encounter, understood choreographically, are never themselves considered to be just 'anybodies'. They are never just bodies that belong to what Despret has characterised as 'some sort of naïve state of nature' (2013:71). Rather, a choreographic perspective assumes what is often ignored by other perspectives on bodily conduct: that every animal, human or not, researcher or subject of research is unique as far as the cultivation of its given corporeal instrumentality is concerned. Intersomaticity is not learned in a day. It does not magically articulate itself into bodily performance by some miracle of nature. It takes years, even lifetimes, of trial and error study (not to mention love) to cultivate an intersomatically attuned body, even a naturally gifted one. Nobody ever emerged from the womb fully equipped to merit the label, 'ballerina' or 'ethologist' for that matter. The same might well be said of bodies that come to merit the label 'hunter', or 'race horse' or 'rescue dog' or 'ethnographer'. Bodies that are appreciated choreographically are always acknowledged as having had to learn whatever expertise they demonstrate in their own particular way, identifying and cultivating whatever gifts they may actually have been given over the course of their lives in relation to their particular worldly calling.

In sum, the great benefit of the choreographic perspective applied to the study of live tourist-animal encounters is that it makes it nearly impossible to fall into the traps of naïve spectatorship that are so hard to avoid from other approaches to bodily study, traps that enable moving living bodies to be seen as mindless, generic, automatons. It foregrounds the reality that no body, not a single one, human or not (scientist or artist or not), comes by their particular way of being with another body mechanically or by fiat. All living, moving bodies have a specific history of practice behind them. To study bodies choreographically is to become interested in processes that communicate unique qualities of cared-for-ness, mastery, gifted-ness, learning, intersomaticity and world-knowledge-making that are always manifest in any given live encounter. To the degree that the nature of these emergent processes can be articulated into a choreographic score, it is possible to learn more about what kind of shared human/nonhuman worlds tourism discloses, how it shapes the lives of all moving in and through them and how it may transform or be transformed in the future. No body, whatever species, is ever just an anybody, choreographically speaking.

The following case in point from a rock-climbing excursion undertaken in May 2010 in Yosemite National Park (YNP) serves as a point of departure for exploring the possibilities of developing a choreographic approach to the study of tourist/animal relations. The Yosemite landscape is a classic example of what Augustin Fuentes, drawing on Donna Harraway (2003), has identified as a 'naturalcultural contact zone' between humans and many species of animals (2010:600). The incident recounted below exemplifies one general kind of trans-species encounter that occurs regularly in Yosemite: unplanned, unsupervised and unwanted close encounters between California Black Bears (weighing on average 200 pounds) and tourists. It illustrates how human and bear bodies, observed choreographically, can serve as emergent, morally charged sites of touristic meaning-making and interpretation.

To stay as close as possible to the occurrence as it actually unfolded, it is presented here as it was initially articulated into field notes. To begin to shift away from the anthropocentric orientation the notes admittedly disclose, however, I would ask the reader to consider the following questions while reading: How do the bodies described move so as to make each other do things? When are the bodies moving like each other? When are they moving *with* each other but *not* like each other? At what moments does the narrative fail most markedly in providing the information that would make these questions answerable? (Figure 3.1).

Figure 3.1 Yosemite Falls of Yosemite National Park, May 2011.
Photo by Sally Ann Ness. [IMG 3574].

Case in point: a bear-climber interaction near Lower Yosemite Fall

Fieldnotes of May 16, 2010

We walked up from the [Valley Loop] trail together.[4] ... In less than 10 minutes, we arrived at the base of the climbs Ray had selected.

They were steep cracks running along a face that went up at least 3 pitches.[5] ...

We were by no means alone. At least two other parties were climbing the harder cracks and ours was the third rope that went up on the face. One other group turned out to be the Stanford Women's Climbing Club; ... They had been up for the weekend and were about to leave to go home.... They had some interesting equipment – in particular a rappelling device that seemed to support and feed the rope more elaborately. Trust Stanford, I thought, to have the latest gear....

Also at the base was a pair of men ...; they turned out to be from San Diego and Orange County; the one from San Diego was a wilderness medic who taught climbing and outdoor excursion classes ...; he was quite a clown and repeatedly joked with the Stanford women, who responded with good humour although no real encouragement ....

Ray started to lead the crack he'd selected for us.... I watched him climb carefully, trying to see how he did the pitch, noticing how he positioned his body when he made a move and trying to memorise it (Figure 3.2).

It was around the time that Ray finished preparing the ropes – Carol may have been climbing or he may still have been climbing, that I heard Dean's voice behind me say, 'Get up, Sally'. The tone was not joking. I got up immediately and Dean pointed up and behind me a few yards, where a large cinnamon-coloured bear had just poked its head around a small boulder. It seemed to be heading in our direction (Figure 3.3)

At first I dismissed it; people had begun to yell at it and I assumed it would wander away soon; it did not.

My next thought was the food in my backpack, which was now several feet uphill from where I'd come to stand. My camera was also there and my notebook; I was thinking about how to separate the food out so that, if the bear wanted that, I could let him take it and still save the other things; at this point, I thought my food might have been what attracted it to the group; a flash of guilt went through me with this thought, but I quickly corrected

Figure 3.2 Crack climbs near Lower Yosemite Fall.
Photo by Derick Fay. From the collection of Sally Ann Ness. [Image DSC02369].

Figure 3.3 The bear.
Photo by Derick Fay. From the Collection of Sally Ann Ness. [Image DSC02378].

(Continued)

myself; people always brought food along and there was nothing in the way of established practice that warned against it.

Several times the bear seemed to retreat, only to return; during these sequences, I managed to reach my bag and find the food, but then saw other people eating bread and cookies and realised I was not the only possible culprit.

Every time the bear reappeared, people got progressively more nervous; after a couple of returns, shouts were sent up to bring all the climbers down off the wall; one of the men made the comment, 'this could get ugly'. It seemed something of an overstatement to me, but I realised later that he was tethered to a climber and had no means of fleeing should the bear attack (see Figure 3.2); that would have made me much more nervous as well; still I remembered that no one had ever been killed by a bear attacking in YNP; I was perplexed and unhappy that the bear wasn't responding to the shouting, but not yet really frightened.

After several unsuccessful attempts to deter the bear's return, the clown finally came forward and asked in a loud voice, 'OK, do you really want to make him go away?' By this time, the climbers were down and all attention was focused on the bear situation; the group responded with 'Yes', so the man directed us all to stand in a big group (which we all did), wave our arms to look as big as possible and scream (which, again we all, to a person, did); we yelled loud and long; the bear just stood there looking at us, an annoyed expression on its face.

I don't know how I gathered this, but I had the clear impression that the bear, while it wasn't showing signs of attacking, was definitely not in a good mood; its manner of nosing around was somehow agitated; I wondered if it had already been sent off its course and was now again being disrupted.

When the shouting didn't produce any result, the group was somewhat at a loss; the bear had come up on its hind legs at one point, but was still being held at bay by the group's antics; it just wasn't showing any signs of leaving.

At this point, Ray had had enough; saying that he'd get rid of the bear, he picked up two large granite rocks went up to a few yards in front of the bear, took aim, and threw the first one so that it hit the bear squarely on the shoulder and clearly hurt it; the bear automatically turned away from the blow and for an instant looked like it was about to leave but then turned back towards Ray, who then threw the second rock at its face; this was enough for the bear, who then turned and went off into the bushes and disappeared from view. The group cheered at the result. I was thankful for Ray's presence.

It took another ten to fifteen minutes for the bear to actually disappear from the area. We saw it move down to the Valley trail, looking back in our direction frequently but staying away. It encountered a family with children in a stroller at the bottom of the trail. I watched in disbelief, standing beside one of the other climbers, while the family moved towards it to take a picture. There was no trouble however. Shortly thereafter, the bear walked on down the path in the direction of the Falls.... We heard no more about it for quite some time, although it did eventually come back around the corner. At this point, however, it stayed down by the trail and lumbered back in the direction of the Ahwahnee[6] and we did not encounter it again.

As all this was transpiring, the other parties of climbers prepared to leave. At first, I told Ray that I wasn't going to climb the route.... I honestly didn't want to be up there and have the bear come back, especially if it was going to be just the four of us there. I didn't think that three of us left at the bottom could defend ourselves, especially if Ray was the one up on the route. I felt responsible for the whole group's safety, and didn't want anything to happen on my watch. It seemed like my call and I determined to err on the side of safety. Ray accepted this decision without much affect, although he was plainly not as worried about the bear as I was.... After a few minutes, however, I changed my thinking. I realised that Ray would not be up on the route again. Some other climbers were showing up as well. I realised that, if we took down the climb, we'd have to live with a spoiled day for the rest of the evening.... Also, the climbers were not hurrying with their leave-taking. It looked now like it would take a while for everyone to actually pack up and leave.

So, I turned around [and] asked Ray, who was now standing right beside me, point blank, 'Can you handle the bear?' He looked me straight in the eye and said, 'yes', in a tone of blunt certainty. 'Alright', I said, 'let's do it'. 'Good', he said. I could tell his respect for me had increased with that decision.

Discussion

This, then, was a multispecies embodied encounter, occurring in a tourist destination famous for such encounters. It should be noted that YNP policies on how best to interact with bears have changed substantially over the history of the park, and this history was definitely present and actively shaping the interaction described. In the park's early years – the late nineteenth through the early twentieth centuries – attempts were made to condition bears to certain (assumed to be) controllable human-centred routines that visitors could enjoy as entertainment. This included feeding bears trash at certain designated areas. Bears were actually encouraged to become a 'commensal' or synanthropic species, rather than remain totally wild (O'Connor 2017:525). They retained a degree of freedom that differentiated them from fully domesticated animals but adapted partially to the park's increasingly anthropic environment through the consumption of provided food. In recent decades, however, park management policies have sought to 'decommensify' bears by separating the overlapping niches previously engineered, attempting to return the bears' diet and life style to something closer to what it was prior to the arrival of tourism. In 2010, for example, every visitor who checked into any accommodation anywhere in Yosemite Valley was required to read and sign a document that certified them as being 'bear aware'. Videos of bears breaking into cars or unsecured food storage containers played continually on monitors positioned over reception areas, making the experience of arriving at the park one in which images of bears performing harmful actions were foregrounded in visitors' awareness. Needless to say, bears were not represented zoocentrically (see Figure 3.4). Visitors were discouraged from seeking them out and were not given any information on how to interpret

Figure 3.4 Bear warning signage in Yosemite Valley, April 2008.
Photo by Sally Ann Ness. [Image 1421].

their behaviour should an encounter occur. On the contrary, park communications profiled bears as a dangerous and destructive species – anonymous, generic bodies with whom humans should avoid contact.

The decommensifying management strategies have enjoyed considerable success. Incidents of bear-related disturbances have reportedly dropped by over 90 percent in Yosemite in the last two decades. The bear's diet has becoming increasingly free of human-made food as well.[7] However, the effort to reverse the course of history has not met with the full approval of the bears themselves. They continue to exhibit commensal preferences, entering campgrounds in search of food, compelling park personnel to find ways to deter them from disturbing campers and damaging vehicles and belongings. The sound of rubber bullets fired in the middle of the night was still a regular part of the camping experience in Yosemite Valley in 2010, as was the sight of particularly unruly bears being trapped and transported to areas in the back country from which they hopefully would not return.[8]

This being the case, literally every visitor who spends any time in Yosemite Valley eventually ends up having at least one unsolicited, unwanted encounter with a bear, as well as a story to tell about it afterwards. The account above is typical of such stories in its anthropocentric orientation. As the narrative unfolds, 'we' humans are represented as succeeding in getting 'it' the bear to move on. The narrative consistently differentiates between a human 'we' and a nonhuman 'it', imposing what Vinciane Despret has termed the 'double we' of anthropocentrism: the two 'we's' in the claim, '"we" know that "we" are different' (2008:123). 'We' are reported as not being attacked, much less hurt, and 'it', the bear, is hurt, making the bear the inferior opponent in the conflict. While it might prove difficult to make a compelling case that this encounter demonstrated the superiority of 'our' tourist/human intelligence, since in the end it was basically brute force that deterred the bear; nonetheless, 'we' tourists did demonstrate a capacity for tool using (Flintstone-era though it was), and 'it' the bear lacked this capability, and, because the bear lacked this, 'it' was compelled to follow 'our' direction. The divisive we/it constructions justify and even celebrate acts of human-led aggression, prompting a very basic question from an animal studies perspective: is this really how 'we' want our relationships with nonhuman animals in national parks to be?

At the motivational core of such anthropocentric renderings of bear-tourist encounters in the Yosemite landscape lies 'deeply embedded' – to return to Desmond's phrasing – a key interest. It is an interest in validating a certain kind of oppositional relation between human beings and what can only be called *wild things*. The wild, the radically uncontrollably natural (the non-cultural, the non-domesticated, the nonhumanly influenced)[9] is represented over and over again as the 'not-us', the other that is destined to be vanquished, or at least disarmed, by 'us' – the civilised, intelligently controlling human/tourist. What continues to replay itself in Yosemite bear stories, including my own, is this narrative of human exceptionalism in relation to the wild. If the bear is sometimes portrayed as clever ('stealing' food, hiding its family, evading rangers' bullets and traps), it is only to show the human as ultimately more clever still. 'We' always get the better of 'it' one way or another. That success story renders sensible the very designating of a 'we' and an 'it'. If the bear were not represented as a radical other, the victories won would begin to ring hollow at best. 'Our' actions taken would have to be understood in relation to a being not wholly unlike us' – a being with cares, interests, attachments and ethical claims of its own.

It is, of course, tempting to move away from this issue by putting the term, 'wild', into scare quotes. Yosemite, after all, as indicated above, is anything but a pristine wilderness, untouched by humankind.[10] Truly wild areas are exceedingly difficult, if not actually impossible, to find anywhere on the planet anymore, and animal studies scholars, among many others, have repeatedly recognised this (Desmond 2017:507, Kalof 2017:16). The bear we encountered in all likelihood had had a tag placed in its ear by park rangers so that they could monitor its activities and exert some degree of control over its behaviour, including its eating habits (Madison 2008, Hopkins et al. 2014). Were it not for the efforts of the National Park Service to decommensify the bear population, the label 'wild' would seem to be a complete misnomer.

Nonetheless, the move to put 'wild' permanently into scare quotes would not itself make much, if any, progress towards achieving a zoocentric perspective on the tourist/animal relationship at issue nor would it serve to change the deeply embedded anthropocentrism motivating the narrative's production. In fact, it would serve to embed the relationship even more deeply inside a human-centred perspective. It would imply that there is no longer any wildness left anywhere in the Yosemite landscape, that wildness has become entirely human-designed and thus by definition non-existent or at best 'pseudo' in character. In this regard, there would be no possibility of authentically anthropo-zoo-genetic relations developing between human and nonhuman animals. Whatever might be marked as wildly non-human would always already have been over-determined by some human construction.

In contrast to such a constructionist move, a choreographic approach would not deny the zoocentric possibility that real wildness can be embodied, even in a landscape as carefully controlled as Yosemite's. It would posit that wildness is conceived and disclosed relationally via intersomatic processes rather than oppositionally constructed via exclusively human semiotic projections and assignments. It is, in fact, precisely when an intersomatic relation is itself established that a character such as wildness can be given the opportunity to come into existence, not only in nonhuman bodies but also in human/tourist ones as well – not symmetrically or identically, but in shared experiences of 'humanly uncontrollable-ness'. Similarly, all bodies involved, regardless of species, may also give each other the opportunity to become available to something other than absolute wildness, moving each other towards relatively domesticated, self-controlling, even touristifying relationships.

To illustrate this perspective, consider choreographically the lead climber, Ray's, series of movements attacking the bear. Were they *not* embodying lesser and lesser degrees of what would count in this context for a (tame) tourist persona as a direct consequence of the bear's responses? Certainly, Ray was departing from any sanctioned park policy for visitor/bear encounters in taking the actions that he did. He confided to me shortly after the incident that he had held back on confronting the bear longer than he would have done had he been acting alone because he expected that the other tourists present would strongly disapprove of his throwing rocks at the bear. He was surprised by their appreciative response. This was definitely 'off script' behaviour, unlike the group noise-making that the clowning medic had had us enact. That collective process had embodied conduct employed by generations of park visitors, although by 2010 it had become increasingly ineffective. Bears had learned to be more assertive in dealing with tourist food supplies by this time. Ray, for his part, had moved towards a more brutal, less humane form of interaction, one that took a form prompted, one might even say disclosed in Despret's terminology, directly by the behaviour the bear was presenting in the interaction itself. This behaviour had communicated to Ray a sense of what was needed to bring about the change desired in the bear's behaviour. Ray's experiment-in-action was not inspired by empathising with the bear but, rather, by attuning to the bear's responses. He learned in so doing what was needed to make the bear leave the area.

Consider the bear's movements choreographically as well. Was it not the bear who demonstrated repeatedly the greatest degree of self-controlled understanding in the encounter, despite being provoked more and more aggressively? While the entire sequence of human behaviour would seem to illustrate a progression towards less and less thoughtful forms of action, the bear, on the other hand, though stubbornly uncooperative, remained stable, never 'losing its head'. The bear's movements demonstrated a clear intention to progress along a remembered route, probably one (it was later learned) that would have led her to reunite with her children in an area on the other side of the Valley. The bear accurately understood the staged noise-making presented to her as non-aggressive behaviour, getting the message that it was a difference that made no difference to her as far as her safety and given interests were concerned. Ultimately, the bear did learn that her way was blocked by bodies who could and would become injurious. Having learned this, the bear did not react in rage, but instead found another way to continue to pursue the activity that had been her interest before the encounter. In all of these respects, the bear's conduct demonstrated a capacity for increasing self-control, interpretive acuity and adaptive decision-making, none of which qualify as hallmark features of 'the wild', humanly conceived. Rather, it presented character traits more akin to those typically identified anthropocentrically with humans/tourists. Again, to adopt Vinciane Despret's terms, the bear performed its acquired expertise of sharing experience with humans, not by turning into a human (anthropomorphising itself), but by articulating movingly a new degree of 'with-ness' via relating intelligently to humans, embodying more of a humans-with-bear bodily identity than its environment had previously disposed it to assume (2004:131).

In sum, all of the bodies involved in this encounter can be observed to have contributed creatively to the unfolding touristic score that eventually developed. All demonstrated the capacity to bring varying degrees of wildness into corporeal existence as well as various contrasting characters. All co-enacted as an ensemble the series of transformations that took place. Despite the 'we/it' constructions employed in the field notes, the movements and actions performed did not, when observed closely, conform to the we/it, subject/object, agent/patient grammatical encodings chosen to represent the bodies involved. The collective encounter would more accurately have been represented choreographically (and zoocentrically) as an *intersubjective* encounter.[11]

Conclusion

Incidents such as the one described above, when articulated choreographically, tend to re-position the nonhumans involved in them in one critically important way. To use Desmond's term, they 'ensubjectify' nonhuman participants, granting subjectivity if not personality to them by identifying in their performance the embodiment of individuating, agentive and affective characteristics that endow them with the ability to act on the world, to exist in self-(other)self relationships coherently, and to make decisions from which they learn and grow in understanding (2016:243).[12] The attribution of subjectivity, Desmond argues, is crucial in shifting from an anthropocentric to a zoocentric perspective (2016:17). It reframes the nonhuman bodies as individual rather anonymous beings and as having lives and life histories that are of social and political value, rather than being characterised as easily 'killable' natural 'resources' (Haraway 2008, Bear and Eden 2011:302), 'animated hides' (Keul 2013:932) or insignificant 'props' in some human drama (Madden 2014:279).

Adopting what I have been calling a choreographic perspective is key to achieving such an ensubjectifying shift. It is this perspective that grants recognition to that which is characteristically subject-producing in humans but not *exclusively* so, to those embodied, significant movements of human (inter)subjectivity and intersomaticity that are relatable to and shared with nonhuman beings. As Vinciane Despret has characterised it, such a perspective redistributes 'the signs that mark the world and that mark the subject', in a way that gives nonhuman bodies 'a chance to be interesting and to articulate other things' besides what anthropomorphic projecting, even in its most empathetic forms, could anticipate and comprehend (2004:125, 128). Rather than isolating humans into a separate (and superior) class of touristic 'embodiers' existing apart from and over all other bodies encountered, the approach foregrounds the living connections and coordinated relationality that the diverse bodies who share Yosemite's environments, however temporarily, can be observed to co-create, co-negotiate, co-perform and even co-interpret through kinesthetically attuned coordinations, mindfully, if not always harmoniously or empathetically embodied.

Looking back, it occurs to me that I may have experienced in my own final decision-making process regarding staying on to climb an acceptance of living with such potentially co-present, co-constituted, not-not-wild touristic bodies – one being the bear and, at the same time, one being myself. Perhaps, there was yet another one in Ray as well. The list could go on. It was acceptance – that change in my tolerance for being disposed towards a greater degree of wildness in bodily co-relating – that Ray seemed to find admirable. In doing so, we entered into a dance-like figure, not only with each other but also with the bear, wherever it had gone to, a figure of increasingly trusting co-action, increasingly responsive, increasingly experimental, increasingly attuned, and increasingly, caringly uncontrolling. Who would become the tamer and who the tamed? Who the wilder still? Could we simply live and let live in closer proximity than had previously been conceivable, knowing we had something now just beginning to approach a mutual understanding of each other's behaviour? These questions had now entered the realm of the ask-able. The real possibilities they put into play were held in a shared balance, ready to change with each new move in the encounter. On we went. In the Yosemite landscape, because it is so heavily controlled to begin with, such dance-like movements of relationality can be experienced as profoundly meaningful, not only for tourist bodies but also for those of animals as well.

Notes

1 Grateful acknowledgement is due to Jonathan Osborn, who encouraged me to present a paper on this topic for a session on animals and humans he organised for the 2016 CORD/SDHS joint conference that served as the basis for this essay and who read and commented on earlier drafts of it. Thanks also Jane Desmond and Barbara Sellers Young for their helpful responses to that paper.
2 See Kalof (2017) and Carr (2009) on the recent growth of interest in animals in tourism studies. On the recent rapid growth of interest in human-animal relations and the rise of 'multispecies ethnography', see Shapiro and DeMello (2010), Kirksey and Helmreich (2010).
3 Dashper (2018) reports a similarly anthropocentric bias for leisure studies.
4 'We' were a party of four: myself, our lead climber 'Ray' (pseudonym) was in charge of selecting climbs and setting up ropes; 'Carol' (pseudonym) was a very experienced climber in her twenties, and 'Dean' (pseudonym) was a less experienced climber in his forties.
5 A 'pitch' is a distance of approximately one rope-length, in this case, around twenty-five meters.
6 The Ahwahnee Hotel (now The Majestic Yosemite Hotel) is the oldest, most expensive hotel located in Yosemite Valley.

7 Reported on the National Park Service Yosemite National Park web page, 'Bear Facts' www.nps.gov/yose/planyourvisit/bearfacts.htm

8 For more information on the management of the 300–500 Black Bears currently inhabiting Yosemite National Park, visit the Park's website: www.nps.gov/yose/learn/nature/bears.htm, the 'Bear Team Blog', www.nps.gov/yose/blogs/bearteam.htm, and the 'Bear Facts' incident report cite for the park at: www.nps.gov/yose/planyourvisit/bearfacts.htm. For information on the changing history of bear/human interactions see Graber and White (1978), Greene (1987), and Madison (2008).

9 Desmond (2017:507) provides a definition of the wild as 'a place outside human influence', aligning her work with Rebecca Cassidy (2007).

10 For more on the construction of wilderness in Yosemite and its consequences for tourists, see Ness (2016).

11 See Michael Jackson's discussion of intersubjectivity for a more detailed articulation of the theory of intersubjectivity employed here (1998). See also Madden (2014:285) and Despret (2008:135).

12 On the role of affect in producing subjectivity, see also Irvine (2004) and Rutherford (2012, cited in Madden 2014:290).

References

Acampora, R. R. (2006) *Corporal Compassion: Animal Ethics and Philosophy of Body.* Pittsburgh, PA: University of Pittsburgh Press.

Bateson, G. (1972) *Steps to an Ecology of Mind.* New York: Basic Books.

Bear, C. and Eden, S. (2011) Thinking like a fish? Engaging with nonhuman difference through recreational angling. *Environment and Planning D: Society and Space*, 29: 336–352.

Bruner, E. M. (1984) Introduction, in E. M. Bruner (ed.) *Text, Play, and Story; The Construction and Reconstruction of Self and Society.* Prospect Heights, IL: Waveland Press, pp. 3–30.

Bruner, E. M. (1986) Ethnography as narrative, in V. Turner and E. M. Bruner (eds.) *The Anthropology of Experience.* Urbana: University of Illinois Press, pp. 139–155.

Bruner, E. M. (2005) *Culture on Tour; Ethnographies of Travel.* Chicago, IL: University of Chicago Press.

Carr, N. (2009) Animals in the tourism and leisure experience. *Current Issues in Tourism*, 12(5–6): 409–411.

Cassidy, R. (2007) Introduction, in R. Cassidy and M. Mullin (eds.) *Where the Wild Things are Now: Domestication Reconsidered.* New York: Berg Publishers, pp. 1–25.

Dashpur, K. (2018) Moving beyond anthropocentrism in leisure research: Multispecies perspectives. *Annals of Leisure Research*, doi: 10.1080/11745398.2018.1478738.

DeGrazia, D. (1996). *Taking Animals Seriously: Mental Life and Moral Status.* Cambridge, MA: Harvard University Press.

Desmond, J. C. (1999) *Staging Tourism; Bodies on Display from Waikiki to Sea World.* Chicago, IL: University of Chicago Press.

Desmond, J. C. (2016) *Displaying Death and Animating Life; Human-Animal Relations in Art, Science, and Everyday Life.* Chicago, IL: University of Chicago Press.

Desmond, J. C. (2017) Staging privilege, proximity, and "Extreme Animal Tourism," in L. Kalof (ed.) *The Oxford Handbook of Animal Studies.* Oxford: Oxford University Press, pp. 506–524.

Despret, V. (2004) The body we care for: Figures of anthropo-zoo-genesis. *Body & Society,* 10(2–3): 111–134.

Despret, V. (2008) The becomings of subjectivity in animal worlds. *Subjectivity*, 23: 123–139.

Despret, V. (2013) Responding bodies and partial affinities in human-animal worlds. *Theory Culture & Society*, 30(7/8): 51–76.

Fine, G. (2004) Review essay. Rats and cats. *Journal of Contemporary Ethnography*, 33(5): 638–644.

Fuentes, A. (2010) Naturalcultural encounters in Bali: Monkeys, temples, tourists, and ethnoprimatology. *Cultural Anthropology*, 23(4): 600–624.

Gmelch, S. B. (Ed.) (2018) *Tourists and Tourism*. Longrove, IL: Waveland Press.

Graber D. M. and White M. (1978) Management of black bears and humans in Yosemite National Park. *Transactions--The Western Section of the Wildlife Society*, 14: 42–51.

Graburn, N. (1977) Tourism the sacred journey, in V. Smith (ed.) *Hosts and Guests; The Anthropology of Tourism*. Philadelphia: University of Pennsylvania Press, pp. 17–31.

Greene L. W. (1987) *Yosemite: The Park and Its Resources – A History of the Discovery, Management, and Physical Development of Yosemite National Park, California*. Historic Resource Study. Denver, CO: US Department of the Interior, National Park Service.

Haraway, D. (2003) *A Companion Species Manifesto: Dogs, People, and Significant Otherness*. Chicago, IL: Prickly Paradigm Press.

Haraway, D. (2008) *When Species Meet*. Minneapolis: University of Minnesota Press.

Haraway, D. (2010) Staying with the trouble: Xenoecologies of home for companions in the contact zones. David Schneider Memorial Lecture at Meetings of the Society for Cultural Anthropology, Santa Fe, New Mexico, May 7.

Hopkins, J. B., Koch, P. L., Ferguson, J. M. and Kalinowski, S. T (2014) The changing anthropogenic diets of American black bears over the past century in Yosemite National Park. *Frontiers in Ecology and the Environment*, 12(2): 107–114.

Irvine, L. (2004) A model of animal selfhood: Expanding interactionist possibilities. *Symbolic Interaction*, 27: 3–21.

Jackson, M. (1998) *Minima Ethnographica: Intersubjectivity and the Anthropological Project*. Chicago, IL: The University of Chicago Press.

Kalof, L. (2017) Introduction, in L. Kalof (ed.) *The Oxford Handbook of Animal Studies*. Oxford: Oxford University Press, pp. 1–21.

Keul, A. (2013) Embodied encounters between humans and gators. *Social and Cultural Geography*, 14(8): 930–953.

Kirksey, S. and Helmreich, S. (2010) The emergence of multispecies ethnography. *Cultural Anthropology*, 25(4): 546–576.

Madden, R. (2014) Animals and the limits of ethnography. *Anthrozoos*, 27(2): 279–293.

Madison, J. (2008) Yosemite National Park: The continuous evolution of human-black bear conflict management. *Human-Wildlife Conflicts*, 2(2): 160–167.

Marchesini, R. (2017). *Over the Human; Post-Humanism and the Concept of Animal Epiphany*. Cham: Springer International Publishing.

Milstein, T. and Krolokke, C. (2012) Transcorporeal tourism: Whales, fetuses, and the rupturing and reinscribing of cultural constraints. *Environmental Communication*, 6(1): 82–100.

Ness, S.A. (1992) *Body, Movement, and Culture; Kinesthetic Symbolism in a Philippine Community*. Philadelphia: University of Pennsylvania Press.

Ness, S. A. (1996) Dancing in the field; notes from memory, in, S. Foster (ed.) *Corporealities*. London: Routledge, pp. 129–154.

Ness, S. A. (1997) Originality in the postcolony; choreographing the neo-ethnic body in Philippine Dance. *Cultural Anthropology,* 12(1): 64–108.

Ness, S. A. (2016) *Choreographies of Landscape; Signs of Performance in Yosemite National Park.* New York: Berghahn Books.

Noland, C. (2009) *Agency & Embodiment; Performing Gestures/Producing Culture.* Cambridge, MA: Harvard University Press.

Noland, C. and Ness, S.A. (Eds.) (2008) *Migrations of Gesture: Dance, Art, and Film.* Minneapolis: University of Minnesota Press.

O'Connor, T. (2017) Commensal species, in L. Kalof (ed.) *The Oxford Handbook of Animal Studies.* Oxford: Oxford University Press, pp. 525–541.

Overend, D. and Lorimer, J. (2018) Wild performatives: Experiments in rewilding at the Knepp Wildland Project. *GeoHumanities,* 00: 1–16, doi: 10.1080/2373566X. 2018.1478742.

Parreñas, R. (2012) Producing affect: Transnational volunteerism in a Malaysian rehabilitation center. *American Ethnologist,* 39(4): 673–687.

Pernecky, T. (2012) Constructionism: Critical pointers for tourism studies. *Annals of Tourism Research,* 39(2): 1116–1137.

Rutherford D. (2012) Commentary: What affect produces. *American Ethnologist,* 39(4): 688–691.

Shapiro, K. (1990) Understanding dogs through kinesthetic empathy, social construction, and history. *Anthrozoös,* 3(3): 184–195.

Shapiro, K. and DeMello, M. (2010) The state of human-animal studies. *Society and Animals,* 18: 307–318.

Smuts, B. (2008) Embodied communication in non-human animals, in A. Fogel et al. (eds), *Human Development in the Twenty-First Century.* Cambridge: Cambridge University Press, pp. 136–146.

Uexküll, J. von (1957) A stroll through the worlds of animals and men: A picture book of invisible worlds, in J. C. H. Schiller (ed.), *Instinctive Behavior: The Development of a Modern Concept.* New York: International Universities Press, pp. 5–80.

Wheeler, W. (2016) *Expecting the Earth: Life/Culture/Biosemiotics.* London: Lawrence & Wishart.

4 Queer bodies and the construction of tourism destination space

Bradley Rink

Introduction: queering Cape Town with the *Pink Map*

Tourist maps such as Cape Town's *Pink Map* can be considered a form of discursive archive that allows scholars a glimpse into the shaping of space. Cartographers seek to 'ground truth' their data by ensuring that the story told through the map – as displayed by symbols, landmarks and physical features – is reflected in the reality on the ground. When applied to tourist maps, cartography serves as a means of defining destination space (Farías 2011) not only in the ways that they mediate way finding and consumption but also as artefacts of tourism destinations and the particular relationships that tourists have with them. In this vein, the archive of the *Pink Map* demonstrates the trends taking place within the city it is meant to portray. The archive of tourist destination space provided by the *Pink Map* reveals that consumption is increasingly depicted as a necessary pathway to citizenship and wellness. It also demonstrates how the body of the queer tourist might potentially engage with other bodies, things and activities. The *Map* provides a touristic guide to an unfamiliar place and ways of living. In its attempt to provide lesbian, gay, bisexual and transgender (LGBT) tourists with a curated reading of the 'pink' touristic landscape of Cape Town, the *Pink Map* also demonstrates the role of embodiment in tourism as the sexualised body serves as a surrogate for the city it is meant to cartographically depict. A discursive analysis of the *Map's* contents in the form of text, image and embodied cartography demonstrates the limited range of bodily representation of queerness, and how sexually 'othered' bodies are used to shape destination space.

With the recognition that as the editors note in the introduction 'embodiment is a way of understanding culture and the self in relation to practices of movement, thinking and sensing' (p. 3), the principle aim of this chapter is to explore how queer[1] bodies are situated amongst a constellation of tourist bodies within Cape Town's *Pink Map* tourist map over the course of its publication. More than simply serving as the container of the tourist subject, the body is represented in the *Pink Map*, on the one hand, as the site of tourism that attracts tourists for pleasure and leisure activities, and, on the other hand, the body serves as a representation of destination space. Through a discursive analysis of the *Map's* contents in the form of text, image and embodied cartography, I intend to take seriously Veijola and Jokinen's (1994) call to engage with '...embodiment, radical otherness, multiplicity of differences, sex and sexuality in tourism' (1994:129) in order to demonstrate how the embodiment of sexual 'others' is used to depict the urban landscape of Cape Town for aesthetic and material tourist consumption. Analysis of the results highlights the need to take seriously the role of other bodies (Johnston 2001) and embodiment itself in the socio-cultural construction of tourism destination space.

Bounding the *Pink Map*: queer tourist bodies and destination space

In my unfolding of the *Pink Map*, I frame the discourse of pleasure and leisure within literatures that focus on the body-tourism nexus of the LGBT – frequently referred to as 'pink' – tourism niche and notions of destination space. Taken together, this framework bounds the understanding of the *Pink Map* as a discursive archive in which queer bodies are represented, consumed and used to shape tourism destination space using the example of Cape Town, South Africa.

Queer bodies

Queer bodies have been historically attendant with 'place', where corporeal geographies are at the heart of understanding intersections of sex, gender, identity and space (Bell et al. 1994). Attentiveness to the embodied nexus of gender, place and culture can be read across feminist and post-structuralist approaches to geographical enquiry as well as the social sciences more broadly (Longhurst and Johnston 2014). Since the nineteenth century, queer bodies have become firmly inscribed onto the touristic landscapes of Mediterranean Europe and North Africa, as the body and sexuality were central to the attraction of gay male tourists to such destinations (Aldrich 1993, Waitt and Markwell 2006, Visser 2014). It is within the context of seeking pleasure/leisure that gay men in nineteenth-century Europe were drawn to the Mediterranean and the Orient by the seductive qualities of the 'sociospatial discourses circulating in the visual and written arts' (Waitt and Markwell 2006:41) and homoerotic orientalist perspectives of those bodies that they might encounter once there (Boone 2014). Such queer quests for mostly white European men were seen as liberating in an age of spatially limited and socially constrained same-sex desire. These journeys were not only typical of the emergent leisure class of the era (Veblen 2009 [1899]) but they were also part of the north-to-south itinerary of homosexual desire that is part of European gay history (Aldrich 1993:4).

The allure for European men of the warmer and seemingly more permissive cultures of the Mediterranean and North Africa was an embodied one, when gay men were attracted as Waitt and Markwell (2006) argue, by mythical homosexual cultures and unbridled sexualities. The importance of the sexualised body thus helped to inscribe such places with meanings filled with desire, pleasure and sexual abandon. Homoerotic orientalism thus relied on sexually othered, racially othered and culturally othered bodies in order to shape tourism geographies of the Mediterranean and the Orient. Bodies and the places in which they were situated become framed as one and the same. The sexualised body thus provides a direct representation of place and helps to signal a queer corporeal turn in tourism studies.

Queer tourist bodies

In the present, gay male tourism in particular is still defined in relation to the body and sex (Waitt and Markwell 2006:27). Waitt and Markwell further argue within the context of tourism and leisure pursuits, '[t]he body is implicated in the pleasures of parades, dance parties, going to the beach, and sexual activity' (2006:27). It is the opportunity for sexual contact, and thus the consumption of the other bodies that help to define place in the context of contemporary gay tourism. In this way, seeking pleasure through the body is part of the liminal experience of tourism (Inglis 2000). Yet, as Clift and Forrest (1999) argue, few studies have actually examined the sexual behaviour of gay men in a tourism setting. In spite of the prominent connections between gay males and tourism, the focus of much of the literature on queer tourist bodies is still implicated in occluding questions of gender and race (Puar 2002). Such gaps, however, do not nullify the power of the tourist imagination in shaping tourism destinations through sexuality and the body. It is not simply the actual contact and the active participation in encounters with other bodies that help to shape tourism destinations, it is also through the imagination of such places where sexuality and the body are critical. As Waitt and Markwell (2006) demonstrate, '...through imagining gay tourism destinations, places serve as contexts in relationship to a priori assumptions about how sexualities, gender, class, and age are inscribed onto the body' (2006:23).

While the north-to-south trajectory of homosexual desire is clearly seen from a gay male European point of view, other perspectives of queer bodies receive less academic attention. Through the framing of homosexual tourism as a white gay male pursuit, other queer bodies are silenced or made invisible (Puar 2002). Although the birth of gay tourism is situated in Europe, the growth and development into the niche known as 'pink tourism' can be seen throughout the world, and specifically in the global South where racially othered and culturally othered queer bodies form part of the tourism attraction. While a growing consciousness of tourism and leisure activities in the Mediterranean and the Orient signals the recognition of queer bodies and same-sex desire, it is not until the late twentieth century when the 'pink' tourism niche begins to grow elsewhere along with mass tourism. Amongst the earliest tourism scholars to focus their attention on tourism within a modern homosexual population were Clift and Forrest (1999) who sought to understand more about the tourist destinations and holiday motivations of gay men using a sample of respondents from the United Kingdom. In his broad review of gay and lesbian tourism practices, Visser (2014) concludes that the discourse of this tourist segment remains framed by the need to be gay 'elsewhere', in spite of the fact that contemporary social and legal environments in many tourism generating regions remain more liberal and accepting than the destinations that attract queer tourists. Queer tourist bodies and their quests for liminality in tourism thus go hand-in-hand.

As Visser (2014) argues, the arc of social change across the world has had an impact on the growth and development of pink tourism globally. Nowhere is the shift as radical as it has been in South Africa between the late twentieth and early twenty-first centuries where the end of Apartheid signalled not only a new political dispensation but also the opening of South Africa to the economic, cultural and geographical changes that come with tourism growth (Dodson 2000). As Dodson further explains, 'The end of apartheid has brought about social and economic freedoms that allow South Africans of all races to avail themselves of local leisure, tourism and consumption opportunities from which they were previously excluded' (Dodson 2000:419).

South Africa's entrance to local and global tourism consumption also reframed how different racialised and sexualised bodies were represented and positioned amongst a constellation of tourist bodies. As the 'new' South Africa emerged from apartheid, queer liberation struggles also began to bear fruit. In representing such victories, it was the bodies of white, gay, urban men who represented progress. Such representation is typical according to Hoad (1999), who notes that,

> Differently classed and gendered national subjects are required to embody these diverging spaces in the emerging nation, where it is usually, but not always, the case that women and rural populations are assigned the representational task of tradition and men, particularly urban men, are seen to embody progress into modernity.
>
> (Hoad 1999:565)

Thus, the gay, male urban body provides an opportunity for South Africa to demonstrate its emergence onto the world stage through tourism and leisure-based consumption which, as Puar (2002) concludes, is an 'ironic marker of an elitist cosmopolitan mobility' made possible through purchasing power of limited range of tourist bodies (2002:942). Yet, the marketing of predominantly gay male 'p/leisure space' in Cape Town, as Elder (2004) points out, continues to articulate limited forms of same-sex desire. Scholars from South Africa (Visser 2002, 2003a, 2003b, 2010, Elder 2004, Rink 2008, 2013) have examined the ways that 'pink' tourism has developed within such narrow terms in the context of Cape Town. These authors contribute to the understanding of embodied experience of tourism and how it reflects upon space and place, at the same time they highlight the androphilic bias of pink tourism which frequently silences queer bodies who are not white, male and able-bodied.

Representing Cape Town, the *Pink Map* must therefore be read within the context of pink tourism in the global South at the turn of the twenty-first century. Although tourism amongst queer individuals has risen throughout the twentieth century, Puar (2002) cautions against conflating economic access to tourism with social progress. As she notes,

> Economic access that is increasingly available to gay and lesbian consumers – often mistaken for "progress" and social acceptance – comes at the cost of more insidious gatekeeping of those who cannot/do not fit into the "good homosexual" image, something made very clear by advertisements from national tourist boards targeting wealthy, white and predominately male queer consumers.
>
> (2002:942–943)

Until recently, there have been few studies within the scholarship of tourism that have focused on the experience of other queer bodies in tourism such as lesbian, bisexual or transgender tourists. Berdychevsky et al. (2013, 2016) are exceptions in their investigations of the embodied and sexualised (2013) experience of female-focused queer tourism. A similar and critical departure from the gay male tourism discourse comes from Ocha and Earth (2012) who explore the experience of transgender sex workers within the sex tourism industry in Thailand. Their analysis complicates the static gender and sexual identities within the context of tourism, and sheds light on the importance of embodiment as a framework for understanding the liminal experiences of the tourist body.

Tourist maps and destination space

The concept of tourism destination space as articulated through tourist maps is discussed by Farías (2011) who argues that tourist maps can also be understood as 'icons' of destination space, by virtue of the fact that the 'maps themselves are taken with tourists upon their return home as souvenirs or mementos' (2011:400). Beyond their role as an artefact of tourism destinations, Farías argues that tourist maps have a more generative and transformative capacity. He asserts that such maps 'perform generative operations that produce tourist spatial extensions' (ibid). These extensions may also be corporeal. Following Nash (1996), the fleshy representation of the body and '...the intimate tactile presence of the body and implicit presence of desire and sexual pleasure [finds itself]...in attachment to a national landscape and cultural traditions' (1996:153). In this way, the tourist, the map and the place merge into one. Thus, in reading the *Pink Map*, the flesh of the body and the landscape of the city become one.

Reading the *Pink Map*

As a geographer, my approach to understanding the *Pink Map* is spatial and thus situated in particular ways. Therefore, the 'situation' presented by the cartography, visual imagery and text of the *Pink Map* is awash with discourses of many kinds. As a result, I utilise Adele Clarke's (2005) Situational Analysis in order to 'draw together studies of discourse and agency, action and structure, image, text and context, history and the present moment to analyse complex situations of inquiry broadly conceived' (2005:xxii). Situational Analysis is more than just a reading of various actors; it allows for the representation of heterogeneity of perspective and thus an understanding of place beyond the assumption of the binary. This study involves 'multisite research' (Clarke 2005:146) in that I have combined multiple forms of data from the 'situation' of the *Pink Maps* as I read them across sixteen editions from 1999 to 2014. These data points come in the form of both narrative and visual texts which constitute or are consequential (Clarke 2005:145). Narrative and visual texts act to convey messages about Cape Town as a place, and the presumed identities and/or positions of those who traverse and consume its queer terrain. Taken together, I wish to examine how these three streams of discourse act to infer, confer, implore and impart/extract meaning to/from the 'place' that is Cape Town.

Coming out: emergence of the *Pink Map*

In parallel with the metaphorical journey of homosexuals as they come out of the closet, the *Pink Map* came 'out' in 1999 as an extension of publisher Philip Todres' focus on special interest touristic maps. It is no coincidence, therefore, that the *Pink Map* emerged onto Cape Town's touristic landscape along with the growth of South Africa's international tourism in the post-1994 environment as discussed by Dodson (2000). The development and growth of a visible and vibrant – albeit decidedly gay/male-centric – queer tourism sector in Cape Town coincided with popular annual events such as the Mother City Queer Projects (MCQP) queer costume party, with the development of gay-owned and focused businesses concentrating in Cape Town's De Waterkant enclave (Rink 2016). While Cape Town Tourism officials and the 1999 version of the *Pink Map* itself credit the MCQP party for putting '…Cape Town on the international Gay Culture Map [sic]' (*Pink Map* 1999), the conjunction of such events along with growing social acceptance of some queer individuals (Tucker 2009), and the city's desire to be seen as a gay-friendly tourist destination (Visser 2003b) meant that it was time for the *Pink Map* to 'come out of the closet' in a similar metaphorical journey of self-discovery experienced by many queer individuals. Although the *Pink Map* is not responsible for metaphorically bringing queer Cape Town out of the closet, at the very least it offered broader visibility to the existence of queer leisure spaces within South Africa's 'Mother City'.

The *Map* is a free publication that relies on revenue from the advertisers and service providers listed within its pages. As a tool for the tourism industry and tourists alike, the *Pink Map* implicitly posits consumption as its central purpose. It is distributed through Cape Town Tourism information kiosks, hotels, guesthouses, clubs, bars and restaurants. More than simply a commercial venture, however, the *Map* also provides relevant information to queer communities that it is intended to serve. That includes information such as the gay, lesbian and bisexual helplines, HIV/AIDS support groups and gay-friendly places of worship. A thinly veiled subtext of the *Pink Map* is the promise to differentiate homosexual space from the 'ambient heterosexual' (Murray 1995), presumably in order to ensure a pleasant stay by filtering out the queer landscape from all the rest (Elder 2004).

Over the course of sixteen editions between 1999 and 2014, the *Pink Map* has located queer tourism amenities at the same time it has charted the ebb and flow of queer desire and belonging. The colourful and often flamboyant cover images feature a variety of queer bodies including, amongst others: an ostentatious peacock with a crest of pink triangle (1999) – one of only two instances of nonhuman animal bodies on the cover; a drag queen holding a pink globe in her/his hand (2000); a chiselled model gazing at his netherregions (2001); a naked, bald but otherwise hirsute chef holding a large fish (2002); and revellers at the aforementioned MCQP costume party (2006). As it locates and catalogues the latest gay-exclusive guesthouses, male steam baths, a host of bars and clubs, and services intended for the queer community and visitors to Cape Town, the *Pink Map* not only helps to define the pink cartographic landscape but also traces the role of queer bodies and the embodied performance of sexuality within the city. Through the uneven terrain of representation that results a range of queer bodies are made invisible, including those of lesbians, bisexuals and transgendered persons. Through its representation of some bodies over others, the *Pink Map* plays an active role in the constitution of queer 'destination space' (Farías 2011).

Queer bodies in the *Pink Map*

Bodies that are evidenced both visually and through textual representations in the *Pink Map* exemplify how the body is a site of tourist consumption and a site of regulation. The queer body as depicted in the *Map* is a site, whereby individuals pursue embodied desire and seek sexual encounters to underpin their own identities. In addition to that, the *Map* evidences consumption *for* the body, where a global gay ideal encourages corporeal self-discipline in bodily regimes.

The body as a site of consumption

In its central role that caters for the needs of tourists, the *Pink Map* organises its listings according to various categories that in some way all involve bodily performance or function that are associated with consumption. These include the following: 'Events' such as the MCQP where a visitor will come into contact with other bodies; 'Cafes & Restaurants' where feeding of the body takes place; 'Shopping' which becomes 'Retail therapy' from the 2006 edition onward; 'Steam baths' which lists a handful of male-only sites of cruising, sexual encounter and relaxation; 'Wildside' which is a category that encompasses male-to-male massage parlours and escort services; 'Adult shops' that sell magazines, videos and sex toys for embodied pleasures; 'Travel Information' where tourists can seek further advice on other consumptive pursuits during their visit; 'Health & grooming' where bodily regimes may be satisfied; 'Accommodation' for listings of places to rest weary bodies; and a range of other categories that come and go across the editions. All, however, support the needs of the tourist and their embodied experience of place.

The inaugural (1999) edition of the *Pink Map* featured a leopard-skin motif serving both as a border to the pages but also a unifying theme to a broader safari-inspired design. The savage and animal-like qualities of the human bodies within this edition are remarkable. Bodies of men – black, white and shades in-between – are seen mingling seductively together: shirtless and gym-toned on the dance floor of 'Bronx Action Bar'; twisted in an erotic masseur and client entanglement at 'Discreet M2M Studio'; enjoying a relaxed drink at 'Domino's Bar'; and sharing a naked dip in the hot tub at 'Hot House', described as 'the latest addition to Cape Town's thriving gay culture' (*Pink Map* 1999). Nudity as displayed in the listing of the Hot House is emblematic of the body as a site of consumption of other bodies. Through the act of stripping bare in the context of a male-only steam bath, consumption is focused on the body itself – in this case the idealised, muscular gay male body. These elements are evident in the *Pink Map* where a naked black man fixes his gaze on the two white men submerged in the water. Although their gazes do not seem to meet in the image, the scene is framed by an aura of masculine desire. It is also ironically one of the rare images in the *Pink Map* where men of different races are positioned in a sexually charged position. Through its use of idealised bodily imagery, this and other early editions of the *Pink Map* mark diffusion of queer globalisation to Cape Town, and touristic scene-setting for the 'global gay' that Oswin (2006) critiques as a product of dominant western ideals of gayness.

The western ideal is firmly situated in the bodies of models and patrons visible throughout the *Maps*. The 2003 edition features images of no less than six underwear-clad or semi-nude men, all with toned white bodies, muscular physiques, and in the two cases where their faces are visible, a come-hither grin. In the same edition, the Hothouse and Steamers gay steam bath advertise their extended hours during the peak tourist/holiday season, at the latter where 'the ultimate cruise venue' awaits. In 2004, like earlier editions, the 'Wildside' section of the *Map* includes entries for M2M (male to male) massage parlours. These venues announce that they serve an 'elite' clientele with 'hot, diverse guys' in a 'discreet' service (*Pink Map* 2004).

Perhaps the most salient example of the body as a site of both consumption and representation lies on the cover of the 2001 edition of the *Pink Map*. On the cover of that edition is the image of a white male, seemingly naked, with dark hair and hairy chest and a 'six pack' of abdominal muscles. Superimposed over the model's image, entangled in the embodied landscape, is a map of an area of Cape Town known as De Waterkant, an urban enclave that has been labelled as Cape Town's gay village (Rink 2016). The embodied map extends from the top of his abdominal muscles to the area above his pubis. The venues depicted on the embodied map are laid-out, grid-like as they are in the narrow cobbled streets of De Waterkant and the bustling main thoroughfare known as Somerset Road. The midline connective tissue of the model's *rectus abdominus* muscle stands in as Somerset Road, while the eye of the viewer is drawn down the bodily landscape from thorax to pubis and includes map references to the Hothouse (a gay male bathhouse); Bronx (a gay 'action bar' that features dancing); On Broadway (a cabaret); Café Manhattan (a gay-owned restaurant and bar); and a variety of bars/dance clubs including Club 55, Detour, Angels, Bar Soho and Bar Code – a gay bar that caters to leather and fetish aficionados that is, perhaps owing to its geographic location or symbolically due to its transgressive sexuality, situated at the lowest point on the verge of the pubis. The cover model focuses his gaze in a 'southerly' direction – both on the actual plane of the map and figuratively towards the nether-regions of his own corporeal geography. In this position, most of the model's face is obscured, lending an air of anonymity while focusing and objectifying the gaze on the contours of his embodied map. The contours of the body become the contours of De Waterkant's landscape, and the journey through both is positioned as one and the same. With this image alone, the body and the touristic enclave are co-constituent.

Silent bodies

Gay male bodies are a visible component of nearly every edition of the *Pink Map*, and as discussed above play a role in situating Cape Town's queer touristic landscape. Lesbian, bisexual and transgender bodies, however, are much more difficult to situate using the *Pink Map*. When a female image first appeared on the cover of the 2000 edition of the *Map*, it was actually that of a drag queen in a blonde wig striking a pose – an image that suggested the female form, but that fell short of representation. In 2003, a listing for that year's MCQP with the theme of 'the Wedding' included a bride with dark skin and luminous pink hair emerging from a wedding cake. In this case, 'she' was also a gender-bending man in drag.

Since its inception, the *Pink Map* has been dominated by venues that cater explicitly to a gay male clientele rather than to lesbians, bisexuals or other sexualities. Of the listings that appear in the map over the years 1999–2008, only eight are from venues, services or accommodations that specifically serve a lesbian or female clientele. Women first become visible on the *Pink Map* in 2001 by way of a female-only monthly event called 'Brenda's Bash'. Until that point, lesbians lacked visibility on the *Map* and thus were relegated to the periphery of the touristic pleasure zone in the heart of Cape Town itself. Brenda's Bash, while fixed in time 'on the first Saturday of each month from nine o'clock until late' (*Pink Map* 2001), represented itself without a fixed space. Following this fleeting instance of lesbian bodies, they reappeared in 2003 in a listing for 'The Habit, stylish hip and happening monthly women's night at the trendy Cohibar' (*Pink Map* 2003).

The body as a site of discipline and regulation

Although it is a tourist publication, the *Pink Map* is not immune to the disciplinary and regulatory regimes that are undergone by the body. Along with the safari theme of the 1999 edition came an oft-repeated section of the *Map* called 'Health & Grooming'. Such bodily practices range from laser hair removal that tames the wildness from the beast (*Pink Map* 1999) to non-surgical face lift consultants that promise to 'reverse the ravages of time' (*Pink Map* 2001). The wildness of images elsewhere in the 1999 edition is counter-balanced by the need to appropriately groom the body in line with a desired 'norm' that confirms to notions of bodily perfection. Over time, however, changes in health and grooming listings in the *Pink Map* suggest that practices become more than utilitarian regimes. Caring for your body later becomes an issue of 'wellness' that involves crystals, pendulums and elaborate settings that feel 'like entering a submarine from the newest James Bond movie' (*Pink Map* 2008) – all the while overseen not by a mere medical practitioner, but by an internationally renowned 'guru' of skincare (*Pink Map* 2008). Wellness also provides for maintaining your sexual performance, as evidenced by a Sea Point-based chemist listed in all editions between 1999 and 2008 that demonstrates the need to care for the failures of the sexualised body, as they advertise 'a good selection of sex aids & poppers' (*Pink Map* 2000). These practices of health care, wellness and grooming fall within the realm of corporeal self-discipline, in the way that Foucault (1977) suggests that citizens invigilate themselves, their bodies and their movements through space. Tourists are therefore not immune to such regimes as evidenced by the *Map*. Caring for the body is both a gateway to wellness and a service to be consumed as part of the experience of the destination.

Conclusion: embodiment and destination space

The literature of tourism maps has been previously excluded from tourism studies due to criticisms, as Farías (2011) notes, 'that they are often considered to be mere representations, irrelevant for the analysis of tourists' embodied performances of space and place' (Farías 2011:398). The embodiment of queer space in opposition to the ambient heterosexual is represented across all sixteen editions of the *Pink Map* from 1999 through 2014. As embodied in the cover of the 2001 edition, the *Pink Map* can be read, following Nash (1996) as a fleshy representation not only of the body, but of '...the intimate tactile presence of the body and implicit presence of desire and sexual pleasure...in attachment to a national landscape and cultural traditions' (1996:153). Although limited in the scope of its representation – by eclipsing lesbian, bisexual and transgender tourist bodies, with an idealised white gay male body, the *Pink Map* nonetheless traces the uneven landscape of the queer tourist city that Cape Town presented to the world at the end of apartheid.

It is perhaps telling that since 2014 the *Pink Map* has ceased to be produced in its printed form. In its place is a static web-based version of the map that remains unchanged since 2012. Rather than freeze queer bodies in-time, the end of the *Pink Map* rather releases queer bodies into the ambient heterosexual touristic landscape, and defines them not by their sexual and embodied citizenship, but by the belonging that emerges through consumption. Queer bodies in the *Pink Map* delineate the boundaries of the queer p/leisure periphery and mark the ways that different bodies are desired and belong. The *Map* is therefore a more accurate reflection of the lived experience of the tourist city of Cape Town than the publishers might have envisaged.

Note

1 In this chapter, I am using the term 'queer' to be inclusive of multiple sexual identities including lesbian, gay, bisexual, transgender, questioning and intersex. The use of this term is not simply a shorthand for sexual others beyond the heterosexual 'norm' but follows Johnston (2001) in recognizing and embracing the power of difference and the sense of belonging that emerges from a broad conception of otherness. My use of 'queer' also follows Tucker's (2009) recognition that same-sex-attracted communities and individuals in Cape Town know/ practise their own type of subversion of the heteronormative.

References

Aldrich, R. (1993) *The Seduction of the Mediterranean: Writing, Art and Homosexual Fantasy.* London: Routledge.

Bell, D., Binnie, J., Cream, J. and Valentine, G. (1994) All hyped up and no place to go. *Gender, Place and Culture*, 1: 31–47.

Berdychevsky, L., Gibson, H. and Poria, Y. (2013) Women's sexual behavior in tourism: Loosening the bridle. *Annals of Tourism Research*, 42: 65–85.

Berdychevsky, L., Gibson, H. J. and Bell, H. L. (2016) 'Girlfriend getaway' as a contested term: Discourse analysis. *Tourism Management*, 55: 106–122.

Boone, J. A. (2014) *The Homoerotics of Orientalism.* New York: Columbia University Press.

Clarke, A. E. (2005) *Situational Analysis: Grounded Theory after the Postmodern Turn.* Thousand Oaks, CA: Sage.

Clift, S. and Forrest, S. (1999) Gay men and tourism: Destinations and holiday motivations. *Tourism Management*, 20: 615–625.

Dodson, B. (2000) Are we having fun yet? Leisure and consumption in the post-apartheid city. *Tijdschrift Voor Economische En Sociale Geografie*, 91(4): 412–425.

Elder, G. (2004) Love for sale: Marketing gay male p/leisure space in contemporary Cape Town, South Africa, in L. Nelson and J. Seager (eds.) *A Companion to Feminist Geography*. London: Blackwell Publishing, pp. 578–589.

Farías, I. (2011) Tourist maps as diagrams of destination space. *Space and Culture*, 14(4): 398–414.

Foucault, M. (1977) *Discipline and Punish: The Birth of Prisons*. Harmondsworth: Penguin.

Hoad, N. (1999) Between the white man's burden and the white man's disease: tracking lesbian and gay human rights in Southern Africa. *Gay and Lesbian Quarterly*, 5(4): 559–584.

Inglis, F. (2000) *The Delicious History of the Holiday*. London: Routledge.

Johnston, L. (2001) (Other) bodies and tourism studies. *Annals of Tourism Research*, 28(1): 180–201.

Longhurst, R. and Johnston, L. (2014) Bodies, gender, place and culture: 21 years on. *Gender, Place & Culture*, 21(3): 267–278.

Murray, A. (1995) Femme on the streets, Butch in the sheets (A play on whores), in D. Bell and G. Valentine (eds.) *Mapping Desire: Geographies of Sexualities*. London: Routledge, pp. 66–74.

Nash, C. J. (1996) Reclaiming vision: Looking at landscape and the body. *Gender, Place and Culture*, 3(2): 149–170.

Oswin, N. (2006) Decentering queer globalization: Diffusion and the 'global gay'. *Environment and Planning D: Society and Space*, 24(5): 777–790.

Ocha, W. and Earth, B. (2012) Identity diversification among transgender sex workers in Thailand's sex tourism industry. *Sexualities*, 16(1/2): 195–216.

Pink Map: Gay guide to Cape Town (1999) Published by A & C Maps, Kalk Bay.

Pink Map: Gay guide to Cape Town (2000) Published by A & C Maps, Newlands.

Pink Map: Gay guide to Cape Town & Surrounds (2001) Published by A & C Maps, Newlands.

Pink Map: Gay guide to Cape Town & Surrounds (2002) Published by A & C Maps, Newlands.

Pink Map: Gay guide to Cape Town & Surrounds (2003) Published by A & C Maps, Newlands.

Pink Map: Gay guide to Cape Town & Surrounds (2004) Published by A & C Maps, Newlands.

Pink Map: Gay guide to Cape Town & Surrounds (2005) Published by A & C Maps, Newlands.

Pink Map: Gay guide to Cape Town (2006) Published by A & C Maps, Newlands.

Pink Map: Gay guide to Cape Town (2007) Published by A & C Maps, Newlands.

Pink Map: Gay guide, Cape Town & Surrounds (2008) Published by A & C Maps, Newlands.

Pink Map: Gay guide, Cape Town & Surrounds (2009) Published by A & C Maps, Newlands.

Pink Map: Gay guide, Cape Town & Surrounds (2010) Published by A & C Maps, Newlands.

Pink Map: Gay guide, Cape Town & Surrounds (2011) Published by A & C Maps, Newlands.

Pink Map: Gay guide, Cape Town & Surrounds (2012) Published by A & C Maps, Newlands.

Pink Map: Gay guide, Cape Town & Surrounds (2013) Published by A & C Maps, Newlands.

Pink Map: Gay guide, Cape Town & Surrounds (2014) Published by A & C Maps, Newlands.

Puar, J. (2002) A transnational feminist critique of queer tourism. *Antipode*, 34(5): 935–946.

Rink, B. (2008) Community as utopia: Reflections on De Waterkant. *Urban Forum*, 19(2): 205–220.

Rink, B. (2013) Que(e)rying Cape Town: Touring Africa's gay capital with the *Pink Map*, in J. Sarmento and E. Brito-Henriques (eds.) *Tourism in the Global South: Heritages, Identities and Development*. Lisbon: Centre for Geographical Studies, pp. 65–90.

Rink, B. (2016) Quartering the city in discourse and bricks: Articulating urban change in a South African enclave. *Urban Forum*, 27(1): 19–34.

Tucker, A. (2009) *Queer Visibilities: Space, Identity and Interaction in Cape Town*. London: Blackwell.

Veblen, T. (2009 [1899]) *The Theory of the Leisure Class*. Oxford: Oxford University Press.

Veijola, S. and Jokinen, E. (1994) The body in tourism. *Theory, Culture & Society*, 11: 125–151.

Visser, G. (2002) Gay tourism in South Africa: Issues from the Cape Town experience. *Urban Forum*, 13(1): 85–94.

Visser, G. (2003a) Gay men, leisure space and South African cities: The case of Cape Town. *Geoforum*, 34(1): 123–137.

Visser, G. (2003b) Gay men, tourism and urban space: Reflections on Africa's 'gay capital'. *Tourism Geographies*, 5(2): 168–189.

Visser, G. (2014) Gay and lesbian tourism practices, in A. Lew, C. M. Hall, and A. Williams (eds.) *The Wiley Blackwell Companion to Tourism*. Chichester: John Wiley & Sons, pp. 435–443.

Waitt, G. and Markwell, K. (2006) *Gay tourism: Culture and Context*. Binghamton, NY: Haworth.

5 Rethinking the body in the touristic scenario

The elusiveness of embodying disability into tourism

Rafael Cruces Portales and Antonio Miguel Nogués-Pedregal

Introduction

This chapter discusses how the different ways of embodying tourist experiences are determined by the close relationship established between the bodily diversity of the tourist and accessibility to the tourist scenario. We regard the tourist scenario as being a set of the following core elements: geographical features such as the sea, mountains and the countryside; the built environment (hotels, means of transport, urban architecture); tourist products (e.g. sport events, musical festivals) and interpersonal relationships (customer services, host and guest interactions).

The research entailed ethnographic fieldwork involving participant observation and in-depth interviews carried out over a period of sixteen months from March 2015 to June 2016. A total of sixty-eight interviews were conducted among tourists of different nationalities, namely British, Germans, North Americans, Swedish and Spanish, all of whom are wheelchair users who had chosen to spend their holidays in either Alicante or Tenerife. In addition, in-depth interviews with six Third Sector representatives (ONCE, PREDIF and CERMI[1]) were carried out and four representatives of the hospitality sector associated with the following hotels *Ilunion, Mar y Sol* and *Scandic Hotels* contributed to the research by answering questions, as well as two local councillors involved in the tourism department in the cities where the fieldwork was undertaken.

The research is theoretically underpinned by a multidisciplinary approach that draws together the anthropology of tourism with central concepts taken from sociology such as habitus and stigma; alterity from philosophy; stereotypes and prejudices from psychology; accessible tourism and accessibility from tourism management; and from the history of the body, with special emphasis on the gaze. Moreover, this chapter employs the concept of aesthetic prejudice as a new lens to analyse, explain and better understand the performance, interaction and role of the body and the embodying experience of the disabled tourist. The connection between the body's image and the power of the gaze operates as a significant categorising and scrutiny mechanism with both individual and social consequences. The remarkable heuristic value implicit in the notion of aesthetic prejudice can be applied to other domains where the body's image plays a distinctive role, for example, gender, migration and ethnic studies.

The tourism industry is continually trying to create in every holiday maker's mind the image of a desirable and idyllic earthly paradise. However, has the disabled body been invited to participate in this purposively designed tourist paradise? Can a disable person's body image become embeded in the touristic scenario mirroring that of a typical tourist? Alternatively, are there factors that determine the disabled body's experience of and relationship with tourism?

The anthropology of tourism needs to pay more attention to the increasing presence of a different tourist appearing in the touristic scenario with its particular body and attached symbolic burden. Symbols represented by the supportive equipment used by people with disabilities such as wheelchairs that surreptitiously suggest to the eye a sort of mismatch with the idealised images of beauty and pleasure promoted by tourism advertising, which almost exclusively utilises young, slim bodies as being the 'right' people to promote tourism. However, other forms of embodying the tourism experience are being revealed, generating new discourses, dynamics and meaningful relationships. The presence of these bodies in the 'tourist sanctuaries' (Jafari 1988:37) is occurring more and more frequently, and the tourism activity carried out within them has brought to light an unexpected yet undeniable structural anomaly in terms of welcoming these tourists. The bodies of tourists with disabilities find physical barriers everywhere and claim to experience discriminatory attitudes along the entire travel chain. However, despite the many difficulties encountered by disabled tourists in their travels, it is striking to see how they keep alive a persistent desire to 'do' tourism (Buhalis et al. 2012).

The body of the disabled tourist yearns to embody the sensations of the tourist experience that spring from the fantasy that surrounds the world of dreams. A world where it is possible to escape from the restrictions of daily life and immerse oneself in the pretence of being able to do what can only be imagined. As illustrated by the conversation with Tim, a British tourist enjoying a cold drink in an accessible part of the *Las Vistas* beach:

> In the week before travelling to Tenerife, one night I dreamed that I could run and play on the beach and swim alone in the sea. With the great realism with which dreams are lived, I could feel the refreshing effect of the sea breeze caressing me while drying the sweat when running through the sand. It was fantastic, there was no wheelchair around because it just was not necessary, but, unfortunately, it was just a dream.

For tourists such as Tim, the image of their bodies is a text subjected to the social hermeneutics of the symbolism embedded in their bodily restrictions. This body image acts in a similar way to that of a wheelchair, stigmatised because of its association with human misfortune and at odds with the highly visual messages of idealised healthy, toned and young bodies promoted by the tourism industry. The idealised version of a tourist body is presented as an archetypal tourist whose body is free of pejorative connotations. This mismatch between the ideal as the norm and the different as disruptive constitutes an aesthetic prejudice, as Anna, a representative of the Third Sector, stated when asked about the *Mar y Sol* hotel in Tenerife, 'I never will choose that hotel plenty of weelchairs, as it reminds me of a hospital instead of a place to happily spend my holidays'.

This aesthetic prejudice filters, classifies and categorises the body of the disabled tourist as ill or abnormal, and therefore unable to get around the destination as a space for pleasure. The body of the disabled tourist is thus subjugated by the social scrutiny that makes the individual feel like an outsider within an environment frequently presented as an idealised space but which all too often is inaccessible and often hostile for disabled tourists. Erika, a swedish wheelchair user, who loves Spain as a holiday destination because of the sun, claims that it is very difficult to find a disabled friendly hotel in Spain. Erika remembered, with a gesture of frustration, a previous disappointing experience in Benidorm, while visiting her sister in Spain. The four star hotel she had booked assured her that the bedroom was fully accessible to wheelchairs. However, the entrance to the terrace had a small step that prevented her moving from the bedroom to the terrace and in the bathroom there was a small but impassable step to get into the shower. Erika also referred to feeling awkward when asking for information at the reception desk, which was not only on two different levels but also the receptionist addressed her sister instead of her every single time as if she were invisible. She responded with an even greater sense of bitterness when remembering how she had to enter the Benidorm Palace nightclub through the back door next to the kitchen as the large staircase in the main entrance was inaccessible to wheelchair users,

> this was the worst part because I felt quite discriminated. I had paid my ticket as everyone but, I had to pass by the kitchen zone through the waiters coming around and stay in a corner where the view was not very good indeed.

A body that becomes either invisible or ignored by the tourist landscape becomes a sort of outsider in the tourist scenario, an odd tourist, an Other tourist, which we refer to here as altertourist.

'Other' ways of embodying the trip

The excitement of flying to a beautiful holiday destination can be accompanied by a certain amount of nervousness and worry, particularly in the critical moments of take-off and landing. This feeling may be quite common and is likely to be shared by a number of passengers. Nevertheless, the combination of fear and concern displayed by Martyn in the following excerpt describing one particular flight, illustrates the specific challenges faced by some disabled travellers. Martyn, who suffers Spinal Muscular Atrophy (SMA), is an electric wheelchair user but he is also an enthusiastic and unflagging worldwide traveller. However, despite being an experienced traveller, he could not get over the hostility encountered on one particular flight:

> Around the time of boarding my stress levels rise. Will the PRM[2] service arrive, with 2 people able to lift me, and with a head support aisle chair? Will I be boarded first (as per the planned protocol)? Will the luggage handlers get my wheelchair in the hold safely? Will I be spoken to by the airline staff or will they act like I'm not there?
>
> Only recently all of the above went wrong. The second PRM guy came late, the airline staff ignored me, and the chair had no head support. Therefore, I was boarded late in front of everyone. This is very undignified because I'm in an awkward position, scared of hurting myself as I'm lifted onto the plane's seat, and people LOVE to stare. Already late for the planned departure time, the pilot announces that we'll be yet more delayed because of the wheelchair not going in the hold. I could feel the gazes and anger!
>
> I wonder. Was it necessary to publicly explain the reason? Moreover, why couldn't they get my wheelchair on, when I had phoned with the details weeks before?
>
> (Disability Horizons 2015)

No one else on the airplane experienced the same fears and frustrations. Tim's experience was solely due to the fact that he was the only person who had and presented a body with special needs on-board. In a somewhat similar vein, the undignified stroll through the aisle exposed him to everyone's staring gaze. This fact was so embarrassing that he unfailingly became a unique, yet stigmatised passenger, because 'the abnormal is a matter of perception, and the stigma is in the eye of the observer'[3] (Goffman in Courtine 2006:252). According to the testimonies of the disabled tourists who we have been in contact with, they normally feel anxious about their journey, knowing in advance that they are going to be fraught with a variety of difficulties both physical and psychological.

Unfortunately, this is not an exceptional case since disabled tourists often find a myriad of barriers they have to cope with from the beginning to the end of their 'tourism adventures'. These barriers may be physical, or in terms of attitudes or a combination of both. In practice, the disabled tourists interviewed encountered these barriers all too frequently either in relation to transport, in accommodation venues, at entertainment events or even more disturbingly at every stage of the trip.

In analysing Martyn's case, we can observe his concern whether aspects significant to him were going to unfold without any incident, for example the safe handling of his wheelchair in the hold, since it is crucial to keep it in a proper state of usage to enable him to get around in the destination. It is easy to imagine how anxious non-disabled tourists might be if someone who they have never met were in charge of looking after their 'legs' and responsible for giving them back in a suitable state of use after the flight. Because, even though it might be very obvious, we should not forget that the wheelchair provides the mechanical function of movement as if it were the disabled person's legs. Therefore, for non-disabled bodies, the wheelchair is either just a kind of vehicle or a useful piece of assistive technology, something superfluous to their needs. Conversely, for the disabled tourist, the wheelchair provides the means by which freedom and autonomy can be acquired. It helps to enhance their senses and offers access to a richer experience. Consequently, the safety of this in-corporated device is of paramount importance as it enables them to access an embodied tourist experience of the sensations that the touristic scenario provides. An in-corporated device becomes essential for achieving a memorable life experience but unfortunately, our findings reveal that disabled people have an extraordinary ability to become invisible to a sizable number of non-disabled people. For instance, there were many reported occasions where a non-disabled person accompanied a disabled person, and when the latter asked for something in the restaurant, the shop or the bank the attendant for no apparent reason responded to the able-bodied companion, rather than the person who actually asked the question.

In relation to Martyn's experiences, there are three important points to consider. First, the airline staff ignored him, as he had feared, and the consequence of being ignored caused him to feel isolated and discriminated against because of his body's condition. Second, the walk through the aisle of the plane, being lifted into his seat exposed him to the gaze of the other passengers. As a disabled person, he became excessively visible and he felt humiliated being carried down the aisle, as if he were in a parade. Third, the pilot's announcement was the official statement, which made everybody aware of the reason for the delayed departure and of who was responsible for it. This experience served to increase Martyn's sense of embarrassment and of being discriminated against both of which contibute to a way of being a tourist that entails a substantially different embodied experience because of the appearance of the body, its limitations and the socially conditioned responses to it.

As Martyn's experience illustrates the rather naive attempt by the cabin crew to 'camouflage' the disabled body highlights the selective nature of the gaze (Urry 1990), whereby the gaze works as a kind of relentless device of social scrutiny. In this sense, Martyn's body image was subject to a process of classification by the rest of the passengers and the aircraft crew, which combined to create the physical, sensorial and psychological elements (Bourdieu

1998) that produced a singular experience that only affected Martyn. The accumulation of unfortunate experiences before the plane had even taken off illustrate that the embodied experience of a disabled person travelling by air is crucially different to that of a non-disabled passenger. The same can be said in relation to other means of transport, such as travelling by train or by bus. Moreover, these essential differences bring to light discriminatory practices, which point to the inequalities within tourism and call into question core claims relating to the importance of service quality generally and specifically in relation to transport.

In the area of the experience economy (Pine and Gilmore 1998), the tourism industry's priority is to design a product that is attractive for tourists, generates positive memories and encourages repeat visits. To achieve this every detail, from the excitement generated in booking a holiday to the anticipation of the next holiday – all intended to cushion the return to the everyday (Jafari 1988) – must be foreseen and tightly controlled. This is the main strategy of the tourism industry, the creation of a continuous desire to travel and in so doing increase the economic benefits of tourism. However, it seems that given the disabled tourists' experiences, the need to accomplish this objective has been overlooked or not taken sufficiently into account.

By way of illustration, we now turn to the lived experience of John, another of our informants holidaying in Tenerife:

> Travelling by plane is stressful itself, so can you imagine when you cannot get up and walk off the aircraft. As I cannot walk, I had to wait on board until everyone else had disembarked but I was forgotten in there for more than one hour. During all that endless waiting time I had to get to the loo since nobody came up to help me, so I had to crawl up the aisle, and it was so humiliating. If I could have walked everything would have been normal, but on the contrary, I felt like dignity was rapidly fading away. In any case, you miss a well-trained staff that could make a difference.
>
> (Conversation with John 29 September 2015)

John's narrative highlights several aspects and moments that shaped his embodied experience. He invites the reader to imagine what it is like to be in his shoes. Then, he expresses his impotence when travelling by plane and reflects upon the stress caused by air travel. This experience contributed to a combined feeling of isolation at being forgotten on the plane; frustration about not being able to communicate and humiliation at having to crawl to the toilet. For John, these feelings resulted in an entirely different embodied sensory experience to that of the other non-disabled passengers. An experience that entailed a huge physical effort and a tremendous psychological cost.

There are several coincidences in the experiences of Martyn and John not least of which are the common physical and attitudinal barriers faced by each informant. The relatively recent literature exploring the intersection between tourism and disability has revealed a large cohort of people who wish to travel and take part in all that tourism has to offer as do non-disabled travellers. Nevertheless, it is noticeable, from the stories included in this literature that the experiences of disabled tourists are very different to those of the majority of tourists. As Daruwalla and Darcy (2005) have shown, disability awareness training is an important mechanism for challenging and changing attitudinal barriers. However, the tourism industry needs to promote disability awareness through training to all levels of staff employed by tourism businesses and in particular, those with direct contact with people with disabilities. We argue that increased co-participation between trained employees and people with disabilities will make a significant difference to the embodiment of disability within tourism.

However, we must not ignore the fact that the embodiment of tourists with disabilities is not a homogenous construct since it manifests itself in a variety of ways, namely, mobility, hearing, vision, learning, sensitivities, and mental health (Buhalis and Darcy 2011). Each one of these embodied expressions is affected by the level of support and the assistive technology required. Both of which help to construct an embodied identity for the individual disabled traveller (Darcy 2012).

In order to protect disabled people from discrimination and from the sort of barriers referred to here, the United Nations enacted the Convention on the Rights of Persons with Disabilities (CRPD 2006), ratified by more than one hundred and fifty of its members. This legal corpus is an attempt to remove barriers and promote dignity, respect, participation and independence. Drawing upon these principles, articles nine and thirty establish access to transportation and tourism as a right for everyone without exception, including disabled people. Despite the entry into force of such legislation, as we have seen here, there is still a long way to go in some sectors of the industry.

Body in paradise or, in the ghetto?

There is a place in southern Tenerife (Canary Islands) called *Los Cristianos* a widely visited 'paradise' for winter tourists from central and northern Europe seeking a warmer winter climate and beaches along the coast. The climate and the health environment were the main reasons why a group of disabled Swedish tourists chose *Los Cristianos* in the late 1950s. At first, when it was only an emergent destination these northern European disabled tourists started recommending *Los Cristianos* through word of mouth publicity. As the decades went by these pioneering tourists grew into a sizable number of people with disabilities, mostly wheelchair users with reduced mobility travelling to spend the winter there. As a result, Tenerife with the enormous contribution of *Los Cristianos* was considered at the time of this research the second destination for accessible tourism worldwide, surpassed only by Florida, USA (Diario de Avisos 2015).

The increasing amount of disabled tourists visiting the location has produced some cultural changes between the local population and the local businesses. Moreover, as verified and observed during the period of our research, a sort of transformation has taken place in the morphology of this touristic scenario due to the considerable presence of wheelchairs on the streets and the seafront. An innovative strategy implemented by the local authorities to expand and promote accessible tourism has brought about a remarkable change in the appearance of the destination, giving rise to what we have referred to as diversity's bodyscape of the tourism environment. This term designates a wider and more inclusive landscape of bodies characterised by a greater expression of diversity in tourist areas initially designed for a standardised mass tourist rather than the specific needs of a disabled tourist.

There has not been an overall change in the position of Tenerife as an important accessible destination, the *Spa and Sports Hotel Mar y Sol* in *Los Cristianos* is an excellent example of what can be achieved. This complex comprises such as a hotel, spa, massage centre, accessibility shop and workshop, carers and assistance services, a user-friendly accessible sports club: scuba-diving, golf. As a result, this hotel is much sought-after by disabled people since it offers the real possibility of a quiet and easily accessible stay, with plenty of adapted activities and events enabling them to enjoy a rich and immersive embodied tourist experience. Scuba diving is one example of the adapted activities offered by the hotel. This activity can be safely practised in the swimming pool as a preliminary experience before going into the sea, always accompanied by an expert assistant. Thereby providing disabled tourists with the opportunity to experience a taste of freedom through movements in water that may not otherwise be possible for them. In addition, the nearby golf club provides a special motorised vehicle, called 'powergolfer', which has a mechanism that elevates the passenger comfortably to the upright position enabling the individual to hit the ball and feel the sensations of practising an outdoor sport.

The hotel has been awarded several prizes and the acknowledgement not only of its distinctive social contribution but as an entrepreneurial, successful business model. In an interview as part of this research Mrs Kraus, the hotel's German General Director, and Mr Fisher, the German owner and founder, explained that the hotel was able to maintain an average occupancy ranging from 75 to 80 percent for its one hundred and sixty fully accessible rooms, all year round. During our stay in the hotel, we were the only non-disabled people apart from the many relatives, friends or assistants and carers accompanying the disabled guests. We were invited to go on a tour through the facilities by a member of the Public Relations staff and we asked her what percentage of non-disabled people stayed at the hotel. Interestingly, she responded that they only did so by mistake.

On the one hand, disabled tourists consider the hotel as a blessing, a kind of paradise where they are finally able to experience multiple bodily sensations and the sense of enjoyment typically experienced by non-disabled guests. On the other hand, a majority of non-disabled guests experienced the hotel as a place designed to marginalise and isolate disabled tourists. So, the question inevitably arises into dichotomous terms, is the hotel a paradise or a ghetto? Fear of the other, stereotypes and prejudice are powerful forces working against the positive integration of difference as an expression of human diversity. As a consequence, two worlds are kept separate by the binary normal/abnormal suggested by Foucault (2003). In this way, bodies that have abnormalities, that show signs which mark them out as different are stigmatised and embody ugliness, misery and undesirability. The tourism councillor of the municipality of Arona stated when we asked him for the reasons why there were not more fully accessible hotels in the area that the majority of the hospitality managers he had talked to about this issue were concerned that too many disabled people in wheelchairs could deter non-disabled clients. In the tourist context, everything is imagined and designed to attract visitors through images of beauty, youth, power and fantasy. These optical illusions are produced to instil the idea of escape from daily restrictions and enjoyment of the extraordinary (Jafari 1985). There is no room for anything that seems to undermine these sacred principles.

The body is the most visible sign of identity, and therefore, its appearance transmits signals that are filtered and classified through the gaze, becoming a prerequisite of belonging or exclusion that contributes at the same time to frame and to be framed in the societal context. Depending on who is looking, at what and how the classifying gaze is individual such that a description of the same place can be completely different. The picture of the Hotel *Mar y Sol* does not escape this categorising judgement which is subject to the stereotyping of disability. The unusually large amount of disabled clients in wheelchairs, in the hotel corridors and lounges, or entering the swimming pool helped by a hoist can have an impact on how non-disabled people perceive the hotel, considering it more like a hospital than a holiday resort. In the process of spatial perception, there is a translation of images from the visual to the cognitive order (Pylyshyn 2002), and in the language of Waskul and Vannini, 'thus, the body as sign vehicle bears the representational traces of culture and power' (2006:11). A body that has to be elevated from a wheelchair and helped by a hoist to enter the swimming pool is culturally marked out as being different to the 'norm'. The combined influence of culture and power is revealed when a disabled body is used to name a hotel as a hospital by those non-disabled who hold the power to classify what is healthy, desirable and strong, and what is sick and weak. As San Martin (2015) noted, this happens because neither sensibility nor spatiality can be thought without the body.

In an interview with Anna, an accessibility manager in one of the most representative organisations of the Third Sector in Spain, we asked for her opinion of the Hotel *Mar y Sol*. She knew the hotel well as she had

undertaken an accessibility assessment of its facilities, which although out-
standing would not encourage, Anna to choose the hotel for a holiday,

> When I go on vacation the last thing I want to think about is prob-
> lems, misfortunes and the like. Of course, much less having to see all
> those 'poor' disabled people around you in the hallways, throughout the
> bars, the restaurant, the pools, everywhere. In seeing all those people in
> wheelchairs so close to you, I can't put up with it and I end up getting
> depressed. Too many wheelchairs together are depressing. It reminds
> me of a hospital. It makes me think that I could be one of them, and just
> imagining so, it gets me extremely stressed and I wanted to escape from
> there quickly.
>
> (Author translation from Spanish into English of an extract
> of the conversation with Anna 22 February 2015)

The perception of the disabled body and the symbols associated with it as
seen above makes it difficult to picture a disable tourist fitting in the socially
constructed image of an archetypal tourist body. To someone like Anna a
disabled person is seen as a sick person, someone who needs either medical
treatment or therapeutic rehabilitation or at least care and support. Those
disabled individuals who require therapeutic and/or medical support tend
to choose clinic style venues where they can be accommodated. This is the
case with *Vintarsol,* in the *Las Américas* beach area, originally a Swedish
clinic for the disabled providing a wide range of health treatments together
with doctor and nursing services is today providing leisure and accommodation facilities, too.

By means of the mechanisms of habitus (Bourdieu 1977), an array of
mental images are shaped and have the quality of becoming sign vehicles
that are interpreted through a process of visual semiosis that, in the case
of disability, transforms the images into stereotypes and prejudice. The
gaze is a subtle yet common expression of human intersubjectivity which
provides very complex but hugely useful information for encountering the
Other. Thereby, the gaze itself becomes a kind of filter installed in the eyes
which captures, sieves, evaluates and classifies the appearance of the images
projected by the Other. Through this unconsciously selective process, the
appearance of the bodies of people with disabilities is pejoratively catego-
rised because of the symbolic burden historically associated with their body
image. As a consequence, this process produces discriminatory effects both
on the individuals and the group (Beriain 2013).

We refer to the prejudice and discrimination attached to images of bodies
that are considered socially Other as aesthetic prejudice. Aesthetic prejudice
judges images and stereotypes the individuals associated with them such
that disability becomes cognitively linked to social futility, abnormality,
lack of personal autonomy and the idea of permanent failure. Stereotyped
images of disability that are emotionally tied to compassion for a personal

tragedy and a dislike of what might be considered 'undesirable' might result in attitudes such as apathy, non-involvement and indifference, if not rejection.

The experiences of Gaizca, the husband of a wheelchair user, travelling to Tenerife as part of a group of disabled people with their relatives from the Basque country in Spain provide an interesting illustration of the range of attitudes and experiences. The group had chosen the Hotel *Mar y Sol* for a holiday, following the advice of a local disability association:

> One comes thinking of having a real time and finds that it looks like a hospital full of wheelchairs. Anywhere you go you will find one or more. This is not inclusive tourism; this is a ghetto for the disabled. Where are the children? One goes on vacation, and kids are usually swimming in the pool and running around. I have already been with my wife [wheelchair user] on other trips of these, for example, in Benidorm where you could see quite a lot of people in electric wheelchairs in the streets, but in the hotel, we were only those of the group, and the rest were 'normal' people.
> (Author translation from Spanish into English of an extract of the conversation with the Basque group, 1 October 2015)

However, Mayte, Gaizca's wife, taking advantage of the fact that the conversation fragmented into several smaller groups, stated that she did not agree with her husband whatsoever, and that the Hotel *Mar y Sol* was, by far, the best she had ever stayed in:

> I was also on that trip to Benidorm, and there is no point of comparison. If I come across other wheelchair users by the hotel, apart from those of our group, it does not bother me at all. Quite the opposite, meeting other people is great; we also went out for that. Besides, the bathroom is great with everything you need; the room is spacious so you can go around it on the wheelchair. The pool looks wonderful with the warm water, its cranes, and its lifeguard that helps you at any time. There is plenty of adapted bathrooms all around the hotel and the friendly and helpful staff is another advantage; I had no complaints at all. For me, it is the best hotel I have ever been in.
> (Own translation from Spanish into English of an extract of the conversation with Mayte 1 October 2015)

It seems that the perception of such facilities, including the evaluation of the staff, is significantly different depending on the self-perception of the individual embodying the experience. The senses involved in the embodiment of being on holiday and of becoming a tourist body by engaging with the facilties and amenities provided, work differently depending upon the body's condition, whether disabled or able bodied (Buhalis and Darcy 2011; Buhalis et al. 2012).

Mayte pointed out, that as a wheelchair user, the hotel was a 'paradise'. However, the same place appeared to Gaizka, her non-disabled husband, either as a hospital or a ghetto because he looked at it 'with the eyes of the distant and near' (Simmel 2009:643). Thus, he perceives reality as captured from the perspective of a stranger, in a sort of social oxymoron, where the near and the distant meet together in space and time. On the other hand, Mayte's disagreement with her husband arises as an expression of alterity. An inverse expression caused by her self-perception as being disabled such that her husband became, in the language of Beriain 'he is with us but he is not one of us'[4] (2013:5). As can be seen, the power of alterity works both ways, but the negative consequences of its social effects are generally asymmetrical.

As tourism is a global social, cultural and economic phenomenon, the apparatus of advertising has a powerful influence over patterns of consumption, consumer motivation and behaviour, aesthetics and so on. In this context, the bodies of the disabled when entering the tourist scenarios find functional and aesthetic mismatches with the images portrayed through tourism advertising. The symbolic messages that accompany them can influence and modify their identity, for example wheelchairs and negative connoatations such as weakness and incapacity become inseparable attributes that can define disabled tourists as different, as Other tourists. There are invisible yet perceptible pre-established social canons which posit and accept certain aesthetic prototypes. The meaningful symbols of disability are embedded in the body image of those individuals deemed to represent a disturbance of the aesthetic precept, who we refer to here as altertourists, because they are relentlessly distinguished as a sort of intruder in the landscape of tourism through a process which we describe as morphologisation of the Other.

In this vein, another illustrative quote from Carling's book *And Yet we are Human* is cited by Goffman, shows the exclusion and discrimination suffered by many people with disabilities because of their stigmatised bodies, which are seen as undesirable images that cause disruption and discomfort in environments associated with fun and leisure:

> I remember for instance a man at an open-air restaurant in Oslo. He was much disabled, and he had left his wheelchair to ascend a rather steep staircase up to the terrace where the tables were. Because he could not use his legs he had to crawl on his knees, and as he began to ascend the stairs in this unconventional way, the waiters rushed to meet him, not to help, but to tell him that they could not serve a man like him at that restaurant, as people visited it to enjoy themselves and have a good time, not to be depressed by the sight of cripples.
>
> (Cited in Goffman 1990:146)

The physical and attitudinal barriers that inhabit tourism make up an adverse world full of difficulties that prevent a disabled tourist from having the same experience as a non-disabled tourist. For example, adequate access to facilities and encountering the apathy of other tourists can cause disabled visitors to feel like true outsiders. Such barriers are preventing disabled bodies from feeling and enjoying the same experiences as a non-disabled tourist, largely because they are seen as fundamentally different to the majority of tourists present, as an 'alien' in the tourist environment.

Accessibility: a prerequisite for embodying tourism

What kind of experience is possible without access? Can we imagine tourism without ease of access to enjoy all the facilities, amenities and attractions? Would it not be considered a form of deception to advertise a destination as a paradise only to find it to be inaccessible on arrival? All these questions highlight the significance of access for disabled tourists. The body of a tourist is fundamentally a sensorial body characterised by a desire to statisfy itself by engaging in as many experiences as possible when on holiday (Veijola and Jokinen 1994, Crouch and Desforges 2003, Merchant 2011). So, accessibility becomes the *sine qua non* condition so that disabled tourists are not left feeling let down and frustrated (Small et al. 2012).

Due to the number of people with disabilities going on holiday, a number of recommendations and regulations have emerged during the last three decades seeking to protect the rights of disabled people. As a result, many of the main Spanish beaches have been equipped with what are called 'accessible points', innovative micro-places aimed at helping a disabled tourist to take a bath. These places facilitate typical tourist activities such as bathing in the sea and socialising with other bathers for tourists with special needs. During our research, we analysed the facilities, quantity and quality of equipment and service performance in two of these new built-in beach spaces, one in *Santa Pola* in Alicante and the other in *Los Cristianos* in Tenerife.

Such accessible beach spaces represent a kind of subset within the larger tourist territory and are characterised by atttudes of empathy and solidarity towards disabled tourists. However, it is noteworthy that a subtle and symbolic separation exists whereby contact with non-disabled tourists is visual rather than physical. Apart from the staff delivering the service, the interactions that take place in these accessible areas are primarily between the disabled tourist, their family and friends. The physical area is demarcated both on land by a wooden floor under a shaded shelter and in the water through buoys that demarcate the space reserved for the disabled bather. Such barriers mark out members of the group based on their body image and contributes to the reproduction and maintenance of stereotypes that stigmatise the disabled as Other inside a bounded enclosure. This enclosure resembles the classic tourist bubble but it is a bubble that facilitates the visual identification of otherness within the tourist landscape. Nevertheless, helping disabled tourists to access, embody and enjoy a beach environment is a hugely positive move forward.

The following testimonies collected through in-depth interviews in the summer of 2015 at two 'accessible points' on the beaches of Levante and Las Vistas illustrate the type of sensations and feelings embodied by the tourists:

> Thankfully things are changing. Nowadays we can find places like this one where you can meet people to help you bathing in the sea, feeling how the waves gently swing your body; salty water on your lips; the sun warming the skin; the sea smell. Magnificent sensations that I can now feel and at the same time also to think you are a bit more like everyone else.
>
> (Author translation from Spanish into English of a conversation with Juan in the 'accessible point' of Levante beach)

Other disabled people, like Juan, also highlighted the positive tangible benefits of such spaces and facilties. Indeed, the increasing emergence of these 'accessible points' represents a remarkable shift in understanding the needs of some disabled tourists. Although the move to address and improve accessibility is certainly welcome, such advancements are scarce and slow to be implemented. By way of illustration, the following comment by Sofia demonstrates a mixture of positive and negative feelings and experiences of an 'accessible point':

> I think it is an excellent opportunity to have a bath in the sea safely. But, we are too many, and most of us want to use the service, and unfortunately, the resources are few. It seems that a single amphibious chair for so many people is not enough and because of that as I would like to share the bath with my disabled friends it gets impossible. The truth is that everything reminds you that you are different. You were coming to do what tourists do, coming to the beach to sunbathe and have a bath or two, and you certainly do it, but it is not the same as those non-disabled who are a few meters away from you.
>
> (Author translation from Spanish into English of a conversation with Sofía in Las Vistas beach)

Despite the scarcity of resources and personnel in the accessible points, the implementation of measures such as these are a step in the right direction, offering disabled tourists the opportunity to experience the sensations and activities enjoyed by a non-disabled tourist.

Conclusion

There is a type of tourist who is increasingly circumnavigating the touristic scenario. By engaging in the activity of tourism, they come across an environment that is not always easy to access. As a result, their embodiment of tourism is marked by having to cope with physical and attitudinal barriers which often result in an unsatisfactory experience. The tourist scenario has not been conceived or designed to welcome the particular bodies of disabled tourists with special needs. This mismatch between the characteristics of supply and demand in the travel chain of mainstream tourism brings discriminatory effects to these active agents who wish to embody the same sensations as a non-disabled tourist. This objective fact highlights a significant structural inadequacy of tourism as an overarching phenomenon that intends to encompass all the elements of a 'total social fact', that is to say, to merge a holistic attitude with the different units of analysis to assemble the organic whole that makes up their interdependent institutions (Mauss 1971:157).

The body image of a disabled tourist carries embedded within it a powerful symbolic burden configured as a subtle but pervasive expression of 'otherness', what we refer to as a process of morphologising the Other. This morphology does not fit comfortably with the idealised images of tourism and contributes to the formation of a negative attitude towards the image of a disabled body of either apathy or rejection resulting in discrimination. Such attitudes are detected, filtered and classified by a sort of 'lookism' that develops an aesthetic prejudice through the vehicle of the gaze as it scans the touristic scenario.

Therefore, it is possible to conclude that without a re-education of the gaze that can free it from the heavy symbolism that accompanies and marks certain images of the body with stigma, it will be enormously difficult to recognise different bodies as an expression of diversity rather than as examples of disruptive abnormality. The present chapter may be located within the domain of both studies dedicated to accessible tourism and studies that are focused on knowing the incorporation processes of embodying tourism experiences from a broad spectrum of cognitive and sensory human diversity.

Notes

1 ONCE Organización Nacional de Ciegos Españoles. A Spanish foundation raising funds to provide services for the blind and visually impaired individuals; PREDIF Plataforma Representativa Estatal de Personas con Discapacidad Física an NGO supporting disabled individuals including support relating to accessible tourism; CERMI Comité Español De Representantes De Personas Con Discapacidad. A Spanish committee representing disabled individuals.
2 PRM refers to Airport Service supporting Passengers with Reduced Mobility getting on and off the plane.
3 Author's translation from Spanish into English of the quotation, 'lo anormal es una cuestión de percepción y el estigma se encuentra en el ojo del que observa'.
4 Author's translation from Spanish into English.

References

Beriain, J. (2013) Encuentros con la alteridad e identidades múltiples. *Arbor*, 189(761): a038. Available at: http://dx.doi.org/10.3989/arbor.2013.761n3006 [accessed 18 May 2015].

Bourdieu, P. (1977) *Outline of a Theory of Practice*. Cambridge: University Press.

Bourdieu, P. (1998) *Practical Reason: On the Theory of Action*. Redwood City, CA: Stanford University Press.

Buhalis, D. and Darcy, S. (Eds.) (2011) *Accessible Tourism: Concepts and Issues*. Bristol: Channel View Publications.

Buhalis, D., Darcy, S. and Ambrose, I. (2012) *Best Practices in Accessible Tourism. Inclusion, Disability, Ageing Population and Tourism*. Bristol: Channel View Publications.

Courtine, J. J. (2006) Historia del cuerpo. La mutación de la mirada. Siglo XX. Madrid: Taurus.

Crouch, D. and Desforges, L. (2003) The sensuous in the tourist encounter. *Tourist Studies*, 3(1): 5–22.

Darcy, S. (2012) (Dis)Embodied air travel experiences: Disability, discrimination and the effect of a discontinuous air travel chain. *Journal of Hospitality and Tourism Management*, 19: 1–11.

Diario de Avisos. (2015) Tenerife, un destino puntero en turismo accesible. Available at: www.diariodeavisos.com/2015/11/tenerife-destino-puntero-en-turismo-accesible/[accessed 10 November 2015].

Daruwalla, P. S. and Darcy, S. (2005) Personal and societal attitudes to disability. *Annals of Tourism Research*, 32(3): 549–570.

Disability Horizons (2015) Accessible air travel: It's good, but needs to be so much better. Available at: http://disabilityhorizons.com/2015/10/accessible-air-travel/ [accessed 10 October 2016].

Foucault, M. (2003) *Abnormal. Lectures at the College de France, 1974–75*. London: Verso.

Goffman, E. (1990) *Stigma: Notes on the Management of Spoiled Identity*. London: Penguin.

Jafari, J. (1985) *The Tourist System: A Theoretical Approach to the Study of Tourism*. Ann Arbor, MI: University Microfilms International.

Jafari, J. (1988) Estructura y función del turismo. *Anthropológica, Revista de etnopsicología y etnopsiquiatría*, 4, 29–50.

Mauss, M. (1971) *Sociología y Antropología*. Tecnos. Madrid.

Merchant, S. (2011) Negotiating underwater space: The sensorium, the body and the practice of Scuba diving. *Tourists Studies*, 11(3): 215–234.

Pine II, B. J., Gilmore, J. H. (1998) Welcome to the experience economy. *Harvard Business Review*, 76: 97–105. Reprint (July–August).

Pylyshyn, Z. (2002) *Seeing and Visualizing: It's Not What You Think: An Essay on Vision and Visual Imagination Scanning*. Piscataway, NJ: Rutgers Center for Cognitive Science.

San Martin, J. (2015). *Antropología Filosófica II. Vida humana, persona y cultura*. Madrid: UNED.

Simmel, G. (2009, [1908]) *Sociology: Inquiries into the Construction of Social Forms* (2 Vols) Boston, MA: Brill.

Small, J., Darcy, S. and Packer, T. (2012) The embodied tourist experiences of people with vision impairment: Management implications beyond the visual gaze. *Tourism Management* 33: 941–950.

United Nations. (2006) *Convention on the Rights of Persons with Disabilities*. New York. Available at: www.un.org/disabilities/documents/convention/convoptprot-e.pdf [accessed 10 October 2016].

Urry, J. (1990) *The Tourist Gaze: Leisure and Travel in Contemporary Societies.* London: Sage Publications Ltd.

Veijola, S. and Jokinen, E. (1994) The body in tourism. *Theory, Culture and Society,* 11: 125–151.

Waskul, D. and Vannini, P. (Ed.) (2006) Introduction: The body in symbolic interaction, in *Body/Embodiment Symbolic Interaction and the Sociology of the Body.* Aldershot: Ashgate Publishing Limited.

6 Yoga as an embodied journey towards flexibility, openness and balance

Amy Speier

Introduction

The serious business of healing is not usually associated with the pleasures of relaxation. However, yoga holidays are sites where the promotion of health and leisure are inextricably linked. This chapter examines the yoga holidays for British and North American women in northern Italy. The yoga holiday is advertised as follows, 'Escape the British weather for a long weekend and spend five days soaking up the sunshine with daily yoga in Liguria, Italy' (Kaleidoscope.com). Pictures of a gorgeous Villa that sits nestled in the Alps with a stunning view of a medieval town evoke images of a natural serene setting for yogis to practise outside on a sunny deck. Those individuals who choose to go on this type of retreat/holiday will benefit from eight yoga classes, three-course vegetarian dinners that include wine, and rooms with a view. It is important to note here that there is a large difference between yoga retreat – which connotes a place for spiritual renewal, detoxing, pure yoga – and yoga holiday which aims to combine tourism elements and yoga.

There are parallels between motivations to travel and to practise yoga. One is to take time away from one's busy schedule. The other is to 'switch off' from one's hectic post-Fordist lifestyle (Schabele 2013). There are health benefits of travelling and of doing yoga, so combining the two grant those who partake an added dimension of taking time for one's self, opening one's mind and body, retuning to one's body and gaining flexibility. In fact, these yoga holidays are a platform for 'empowerment' for female yoga travellers (Newcombe 2013:69). This chapter examines tourism and embodiment through the lens of yoga holidays to deconstruct the ways that health, yoga and travel intersect for women in northern Italy.

Methods

Late during the spring of 2014, a yoga teacher friend of mine Adele announced on Facebook there was one spot left for her Italian yoga holiday. Since I was doing research in Prague for the summer, I decided to conduct a pilot study of yoga holidays as a form of health tourism. I have studied various facets of health and medical tourism in Europe over the past fifteen years, examining Czech health spas (Speier 2008, 2011a) as sites of health tourism for retired German patients suffering chronic ailments associated with aging, as well as North Americans who travel to the Czech Republic for assisted reproductive technologies (Speier 2011b, 2011c, 2015, 2016).

During the summer of 2015, I conducted an ethnographic study of a yoga retreat in Liguria, Italy. I conducted participant observation as well as semi-structured interviews with the nine British and North American women who also attended the yoga retreat, Adele, and the owners of the Villa. I participated in yoga sessions, outings to the medieval town and to dinner one evening, and numerous casual conversations over the five days in Italy. This study examines why women practise yoga, chose this yoga holiday, their notions of health as they relate to both travel and yoga, and their bodily and mental experiences of yoga in Italy. Pseudonyms have been used for all participants.

Literature review of health tourism

In much of the anthropological literature of tourism, the majority of attention has focused on cognitivist understandings of tourism, while not enough has focused on the tourists' embodied, visceral experiences (Veijola and Jokinen 1994; see also Foucault 1978, Butler 1990, Castenada 1991, Game 1991). The literature also discusses the 'tourist gaze' (Urry 1990), which constitutes the primary vehicle of sensory experience as the tourist breaks with established routines. When scholars only analyse the tourist gaze and responses to visual perceptions, the sensorial experiences of different places and cultures become overlooked (Bruner 2005).

Medical tourism can be defined as 'the practice of patients seeking lower cost health care procedures abroad, often packaged with travel and sight-seeing excursions' (Senate Committee on Aging 2006). There has been an increasing proliferation of medical or health tourism in today's global world. Tourists who embark on medical or health tourism are a perfect lens through which to examine the embodied experiences of travellers. Merchant defines sensorium as the 'sum of a person's perceptions, or the seat of sensations; of their interpretation of their environment' (2011:215). Subsequently, there has been a burgeoning scholarly interest in medical tourism over the past decade, paralleling the industry's growth. Special issues 'Medical Travel' (Smith-Morris and Manderson 2010, Whittaker and Speier 2010) in *Medical Anthropology: Cross-Cultural Studies in Health and Illness* and 'Healing holidays?' (Naraindas and Bastos 2011) reveal the new directions medical anthropologists are beginning to take to theoretically examine this global phenomenon. Yet, the many links between health and tourism remain unexplored.

I am arguing for a refined category of analysis called health tourism within the anthropology of tourism. By looking at health tourism, we can begin to look at the embodied patient tourists who are breaking with routines by crossing into new 'therapeutic landscapes' (Hoyez 2007). This study incorporates medical anthropological analysis of yoga and its effects on the body within the context of health tourism. By looking at health tourism, we can begin to look at the embodied patient tourists who are breaking away from a consumer-driven lifestyle.

Travelling yogis in therapeutic landscapes

My sample consists of nine women: Adele was the yoga instructor, two mother daughter pairs: Meredith and Leila and Patricia and Sarah, close friends Elaine and Gina, a single woman Iris, and an American woman Evelyn. The owners of the Villa, Steven and Eunice, spoke to me about hosting various kinds of yoga holidays throughout the year. Based on my sample size, women's ages ranged from early twenties to early sixties. They have the means, the time and the desire to prevent various problems that are associated with aging. They are mobile in their global quests for health and relaxation. The women varied in the extent to which they had been practising yoga: some were fairly new to the practice, whereas others have been practising for decades.

Hoyez (2007) has written about yoga centres as global forms of therapeutic landscapes. 'Yoga is supposed to be practised in an ideal place... "natural" elements are very important' (Hoyez 2007:116). The owners of the Villa where Adele's Italian yoga holiday took place had envisioned their Villa to host yoga retreats when they began construction a decade earlier. Steven said, 'I think it's helpful to those who are taking part in yoga courses that they feel that they are in the middle of nature with mountains, greenery and trees. It's conducive to their practice, we hope'. This chapter focuses on Italy as a therapeutic landscape, which contrasts with yoga holidays and retreats to India (Nichter 2013).

The women from my study were primarily from Newcastle, UK, where Adele teaches classes regularly. A few of them imagined a yoga holiday to be something posh. Leila, a twenty-one-year-old university student who came with her mum Meredith, remembers her classmates 'ooh-ing' and 'ahh-ing' asking her, 'Why are you going on a yoga retreat? Who do you think you are? With your little posh weekend getaway?' Sarah, a thirty-seven-year-old woman who was also travelling to Italy with her mother Patricia, also thought it sounded 'a bit posh, like very fancy going on a yoga retreat'. However, their yoga holiday was seen as affordable and simple in its accommodations, with emphasis being placed on the natural surroundings of the mountains.

Adele is an American who met her British husband on a backpacking trip in South America. She has never quite adjusted to the cold climate of England. When she creates her yoga holidays, she simply thinks it is better to be anywhere else practising yoga, 'well the sun is a big thing, so it's nice to be able to do it outside, and it's nice to get some vitamin D. I wouldn't say it's Italy per se, it's just being somewhere else'. Scholars of tourism have noted how we travel seeking something opposite from where we live (Graburn 2010).

For those who live in a cold, Northern city, travelling to the mountainous countryside of Italy was one motivating factor – particularly for the warmth they imagined Italy to offer. Iris said she was particularly drawn to the 'countryside setting', whereas Patricia, Sarah's mother, thought, 'I'll enjoy the warmth of it, I've never been to this part of Italy as well and it sounded good'. The Americans travelling to Italy may have had grander imaginations of Italy. As Steven of the Villa said, 'I think that people look at Italy as the land of culture, of sunshine (because it's Mediterranean), of good healthy food. It is much healthier food than most Northern European food. So, it's a combination of all those things'.

Two predominant images of yoga retreat came to the mind of my informants when I asked them how they imagined it before their departure. Some imagined a restrictive, vegan, regimented space to detox. Iris, a forty-seven-year-old, single, mental health worker said the usual cliché is 'hippie, vegetarian or vegan… chanting, calm, quiet'. However, Adele wanted to create something much more pleasurable, 'that's not what I want in terms of my retreats or holidays. I think it's good to have that, but sometimes people just wanna be 'free' to have a weekend with their friends and do some yoga and have a glass of wine'. Adele's website was the starting point of these women's imaginations of what this particular Italian yoga retreat would offer them. There were pictures of the countryside, the Villa, as well as the yoga deck and the pool.

The women were drawn to the fact that yoga would be outside and that the Villa was secluded. Patricia, a sixty-two-year-old retired school teacher was drawn to the gardens of the Villa,

> I think it's secluded, it's got beautiful gardens, fantastic views. Plants are good as well. Also, the wildlife as in grasshoppers or crickets or whatever they are…frogs, bats and the swallows in the daytime have been lovely, watching the swallows. It's a very tranquil place.

She continued talking about the joy of doing yoga outside, as opposed to on a cold church floor, where Adele's class was in Newcastle,

> I just think that I love the outside. To do yoga in the open air I think is fantastic, with the insects around and the noises and the breaths of the air, just little breezes where you go, and the warmth of the sun, and having to get out of the sun into the shade I think it's not distracting, it's sort of beneficial.

The idyllic, natural setting drew these yogis to pursue the healing benefits of yoga in a therapeutic landscape.

Therapeutic qualities of yoga

People practise yoga for various reasons, reasons that are often linked to notions of the mind/body as well as personal health. Scholars have noted that it is now an individual's moral responsibility to practise good health, and so those who do yoga are good citizens who are seeking improved health. Hauser writes, '[t]o keep oneself fit and free of disease is considered an obligation and thus a matter of morality. In recent decades, this duty has seemingly expanded to also include notions of emotional balance, mental flexibility, and self-care' (2013:111). Those who decide to venture abroad on a yoga holiday or retreat are good citizens consuming a health-promoting holiday.

I asked the women in Italy why they thought yoga was healthy. Four women used the metaphor of 'switching off' to describe the health benefits of doing yoga. Iris said,

> It's a little bit of something that is just for me. I have to say after a long day at work, when it's all been crazy mad and even if I am just lying down and doing a few twists, I just automatically just feel calmer and energised and switched off.

Similarly, Leila said,

> It's quite nice to do something different, because you don't really get to sit and just think. You know, normally I've got to do this, I've got to go here, I've got to go there, I've got to write this essay, I've got to sort this bloody power point out. You don't get time to just sit and not think about anything. It's quite nice actually. It's still quite nice to sit there and just kind of switch off from it.

Meredith is more particular about what exactly she is switching off:

> Well, personally for me, it's more of a mental thing, you know? It's more we're so busy at home on a day-to-day basis it's just nice to have a bit of 'me' time. It's all about me. That hour and a half of class when we do yoga I really actually don't think about anything. I get the breathing right, I can switch that voice off in your head that's saying, 'you should be doing this, you should be doing that', and I really enjoy the fact that I can switch off. I can just not think about anything and that's important to me, because at home the phone's ringing, the kids are like, 'mum this, mum that, get me this, get me that'. You know, at work it's, 'do this, do that', and it's just lovely to not have that business in the background.

All this business includes daily demands that come from work, school as well as family. Women are demanding time for themselves.

During that time when they are switched off, they can obtain a feeling of calm by practising yoga. Patricia remembered when she first started yoga,

> I joined [a class] and the teacher was very gentle, very calming and it was good after a stressful day at work. The poses reminded me of when I was very little, I would hang upside down on the sofa. It was just very, very calm and felt good.

Patricia seems to hearken back to the embodiment of her childhood through yoga. There is a sense that the voices or demands of life are drowned out by utter concentration yoga demands of its practitioners, which Elaine intimates:

> I would probably say [yoga is] a series of poses and shapes and putting your body into positions in order to connect with your breath. By doing that, you can manage to switch off. The very fact that you're doing all of these poses frees up your mind more than exercise does, because all you can think about is the next place that you turn. You're trying to get into a position, all you can think about is, 'am I breathing right? Are my legs in the right place?' So, by the time you get to the shavasana pose, you're less stressed and you're empty of thoughts and it enables you to relax.

Yoga demands that one focus on the pose along with the breath, so women enter a new realm of embodiment. 'The ability to transcend the body and focus the mind remains a central element of their practices' (Newcombe 2013:73).

Other ways that women clarified health benefits of yoga that relate to this notion of switching off is being present. Elaine said,

> I think you get the mind thing, everybody has worries, everybody has anxieties, various things going on in their lives, maybe it's work, maybe it's family... but maybe the ability to perhaps slow down, be a bit more in the moment.

It is the everyday work life of family and work that cause stress, and yoga eases that stress for women in their daily lives. As Leila said, yoga causes clarity, it is a mental exercise that removes stress,

> I think seeing things in a different way is a health benefit as well. When you can sit down and clear your mind, to get away from the stress. I am sure people get stressed at university, I get stressed for my kind of thing.

Meredith, her mother, agrees with the ways that yoga relieves stress, 'It's good for stress. I mean, it's more of a mental thing for me than the strength. I go because I can just zone out everything'. Again, women turn to yoga to be present with their bodies, their breath and to clear their minds.

Even further, they are not totally switching off, but they are re-connecting to themselves. According to Iris,

> I would describe yoga as a means of connecting to yourself, a means of acknowledging your own mind body, being able to join that together but also to be able to separate the two so you can concentrate on your body and your breath while quieting the mind.

They are reconnecting with themselves to re-energise themselves, to be able to go back to the daily grind and stress and have more energy to do so. Sarah said that her noon-time class at work 'was actually really refreshing, like you went back to work and you felt so much better than just sort of hunched over your sandwich, so it was actually really nice'. Leila, a student similarly said,

> I'd just say it's the odd hour where you just take the time to yourself. You get your bit of exercise in a way that you're stretching, you can feel your body working, but it's not too like, 'Oh my God I'm out of breath, oh my God I'm going to die, this person is trying to kill me'... It's very chill and I really, really enjoy it. It gives you a different feeling when you're finished. You're more awake than sweaty and half dead. I think it's really good for you.

Often, women would compare yoga with other types of exercise, and a distinguishing factor is that it is calming, yet also energising. After yoga, a woman feels more present in her body, more cognisant of her body and its breath.

Clarity is gained through the practice of yoga. Iris says, 'it gives me kind of clarity, it makes me appreciate my body more, it enables me to listen and tune into my own intuition, what my body's telling me and flexibility'. Similarly, there seemed to be a closer listening to one's body with the quieting of the mind, at least according to Sarah,

> I think it makes you more supple, good to stretch more, helps your core a lot which helps everything you're doing. But also, because you are concentrating on what your body is doing, and I think just it's beneficial for your mental health. Again, it's just having that time to think about your body when you might not normally do that.

Running throughout these comments is this realisation that yoga allows women to disconnect from their everyday demands but also to reconnect – particularly with their bodies. They intimate that they begin paying attention to their bodies and listening to them.

Flexibility or suppleness is another health benefit of doing yoga for these women. I asked why flexibility was a good thing, and I was surprised to find the ways that flexibility and suppleness were linked to mobility. Iris said,

'I think if you've got a flexible body and a strong spine, then it keeps you going'. Sarah also thought yoga makes you supple. Her mother, Patricia, says,

> Well for me it's a way of keeping the body supple and letting you do more with your body than you thought you could just by breathing and calming the whole body. To do different poses, to meditate and just feel some sort of inner peace.

However, to remain supple also guarantees that you will be mobile. Patricia adds, 'I think the stretches keep your body flexible...I think you stiffen with age, and I'm conscious about a lot or a few of my friends having health problems, and so I want to keep as healthy as I can'. Other scholars have noted how we can see 'yoga as an elixir of youth, as a method of healing, and for psychological empowerment' (Newcombe 2013:69); it can also be seen as a mode of empowerment for women to fight aging.

For those women approaching their fifties and sixties, and as they witness parents passing or older relatives with limited mobility, they are practising yoga as a form of preventative health care – to ensure their mobility so they can continue to take trips like this yoga holiday in Italy. Emily Martin (1994) talks of flexibility and yoga enables flexibility and mobility, but at the same time it enables one to calm down and to slow down, be in the moment. 'The flexibility required on the employment market is practiced in yoga' (Schnabele 2013:141).

Yoga holidays and wellness

The act of travel is deemed something that has health benefits in terms of mental health, making someone more 'open' to different customs. It was actually while Elaine had been vacationing in St. Lucia that she discovered yoga:

> I was on holiday in St. Lucia, and I'd never tried yoga before, because for me exercise was about getting sweaty and burning calories. It was a nice resort and they offered sunrise yoga and sunset yoga. It was a lovely setting on a beach on a wooden pier and I did it that first day and I was hooked. I felt great afterwards, so I did it every day for a fortnight. So, when I came back to England, I set about trying to find a class with an instructor that I liked. So that was my introduction.

Elaine correlates the act of travel with doing yoga. In fact, she intimates she is more disciplined while travelling:

> Remember when I said I first fell in love with yoga in St. Lucia doing it looking at the sea? So, I'm fortunate. I do have a lot of holidays, and

wherever I go now I actually check to see that there's some yoga, because- where was I last year? Mexico, Colorado, Jamaica, and I would check that there was yoga in the hotel that I took with my husband just because I know if I can do that... I wish I could practice at home. I'm not as disciplined as I should be.

I want to examine this connection between yoga and travel, and the ways that yoga and mobility inform one another as they both heal.

Travel, even when it may not entail yoga, is usually thought to be something 'good' for you. Some of the women I met spoke to the healing properties of travel. When Patricia and I sat in the Villa's front room after breakfast one morning, she said, 'Well they say travel broadens the mind, doesn't it?' I think just to experience new surroundings, landscapes is healthy. Echoing this sentiment, Elaine also said regarding the positive benefit of travel:

> To travel and to go to different places and to experience different cultures ... having seen different things and respecting other customs like cover up your hair here. It could be something as simple as going to a completely different culture like Thailand, where they value completely separate things. I think it expands your mind a little bit. And anything from skiing to going to a beach holiday, having experienced either the food, the way of life.

In these comments, the healthy benefits are about broadening the 'mind', yet Elaine also mentions skiing, or a beach, or the food – all differences that are experienced bodily. As Iris says, 'I think it's very healthy for the mind. I think it's it opens your world up'. Travel entails stretching and opening oneself to other ways of life but also opening your embodied sense of the world.

Yoga abroad is thought to have similar healing effects. Elaine finds further fulfilment in doing yoga in other places,

> When you do yoga in different places, and your view is different, it's not perhaps inside a gym, just for me, I'm more open to the ritual side of yoga, so I really appreciate all the view and the trees and I just feel more... we have climate in England where you are not often outside, you are not in tune with nature.

In fact, I heard many women speak of how the yoga holiday pushed them out of their comfort zones. Iris, who had completed a teacher training like Adele though never used it, typically practised at home. She spoke of this broadening:

> It's challenged a lot of my barriers. The yoga itself, I'm out of my comfort zone. When you practice at home, you're staying in your comfort

zone. And when you practice in a class, you're there to follow the instructions and it's pushed me out of my comfort zone... because you do stay in your comfort zone – the postures that you feel comfortable with and you have that flexibility. You shy away from the postures that you find difficult or uncomfortable or just plain nauseous. I knew I would be challenged by Adele; I knew that it was going to be a challenge, so it was great but it was bloody rock hard sometimes.

In Schnabele's study of yoga, the author touches upon the way yoga constantly pushes against limits – yogis become aware of limits in order to overtake them, 'creating awareness of limits enables overcoming them' (Schnabele 2013:147). Similarly, by going on a yoga holiday, British and North American women are not only expanding their minds but also their bodies. Women are seeking a challenge, by attending a holiday where they must get up early to practise yoga before breakfast. They are stretching their own yoga practice, and hoping to bring that back with them when they return home. As Irish continued,

Which is good for me, because I'm getting out of that comfort zone, and when I go back home I think I need to up the game. Yeah, you've been coasting here, you know you're not going to progress if you keep in your comfort zone. You need to up the game somewhat. So that's been a good thing, really. I think that's one of the main reason of coming here, a kick up the ass, a bit of a boot.

Health benefits magnified

Some of the health benefits of yoga at home became magnified by travelling for yoga and these benefits include flexibility, switching off and connecting to something else. Even more, yoga becomes more emancipatory and empowering for those women practising it.

On our second day of the yoga holiday, the group was boisterous and full of excited energy. About eight of the group walked several miles down a winding road to explore the small centre of town. Quickly, women paired off by speed. As we started our day trip, I interviewed Elaine and Gina. Elaine is a regular student of Adele, and Gina was a good friend who was thinking about returning to yoga. We would stop to admire a donkey in a yard, or to let a car pass as we chatted. They talked about flexibility being one of the main health benefits of doing yoga. Elaine said, 'To maintain movement and increase your range of movement so that things like hamstrings don't stay tight. Yoga is something hopefully you can do when you're 80'. At that point, Gina mentioned seeing a seventy-five-year-old woman who looked great and was in shape and she did yoga, saying 'I think it's all about keeping you moving and keeping you flexible. You don't want your hips to go, you don't want to be not mobile, and yoga isn't strenuous on your joints but it will keep you'. Gina continues, 'Flexibility, mobility as you get older. You know I'm going to be fifty soon I can't just...', she drifts off talking about the side effects of aging and the ways that stretching can keep a body moving, rather than simply shuffling along.

The switching off that occurred for Leila in the gym was even more intensified in Italy, 'Here it's just crazy because you just sit in your little shavasana at the end, and it's just birds tweeting. There's no washer going, people talking, it's great'. She later says about the switching off in Italy:

> Being able to switch off and not having to...Like if we go to yoga at home, I mean I've not many responsibilities, but obviously my mum, you know, you get home then you've got to make tea, you've got to sort something else out, and you just switch. I mean I'll go to yoga at uni and you get after the class you switch straight back into student mode and it's like 'Oh Christ what report have I got to write now? Or what am I going to have for tea? What do I have to buy from the shop?' You know, you officially get to switch off – it's great, it's great.

Even more, women found themselves less consumed with social media and their phones, given that there was restricted wi-fi access. Adele added the health benefits of doing yoga in Italy, 'I also think it's really good to train yourself to focus on just one thing at a time and taking time to get away from technology and just being with yourself, which we don't often do anymore'. Italy encouraged the women to do this. Yoga, rather than work, became their priorities while they were at the Villa, as Sarah says:

> Because it is a yoga holiday, it is just holiday-ish. The warmth is very nice. Doing yoga outside is nice. So, I think that all adds to the general feeling of contentment, because you're having a proper break ... I think if it's just a class it'd be the latter part of your day that's just one thing of many things that you're doing. Whereas this is, instead of your work being the main thing of the day, actually yoga is the main thing. It's just different priorities.

Yoga helps one connect with oneself while at home. Yet, travel also makes people connect with one another. Scholars who liken tourism to a ritual (Graburn 2010) write about the liminal aspect of travel and bonding that happens amongst fellow travellers. They experience a form of communitas (Graburn 2010). Meredith, in particular, kept repeating how astounded she was at the great amount of fun that had been had amongst this particular group of women:

> And I can't believe how much of a laugh we've had, because I certainly didn't expect to laugh as much as we have laughed. It's just been

amazing. It's definitely more than a fun factor. Definitely more than I imagined, because that's really all about the people that you meet, isn't it? I love going to different places and meeting different people and not knowing what to expect. Everybody's got different life experiences, and I really like swapping stories. And every journey you go on in your life, it is all about the people that you meet. And if we had come here and people just didn't interact or talk or get on or have a good laugh at dinner…That would have not been the same. But we've all got on, we've all had a laugh, we've all been open and it's just been really, really good fun, really good fun.

Not only did the women appreciate the communitas of the holiday, they also appreciate the non-competitive nature of yoga. Elaine said, 'I quite like in yoga the way that you're not competitive. There's only you and the mat. So, it doesn't matter if I can't get my arm up, or my leg doesn't go that way, or if I can. Not sort of think 'Ooh look at me, I can put my leg there', or, 'Oh shame on me I can't put my leg there'. Iris, who practises at home and whose boundaries were pushed with Adele's class, also spoke of how nice it was to feel the energy of the other women:

Doing it in a group as well. Obviously, that's different, because I don't go to classes very often. But I think that's quite nice, because you see different people at different stages with different body shapes with different flexibility with different bodies, how they work. It's just re-alizing that we're all different and we're all just doing what we can, what's right for us. It's nice having shavasana and you get a kind of nice energy from everyone, which you don't obviously get when you practice on your own.

The women are all basking in connecting to themselves while doing yoga but also soaking up the energy of each other. Their communitas is embodied.

Hauser noted the 'choice of yoga practice as an individualized strat-egy for coping with the pressures of a post-Fordist labor market' (Hauser 2013:6). While the flexibility of yoga may enable one to function in a flexi-ble work environment, there were elements of resistance that I detected in some women's descriptions of yoga. Yoga is resistance to, a counterbalanc-ing of our post-Fordist workplace of flexible work. Not only do the asana poses counterbalance our bodily postures during work, as Elaine says, 'I have got in my head that [yoga] will counterbalance even if I am hunched over my desk all day, you know that kind of counterbalances that'. Simi-larly, Sarah also saw yoga as a way to counter work postures, 'you do a lot of stretches using muscles that you might not have known you had, mus-cles that haven't been stretched that way, particularly if you're doing office work or whatever'.

However, I witnessed an even stronger critique amongst the women against modern lifestyles. The non-competitiveness of yoga was rewarding, to remind Gina that she does not want to compete in life either:

> Sometimes I think going away, especially on this type of holiday, you then realise, 'Hey, there's more to life than the rat race and this or that and doing realistic things and clawing away'. It's like, 'hey, just simplify everything', Isn't it? Chill, we're not rushing around. You know you hit an age, like where I'm at, and it's like all I want is to be happy and healthy and have no worries. You know, it's not all about more, more, more. And you come to realise that the world is a big place and there's loads of other places to see than to sit in your gym.

Latent in Gina's statement is a critique of gross, reckless, blind consumption. Also, we must be mobile to recognise the world and all the various places it entails. 'The body becomes a sanctuary and a place of resistance against pervasive demands of consumer society' (Schnabele 2013:148).

Conclusion

The overall effect of yoga holidays was a tired energised feeling. They had pushed themselves, but at the same time they re-energised themselves so that they could return home. As Leila said about doing yoga in the morning:

> Apart from being a bit sore, really good. Actually awake, surprisingly, and I even think it's a bit strange when you do the breath, the calming breath, like it actually works, like you feel you've got more energy. You feel like when you wake up and you've done your lesson, you feel like you've got enough energy to carry on during the day.

Many of the women were surprised by how achy they felt over the holiday, like Meredith, 'But I'm aching more than I expected to ache, and I'm more tired more than I expected to be'.

Women who travel to Italy to experience a yoga holiday are seeking the health benefits they usually associated with yoga at home. They hope to embody mindfulness, presence, yet also expand their bodily limits through practising a new type of yoga in a new, natural setting. They are connecting and broadening their minds and bodies, reframing their own lives as they encounter other ways of living. Sarah felt like she may even have enough energy to return home with that health kick in mind. Women return home energised to resume or start a new health kick, embodying the welcome tired achiness that accompanies the weary yogi traveller.

References

Bruner, E. M. (2005) *Culture on Tour: Ethnographies of Travel*. Chicago, IL: University of Chicago Press.

Butler, J. (1990) Gender trouble, feminist theory, and psychoanalytic discourse, in L. Nicholson (ed.) *Feminism/Postmodernism*. New York: Routledge, pp. 324–340.

Castenada, Q. (1991) *An 'Archaeology' of Chichén Itza: Discourse, Power and Resistance in a Maya Tourist Site*. Unpublished doctoral dissertation. Albany: State University of New York.

Foucault, M. (1978) *The History of Sexuality: An Introduction*. New York: Vintage Books.

Game, A. (1991) *Undoing the Social: Towards a Deconstructive Sociology*. Buckingham: Open University Press.

Graburn, N. (2010) Secular ritual: A general theory of tourism, in S. Gmelch (ed.) *Tourists and Tourism: A Reader*. 2nd ed. Long Grove: Waveland Press, pp. 25–36.

Hauser, B. (Ed.). (2013) Introduction: Transcultural yoga(s): Analyzing a traveling subject, in B. Hauser (ed.) *Yoga Traveling: Bodily Practice in Transcultural Perspective*. London: Springer, pp. 1–34.

Hoyez, A. C. (2007) The 'world of yoga': The production and reproduction of therapeutic landscapes. *Social Science and Medicine*, 65(1): 112–124.

Kaleidoscope.com. Available at: www.kaleidoscopeyoganewcastle.com/retreats.php

Martin, E. (1994) *Flexible Bodies: Tracking Immunity in American Culture from the Days of Polio to the Age of AIDS*. Boston, MA: Beacon Press.

Merchant, S. (2011) Negotiating underwater space: The sensorium, the body and the practice of scuba-diving. *Tourist Studies*, 11: 215–234.

Naraindas, H. and Bastos, C. (Eds.) (2011) Healing holidays? Itinerant patients, therapeutic locales and the quest for health? *Anthropology and Medicine*, 18(1): 1–6.

Newcombe, S. (2013) Magic and yoga: The role of subcultures in transcultural exchange, in B. Hauser (ed.) *Yoga Traveling: Bodily Practice in Transcultural Perspective*. London: Springer, pp. 57–79.

Nichter, M. (2013) The social life of yoga: Exploring transcultural flows in India, in B. Hauser (ed.) *Yoga Traveling: Bodily Practice in Transcultural Perspective*. London: Springer, pp. 201–224.

Schnabele, V. (2013) 'The Useful Body': The yogic answer to appearance management in the post-Fordist workplace, in B. Hauser (ed.) *Yoga Traveling: Bodily Practice in Transcultural Perspective*. London: Springer, pp. 135–151.

Senate Committee on Aging. (2006) *The Globalization of Health Care: Can Medical Tourism Reduce Health Care Costs?* Washington, DC: U.S. Government Printing Office.

Smith-Morris, C. and Manderson, L. (2010). The baggage of health travelers. *Medical Anthropology*, 29(4): 331–335.

Speier, A. (2008) Czech Balneotherapy: Border medicine and health tourism. *Anthropological Journal of European Cultures*, 17: 145–159.

Speier, A. (2011a) Health tourism in a Czech health spa. *Anthropology and Medicine*, 18(1): 125–136.

Speier, A. (2011b). Brokers, consumers, and the internet: How North American consumers navigate their infertility journeys. *Reproductive Biomedicine Online*, 23(5): 592–599.

Speier, A. (2011c). 'IVF Holiday': Contradictions of patient care abroad. *CARGO: Journal for Cultural and Social Anthropology*, 9(1–2). http://cargojournal.org/index.php/cargo/article/view/45

Speier, A. (2015). Czech hosts creating 'A Real home away from home' for North American reproductive tourists. *Anthropologica*, 57(1): 27–39.

Speier, A. (2016). *Fertility Holidays: IVF Tourism and the Reproduction of Whiteness.* New York: New York University Press.

Urry, J. (1990) *The Tourist Gaze*. London: Sage.

Veijola, S. and Jokinen, E. (1994) The body in tourism. *Theory, Culture & Society*, 11: 125–151.

Whittaker, A. and Speier, A. (2010) 'Cycling overseas': Care, commodification and stratification in cross-border reproductive travel. *Medical Anthropology: Cross-Cultural Studies in Health and Illness*, 29(4): 363–383.

7 Yoga-scapes, embodiment and imagined spiritual tourism

Patrick McCartney

Introduction

In relation to the anthropology of tourism and the tourist's body, this chapter explores how subjective, embodied experience is mediated through one's expectations, goals and imagination. It challenges us to reflect on the different ways yoga-inflected lifestyles embody tourism, both within and beyond one's self; and, how through pilgrimage, one's own body is potentially transformed through this imaginative consumption. In the two main parts that follow, I explore the imaginative consumption of both physical and metaphysical 'pilgrimage' within the global wellness industry; not only in relation to global yoga and spiritual tourism but also through the idea of how divine presence represents civilizational embodiment through the incarnation of cultural essence as the vehicle of civilisation and the process of cultural re-territorialisation (Jain 2007:93).

The *yātra-sādhana* (performance of pilgrimage) is central to many South Asian religious traditions and involves both internal and external forms (Singh 2002). The imagined embodiment of the global yoga consumer, the devout Hindu pilgrim and the advanced tantric practitioner share similar ideas and practices. While the medium of pilgrimage, and popular usage of this term, is used in secular, spiritual and institutionalised environments, this chapter articulates some of the ways in which complex local and pan-national pilgrimage culture is expressed and rarefied through a globalised filter (Reader 1993:5). Appreciating that the traditional tantric practitioner has disdain for the diluted ideals and practices promoted in the global yoga/wellness industry, it is necessary to keep in mind that the *sādhu/yogin* does not join commercial tours. Therefore, not all 'pilgrimages' are 'spiritual tourism'. Also, not all pilgrimages or tourism are physical.

Through processes of embodied, imaginative interiorisation, the esoteric practices of the Śaiva-Śakta and tantric Buddhist traditions generate an internalised sacred-scape that creates a 'living', coherent, metaphysical body of the *devī* (divine feminine) (Singh 1995). These symbolic projections of the cosmic are mental reconstructions of the creative processes of expansion and absorption back to the original source, which enable the practitioner to identify with what some regard as the 'ultimate reality' (Heilijgeers-Seelen 1994:17).

This contemplative culture extrapolates an internal, imagined-*scape* onto an external, physical network of 'sacred geography' related to the physical *śakti-pīṭha*-s ('places of power'; *pīṭha* means 'seat'; *śakti* relates to 'divine feminine energy') that mythology links across South Asia. The *śaktī-pīṭha*-s are physical places where parts of the corpse of Śiva's wife, Satī, are said to have fallen while Śiva carried her corpse after immolating herself in protest upon her father's ritual fire. As a result, these places are also referred to as *satī-pīṭha*-s. This leads to movement between the *antara-* (internal) and *bāhya-* (external) *pīṭha*-s.

While the Yoginīhṛdaya, Ambāmatasaṁhitā and Manthānabhairava suggest fifty sites (Dyczkowski 2001); the Matsya, Skanda, Padma and Devībhāgavata Purāṇa-s place the number at 108 (Feldhaus 2003:131). According to Sircar (1948:3), the Pīṭhanirṇaya/Mahāpīṭhanirūpaṇa, which is a section of the larger Tantracūḍāmāṇi, provides a list of the 51 *śakti-pīṭha*-s, in: India (41), Bangladesh (4), Nepal (3), Pakistan (1), Sri Lanka (1) and Tibet (1). Through visiting these places, one connects to 'the ever-awake Energy of the universe. All these places, in other words, become the microcosms of the universe' (Mukhopadhyay 2018:59).

The esoteric Kubjikāmata school of Śakta-Tantra Hinduism (*circa* eleventh century CE) occupied itself with worship of the goddess, Kubjikā ('bent', 'curved' or 'contracted one'), which is an alloform of *haṭha-yoga*'s *kuṇḍalinī* (Goudriaan and Schoterman 1988:3; White 1996:79). It outlines strategies for interiorising sacred geography and inscribing the 'yoga body' with sound (Dcyzkowski 2001:45), creating a dialectic interplay between the internal and external realities while giving 'name and form' (*nāma-rūpa*) to the inner world through the interiorisation of the external; and, through embodiment, it creates a pure, ideal, sacred-scape.

The subtle, yoga body of tantric yoga is a multi-vocal set of traditions and practices linking tradition-specific metaphysics and ritual schematic traditions, which emphasise visualised installation on, or within, the physical body of the practitioner. Based on certain texts, the *cakra*-s are not considered to have an ontological reality of their own (Mallison and Singleton 2017, chapter 5); even though, over the past century, they have become a 'real' component of global yoga's imagination. Heilijgeers-Seelen (1994:17) explains how the *cakra*-s also symbolise the cosmic processes of emanation and re-integration through the six levels of *cakra*-s, upon which each letter of the Sanskrit alphabet is assigned to one petal of the *cakra*-s, visualised as lotus flowers. Also, various gods/goddesses are said to preside over different parts of the alphabet. For instance, the sixteen *pīṭhādhipa*-s (Rulers of Seats) are worshipped within the sixteen vowels (Goudriaan and Schoterman 1988:484, Goodall and Rastelli 2013:465), which are each assigned to one of the sixteen petals of *viśuddhi cakra* imagined at the throat. Figure 7.1 demonstrates the imagined location of each letter. Starting at twelve o'clock, moving clockwise, the vowels are uttered, and the deities, as well as Satī's body parts, are honoured.

Figure 7.1 Viśuddhi Cakra.
Source: Atarax42 (2014).

Even though the historical development of various *cakra* systems detailed different numbers – six, nine, twelve, or twenty-seven, some of which exist external to the body – of configurations and locations (Kaviraj 1963:229–237), it was Vidyāratna and Avalon's (1913) translation of the Ṣaṭcakranirūpaṇa ('searching for the six (*ṣaṭ*) *cakra*-s; from *mūlādhāra* to *ājñā*) that is best known as the 'true' representation of the *cakra-tantra* (chakra-system). The global imagination regarding the ontological veracity of *cakra*-s can be understood in the way factoids represent what *ought* to be true (Mailer 1973, Rostron 2012). The insidiously unbiological nature of factoids means that, the more often a non-arbitrary truth claim is repeated, the hypothesis comes closer to attaining the rank of established fact (Maier 1985:332). In the global wellness industry and New Age movement, this is evidenced by the belief that, not only are *cakra*-s real in an ontological sense but also at an outlier fringe level, there is a supposed 'reptilian conspiracy' involving 'alien implants' (the *cakra*-s) and 'reptilian masters' that 'possess your soul' (*ThunderWizarddotcom* 2016). Also, one's 'energetic system' can not only be 'tuned', 'cleansed' or 'activated'; it can also be completely removed (*ChakraWings* 2014). Charting these ideas influences our understanding of 'tourism'. As one is able to vicariously enter different New Age/yoga-related social worlds through different platforms, we find another way of contemplating how reconstituted yogic ideals can inspire journeys and imaginative embodiment.

Spinney (2006) discusses how a sense of belonging is created through experiences collected during geographical exploration, which enables the creation of meaningful spatial relations. 'Geographical exploration' occurs during contemplative meditation; and, from within the global yoga industry, these two 'traditional' forms of internal and external pilgrimage are consumed in reconstituted ways by global yogis through the pursuit of yoga-inspired leisure (i.e. *serious* contra *casual*) (Stebbins 2014).

Regardless of one's soteriological aspirations, many yoga retreats and workshops offer ways to embody this 'sacred feminine' geography without travelling to India or knowing anything about tantric traditions. The consumption of yoga-related tourism through pilgrimages to 'yoga festivals' is similar to multi-day music festivals like Glastonbury or Burning Man; particularly how a sense of re-enchantment through 'the globalisation of intermittent co-presence' is facilitated (Urry 2002:264). Global yogis, particularly within the less constrained parameters of global yoga festivals, are swayed by proselytising rhetoric to consume portable, yoga-inspired lifestyles (Lucia 2018:37).

Yogaland is an emic euphemism used by global yogis to describe the utopian-inspired meta-space where life is celebrated, and various yoga-inflected lifestyles are promoted as the antithesis, or a distraction to, perceived disenchantment. The irony is that the multibillion-dollar global yoga industry is modelled on neoliberal ideology, which the Indian state blends with the guru-devotee relationship in the pursuit of certain ends (Copeman and Ikegame 2012, Gooptu 2016). For many of its citizens, Yogaland exists in a local, quotidian experience of 'community' nestled around parochial consumption of different yoga brands. It is a metaphor or psychological entity in the minds of those who describe their yoga tribe as being a part of something greater than the sum of its parts. The idea of 'yoga-related' *tribes* is not entirely new, as early Aryan tribes viewed life as one typified by the dichotomy between *yoga* (see derivatives of roots √yudh-, √yuj- and √yā, which refer to war and movement) and *kṣema* (√kṣi-, which signifies resting, 'staying over' and intervals of settled life) (Palihawadana 1968:185). The idea that pre-Vedic (Harappan) and Vedic people were the same civilization, and also peaceful people practising yoga, is a popular factoid within Yogaland. Lauren (2015) and Tribe Yoga (2017) reveal that the twenty-first century 'yoga tribe' promotes yoga-inflected lifestyles within a pilgrimage tourism paradigm. An example is the yoga 'master' teacher, Sianna Sherman, who explains in the prominent Yoga Journal magazine that the 'hope for humanity rests with our 'collective heart tribe' (Sherman 2017). We can see how this rhetoric promotes an aspiration for embodying a 'collective' sense of interconnectedness.

The article is an advertorial plugging her online 'Goddess Yoga' course, which is Tantra-lite. It will 'transform your practice – on and off the mat' by helping you 'find your inner goddess and deepen your yoga practice' (AimHealthyU, 2017). This idea of finding the goddess relates to metaphysically embodying the power of the *kuṇḍalinī śakti* believed to exist in the physical *śakti-pīṭha*-s and metaphysical *cakra*-s mentioned above. Therefore, it is worth again considering what we mean by 'tourist' and 'pilgrim', how far an individual needs to travel for a journey to be considered a pilgrimage, and whether this type of journey relates only to the physical, or also to the metaphysical.

Movement and pilgrimage (*tīrtha-yātrā*) have been important cultural performative markers within South Asian religions for a long time (Singh 2013:10). In contrast, Margry (2008:28) questions whether *movement* is a universal phenomenon (for the Christian pilgrimage, at least) and 'the primary constitutive element of the pilgrimage'. The Aitareya Brāhmaṇa (7.15) exhorts people to travel for expiation of their sins; as, in many instances, *tīrtha-yātrā* is associated with *puṇya* (merit) and *śuddhi* (purification) (Kaur 1985:23). Also, *yātrin*-s (pilgrims) are attested in both epics, the Mahābhārata and Rāmāyaṇa, and several Purāṇa-s (Madan 2009:30), and *paryaṭaka*-s 'tourists/wanderers' are found in the Mṛcchakaṭika.

Singh (2013:305) contemporises 'pilgrimage tourism' as a rational, post-modern strategy for overriding the sacred-profane dichotomy through 'heritage awakening, deeper experiences and transferring the religiosity into global humanism and spirituality', which results in combining religious devotion with sightseeing by choosing a holy place as the destination (Madan 2009:30). As the internalised tantric pilgrimage does not necessarily require the pilgrim to physically journey to geographical places, as some texts reserve the interiorisation as a part of a ritual to purify the practitioner, help ward off fear or gain boons, the sacred geography is creatively imagined within the practitioner's body.

How ought we best approach this type of embodied pilgrimage methodologically, epistemologically and ontologically? Trying to typologise the internal pilgrimage as a metaphorical or allegorical journey, as a pilgrim can be understood as 'one who journeys to a place of importance to himself alone' (Morinis 1992:4), perhaps does epistemic violence to the tantric practitioner's local knowledge system. As this journey is much more than a metaphor. It is a literal co-mingling of external and internal realities that energise each other within the body of the practitioner. Surely, the same could possibly be said for the Tantra-lite consumer of global yoga as well.

Margry (2008:17) defines pilgrimage as a journey

> based on religious or spiritual inspiration, undertaken by individuals or groups, to a place that is regarded as more sacred or salutary than the environment of everyday life, to seek a transcendental encounter with a specific cult object for acquiring spiritual, emotional or physical healing or benefit.

Seemingly, this definition covers both internal and external movements or journeys, which are also made by pilgrims, tourists, consumers and practitioners.

A productive way to view contemporary spirituality, and these internal-external variants, is through what Bowman (2008:244) refers to as *interconnectedness* and *synchronicity*. Interconnectedness occurs through individuals coming together at yoga festivals, meditation classes, or while sitting on a tour bus, people can feel connected, in a holistic way and not just to each other, but to other species of animals, the planet, and through and beyond dimensions of time and space. The same can be said for the tantric practitioner. While synchronicity refers to the self-authentication process where individuals find meaning, purpose or answers, and, which is also possible even without seeking.

Spiritual tourism might awaken an individual's 'quest and feelings to realise the serene and divine message of the spirit of place, i.e. meeting of humanity and divinity through ecospirituality' (Singh 2013:308). This relates to place-making and how cultural representations enable or frame places as 'sacred' (Spinney 2006:710). While the anthropologist might be interested in theoretically contemplative meanings, spiritual tourists to India or yoga retreats/festivals, and tantric practitioners sitting quietly alone in a temple, cave or home, are more interested in embodied notions of 'doing' *yoga*, as opposed to thinking about it. Yet, even though *yoga* is polysemic, the popular definition reduces to the attempt to correct one's understanding about the non-dual unity of the individual microcosm and the macrocosm, and how to embody it.

Creating meaning in place through rhythm in Yogaland relates to the popular flow of modern postural yoga and the practice of rhythmic breathing (*prāṇāyāma*) linked to the higher stages of the rarified, contemplative process. Spinney refers to the production of rhythms as central to the process of re-embodiment, which enable, through intense feelings of muscular 'kinaesthetic burn', the objective reality of nature to become internalised. The modern postural yoga *flow* is emblematic of global yoga's commodified state. It generates a (meta)physical connection through the hybrid interconnectedness of the individual's yoga mat and physical body. This movement, on the mat, becomes a potent metaphorical vehicle to self-authenticate one's interconnectedness and synchronicity through the combination of the group movement, focused breathing and creative visualisation (i.e. meditation that normally occurs at the end of the class).

Yogaland has a fertile spectrum of opinions regarding yoga's history and purpose. Because global yoga generally serves as an instrument to counteract a perceived sense of disenchantment, the predominant narratives in the marketing of wellness and yoga quite often express romantic, anarchist-lite, eco-sensitive, utopian-idealised, post-national representations. An example comes from an article in Yoga Journal that explains how to harness the power of Hindu deities (Eichenseher 2017). Yoga, ostensibly, is applied rationally as a technology for empowerment (Black 2015), which, combined with a Tantra-lite approach to 'finding one's own goddess', becomes clearer why global yoga is so popular, particularly amongst middle-class women, and why yoga-related spiritual tourism is exceptionally popular (McCartney 2016, 2017).

Another representative example of how the rhetoric of global yoga promotes ideas related to reconnection, empowerment and metaphysical embodiment, follows:

> As women we spend so much time caring for and loving others. We nurture
> our families and friends, strive to improve the lives of those around us and
> rarely stop to appreciate ourselves. This divine two hour workshop will find
> us re-exploring the inner Goddess, empowering ourselves to be stronger,
> gentler and more in tune with our own needs. [The yoga teacher] will be
> leading us in gentle, restorative poses with her strong and magical voice.
> We will sink deep into our asanas as we release tension and prepare our
> hearts for reconnection to self. [The yoga teacher] will be giving treatments
> to each participant, with Essential Oils. As she applies the oils to your tem-
> ples, heart and center chakra, you will feel the energetic connection to self-
> worth & love as you gently release what no longer serves you.
>
> (Tribes 2017)

This *Sister Chakra Workshop* is an event marketed specifically to women in
what can be described as a Tantra-lite approach of internal creative visualisation, which aims to empower, through inscribing sound (*mantra*) within the
physical body, embodiment of the goddess. We can assume from Figure 7.2,

Figure 7.2 Location of Chakras.
Source: Giel (2005).

which is a generic image of the proposed location of where the *cakra*-s are to be visualised on the physical body, that the primary focus of this *Sister Chakra Workshop* is a journey through the 'seed sounds' (*bīja mantra*-s) attributed to the main *cakra*-s. The tantric practice, *ṣat-cakra-bheda* (six-chakra-piercing), evolved out of the sixth century CE Netra Tantra, which is the first known work to teach the 'six-chakra system'. The tenth century CE Kubjikāmata Tantra is the first text to systematically teach this process. Dyczkowski (2001:46) mentions that, according to primary tantric texts, like the Kubjikā Tantras and the Bhairava Tantra, the Niśisaṁcāra, the goddess *is* sound. However, more importantly, the Tantra-lite, or even advanced postural yoga-meditation teacher generally has very little to no practical understanding of tantric cosmology and practice. If they do, then it has typically come through New Age popular culture and not by reading the primary Sanskrit texts mentioned here.

Before we talk about metaphysical tourism in Yogaland, let us discuss physical pilgrimage in more detail.

Physical pilgrimage in Yogaland

This section has two parts. The first discusses the 'pilgrimages' of the global yoga consumer-practitioner. The second part discusses the domestic, Hindu pilgrimage throughout sacred geographical places related to the mythical story of Satī, which is available to the paying customer, who can join packaged holidays to explore the 'sacred geography' of the *śakti-pīṭha*-s.

Pilgrimage in global yoga

Multi-day festivals, like Glastonbury or Burning Man, facilitate the creation of a sense of re-enchantment through 'the globalization of intermittent co-presence' (Urry 2002:262–264). Urry's three-tier typology of co-presence includes: *face-to-face*, *face-the-place* and *face-the-moment*. *Face-to-face* refers to the intense commingling which facilitates feelings of interconnectedness (see a Turnerian 1986 sense of *communitas* and heightened feelings associated with Durkheim's collective effervescence, which is contrasted to the normal state the individual experiences when alone) through being within a group of like-minded people. This occurs through identifying with the group mentality, which ultimately leads to the feeling of collective effervescence (Law 2011). While Weber argues that unthinking emersion in a group was a response of lethargy, Durkheim argues that participation, and the sense of self-loss in the community, is validated by the immediate sense of transcendence and ecstasy it offers (Lindholm 2002:294). *Face-the-place* refers to physically walking, seeing, touching, doing, being, etc., which is a self-evident part of pilgrimage. *Face-the-moment* refers to the 'timing' of travelling to and being at a 'live' event. Wanderlust is a perfect example of a globalised, syndicated yoga festival, which occurs in several locations around the world, offering an 'endless summer of yoga', in which it becomes the context for 'conscious living' and 'guilt-free partying'. Wanderlust explains that, it 'is a leader in the yoga lifestyle space-encompassing events, centres, and media' (Wanderlust 2017), which focuses on cultivating a yoga 'practice to inspire connection' (Mishler 2017). The popularity of this growing number of globally available yoga festivals is neatly summarised by the following:

> There's nothing quite like a good yoga festival to reignite your passion for your practice. The sense of belonging that you feel with others around you from all over the country (or even the world) really brings the uniting practice of yoga to the forefront. We all care about this practice, and it has changed all of us in ways we could never imagine. Being present at a yoga festival allows us to celebrate that fact with other like-minded people, while celebrating the wonderfulness of the practice itself.
>
> (DoYouYoga 2017)

Interestingly, several attendees whom I spoke with view yoga festivals as the antithesis of a pilgrimage. This is mostly due to the hyper-commercialised context in which these events operate. Rather, they see themselves as consumers and participants in cultural festivals that allow them to experience the sociability of being amongst fellow yoga practitioners. As one respondent mentions,

> I come from a religion in which pilgrimage is sacred and I can't really wrap my head around going to a highly commercialized yoga event as being the same thing. And that doesn't mean I don't think one's yoga practice can't be their spiritual practice, that just means I don't see a highly commercialized yoga festival like wanderlust as a sacred destination.
>
> (Personal Conversation 22 September 2017)

However, some people do view such journeys and experiences as quasi- or pseudo-pilgrimages, as another respondent noted:

> I went to Wanderlust. It was sort of a pilgrimage because it was a three-to-four-hour drive. I went because it looked fun to do yoga with so many people. To be a part of a bigger thing that unified us all. I guess anything more than a three-hour trip is sort of pilgrimage.
>
> (Personal Conversation 22 September 2017)

The Yoga Journal frames individual or group journeys to India to consume yoga-related products and services by suggesting that a 'pilgrimage to India promises an adventure like no other' (Brown 2015). This is reiterated by

Natural Yoga's advertisement about their yoga tour to India. Notice how the same, essentialised, romantic, nineteenth-century narratives are used to create an image that India is a 'sacred', 'spiritual', 'mystical' place, where one *should* be a pilgrim rather than a tourist:

> Join us on a trip to some of India's most amazing spiritual places. We will practice yoga and meditation on the banks of the sacred Ganges, as yogis have done for thousands of years. We'll meet with sadhus, visit ancient temples, meditate in sacred Himalayan caves and dive deep into the wonders of Yogic India – most of them off the beaten tourist track. We will explore the main schools of yoga (hatha, karma, jnana and bhakti), and discuss the relevance of yoga in our daily life. Mystical India will be a pilgrimage towards discovering our authentic Self. It is not going to be a sightseeing tour or a shopping experience. Yoga is a path that is supposed to lead us to Freedom and Joy. How do we embody these qualities in our life? What is preventing us from truly embracing these qualities? And what can we do to remove the obstacles that prevent us from living this truth? All the places we will visit have a strong meditative power, that can really help us in connecting with our divine essence. We will use tools from the yoga tradition to help us develop a framework for transformative practice.
>
> (NaturalYoga 2016)

Yoga-related spiritual-pilgrimage-tourism linked with sacred geography appeals to anyone inclined towards sacred, feminist-inspired ideology, which seeks to empower both women and men through an ecofeminist ethic that places the feminine principle at the centre of the cosmology. Singh (2013:152) explains that the tantric system represents manifestations of goddesses that cross the narrowness and strictness of orthodox Hindu traditions. This is one reason how it also makes it more appealing to the global yoga consumer.

While it is easy to be cynical and sceptical about tours not being 'authentic' or 'traditional', they do provide potentially vulnerable individuals a safety-in-numbers opportunity to travel, possibly for the first time, as a group, in a country that is infamous for rape, theft and illness. Without this type of tour package, many people would possibly not travel to India as (spiritual) tourists.

As we discuss in the next section, this commodification and essentialist rhetoric is not just something that actors within the global yoga, spiritual tourism and wellness industries engage in; it is also the domain of domestic spiritual tourism operators.

Pilgrimage to the 'Places of Power'

In response to joining a group tour on a bus trip to different sacred geographical sites through the Indian Himalayas, Lochtefeld (2010:203) asks,

'Was it a pilgrimage, was it a vacation, was it cultural tourism – a vacation trip to places with historic or religious significance – or was it some of each?'

The commodification of spiritual tourism includes tours available for the more intrepid tourist-pilgrim, which includes several group and individual tours to some, or all, of the 51 *śakti-pīṭha*-s. For instance, Holiday Travel (2017) offers packages and information on a state-country basis. This includes basic information about trekking, distance, mythological significance, transport, accommodation, etc. However, most tour companies only provide tours that include the *śakti-pīṭha*-s within one state, region or country.

For the international pilgrim, Adieu Holidays (2017) offers an eighteen-night package from the United Kingdom, which includes flying return from Heathrow to New Delhi, and visiting some of the more significant and popular *pīṭha*-s on the circuit. As an example, Dey (2017) writes about the 'Must Visit Shakti Peethas in India: The Divine Seats of Cosmic Power' on Tour My India's blog. Through email, this company detailed a ten percent mix of international tourists and non-resident Indians (NRIs) normally combines with an overwhelming majority of domestic clientele on their thirty-day 51 *śakti-pīṭha* tour.

Holiday Travel (2017) lists the main four (*ādi-śakti-pīṭha*-s) as (1) Kāmākhyā, Guwahati, Assam – represents Satī's womb/vagina [Kulacūḍamāṇi Tantra 5.1 mentions the *yonī* (vagina) and 5.36 claims it to be the principal *pīṭha*]; (2) Bimala Temple is located inside the Jagannātha Temple, Pūri, Odisha – represents Satī's feet; (3) Tārā Tāriṇī is located near Berhampūr, Odisha – represents Satī's breasts; and (4) Dakṣiṇa Kālikā is located in Kolkata, West Bengal – represents Satī's right toe. For the more intrepid and less group-oriented tourist, one can organise the itinerary themselves. There are many online groups devoted to sharing information relevant to the pilgrimage. One such site is Shaktipeethas (2017).

Ultimately, it depends on one's inclination and budget. As visiting all 51 sites requires travelling to several SAARC countries (South Asian Association for Regional Cooperation: India, Pakistan, Sri Lanka, Nepal, Bangladesh, Afghanistan, Bhutan and Maldives). This is one reason why the 51 Shaktipeeth Circuit (2017) claims it is theoretically possible to develop 'progress in tourism, cultural development, economic growth, communal harmony and peace thereby finish terrorism and harmonise foreign relations' through promoting this Shaktipeeth Circuit. Figure 7.3 displays the location of the international circuit [see Shaktipeethas (2017) for an interactive map].

The entire circuit would take significant resources, time and effort. Typically, people complete legs of the circuit in a state-by-state sequence. One alternate option includes a five-day pilgrimage that incorporates, as a representative mesocosm, all the 51 *śakti-pīṭha*-s within it. According to Singh (2013:140), the Vindhyachal Kshetra is located eighty kilometres west of Varanasi, and is first described in the non-standard eighteenth century, Autsanash Purāṇa.

Figure 7.3 51 Shaktipeeth Circuit.
Source: Singh (2013:135).

Another shorter pilgrimage involves the miniature, yet physical, rep-resentations of the pilgrimage at the 51 Shaktipeeth Circuit temple just outside Lucknow, Uttar Pradesh, which houses physical remnants of the 51 *śakti-pīṭha*-s in one convenient location. Singh (2013:149) explains that the 'temple is arranged in a glass cascade that exhibits the 51-*Kalashas* [Sanskrit: *kalaśa*, mud water-pots] possessing the sacred soils' from all the *śakti-pīṭha*-s, which gives 'a way to experience the universality of the divine mother spirit through micro-cosmic representation'. In relation to this, Diane Eck discusses how the Hindu term *darśana* does not only signify 'seeing the deity' but also includes the 'seeing of truth' (1998:4). The visual aspect of seeing the divine form is an intimate occasion that places emphasis on a personal encounter. Various forms of *darśana* are heightened modes of perception that focus attention. This 'attention is the closed telescope when the gaze is upon the deity' (Sanzaro 2008:16).

The 51 Shaktipeeth Circuit asserts that

> The images of trio-force goddesses representing Mahasarasvati, Mahalakshmi and Mahakali are installed at the ground floor, and at the second floor all the 51 Shakti images along with the associated Bhairavas and the parts of body fell there, are arranged clock-wise symmetrically in the sequential order in the circular-form inner sanctum.

Through circumambulating the three-storey temple, the pilgrim internalises this cosmological representation and embodies the fallen body parts.

Having given a brief overview of the ways in which domestic and international spiritual tourists travel and embody the goddess in India, I now move to the final section which briefly looks at the metaphysical pilgrimage and embodiment.

Metaphysical pilgrimage in Yogaland

Above, I explored the outward physical journey. In this section, I discuss the journey to the inner world of Tantra, where an internal, embodied, sacred-scape is created using contemplation, sound, breath and abstract meditation, which creates a metaphysical body of the goddess within oneself (Zangpo 2001). However, even though this journey is available in a countless array of superficial Tantra-lite options, the experienced practitioner engages in a much deeper level of visualisation, embodiment and pilgrimage. While the underlying premise is the same – to create a space within one's physical body where an imagined, yet 'living', coherent body of the *devī* can be embodied – the advanced practitioner inscribes the 51 *śakti-pīṭha*-s within their own body using the sounds of the Sanskrit alphabet. Sanskrit's phonemic inventory includes the following: sixteen vowels, twenty-five consonants, four sibilants, four semi-vowels, plus a couple of extra conjunct sounds.

The Tantra-lite versions typically engage with other New Age modalities and goddess worship from other cultures (Javaid 2017). This introductory level of 'awakening the goddess within' typically involves learning how to 'balance the chakras'. This might involve a sequence of modern yoga postures or intoning sound (*mantra*). The popular, basic sequence involves reciting 'seed sounds' (*bīja mantra*-s) associated with each *cakra*. The six-chakra system includes focusing attention at points along the front of the body, for instance, at the eyebrow centre, throat, sternum, navel, pubic bone and pelvic floor (Figure 7.2). At each location, a one-syllable *mantra* is recited in descending and then ascending order: *oṁ, haṁ, yaṁ, raṁ, vaṁ, laṁ*. An even simpler version uses *oṁ* for all the *cakra*-s. Both advanced and novice practitioners link the movement of the breath up and down the front of the body while visualising any number of things, such as a small candle flame, a ruby, a simple flower and so on.

However, these simple versions of the practice are based upon a much older and more complicated series of techniques. A seminal reference related to the historical development of the chakra systems' theories and practices is located in Śārṅgadeva's thirteenth-century musicological text, known as the Saṅgītaratnākara. Verses 2.120–145 contain an intimate description of a particular emotional state or mood (vṛtti) linked to each petal. While the New Age practitioner might use these moods as contemplative devices, these moods are said to arise from situating the self in each petal (Kitada, 2012:28–303). For instance, the svādhiṣṭhāna-cakra imagined at the base of the genitals has six petals; which each correspond with the following moods: modesty, cruelty, destruction of pride, stupefaction, disrespect and suspicion (See Mallison and Singleton 2017:516–524 for an easy to read list).

Bühnemann (1991) explains that the fifteenth-century Kulārṇava Tantra (15.48–49) describes how to garland oneself with a 'necklace of imperishable sounds' (akṣamālā), which should be counted in regular and reversed order [see Avalon and Vidyāratna (1913:225) 15.49cd: *anulomavilomābhyām gaṇayen mantravittamaḥ*]. The Lalitā–sahasra–nāma-stotram (The Thousand – names of Lalitā Song), explains that Mālinī is the name of the 51-lettered deity who is the goddess of energy (*prāṇeśvarī*), the giver of energy (*prāṇadātrī*) and the one whose form is the 51 *pīṭha*-s (*pañcāśat–pīṭharūpiṇī*) (Sastry 1951:236; Giridhar, 2013:14). This forms the basis of the simple technique, but the advanced practitioner uses it as a base to create much more complicated forms of imagined embodiment.

Dyczkowski (2001:46) highlights that each of these imaginary lotus petals represents one of the sacred physical *pīṭha*-s mentioned above. While both the dynamic and resting breath are the *loci* of projection where, combined with sound the transcendent becomes immanent, there are many other ways to embody the goddess in her various manifestations along this internal pilgrimage. The Yoginī–hṛdaya Tantra (8.32–49, 57–71) explains the process of interiorisation of this metaphysical journey. It involves mentally moving from spatial/visual domains to subtle oral ones (Kaviraj 1963:206–229, Padoux and Jeanty 2013:102–103). Some discrepancy exists between Kaviraj's and Padoux and Jeanty's translations of this text. Their verse numbers are out by three. For example, verses 8.35ab and 8.32ab, respectively, explain how the metaphysical journey around and within the practitioner's own body should begin with the right foot (*dakṣiṇaṃ padam ārabhya*) and end with the left foot (*vāma–pāda–avasānakam*) (Kaviraj 1963:206, Padoux and Jeanty 2013:102). The following verses (33–40; 36–43) begin with explaining how the names and locations of the *pīṭha*-s will be given. We then end up with a list, such as this, in Table 7.1.

Two, final, examples (Figures 7.4 and 7.5), both of which contain the Sanskrit alphabet within different but related geometric diagrams, relate to the incipient way that distant and complex tantric rituals are adopted, reconstituted and localised by non-experts within Yogaland.

Table 7.1 List of Mantras, Locations and Body Parts

Letter	Mantra	Location	Body Part
a	*aṁ kāmrūpāya namaḥ*	Kāmarūpa	Top of head
ā	*āṁ vārāṇasyai namaḥ*	Vārāṇasi	Face
i	*iṁ nepālāya namaḥ*	Nepāla	Right eye
ī	*īṁ pauṇḍravardhanāya namaḥ*	Purandra Kardhana	Left eye
u	*uṁ purasthitakaśmīrāya namaḥ*	Purasthita Kashmir	Right ear
ū	*ūṁ kānyakubjāya namaḥ*	Kānyakubja	Left ear
ṛ	*ṛṁ pūrṇaśalāya namaḥ*	Pūrṇaśaila	Right nostril
ṝ	*ṝṁ arbudācalāya namaḥ*	Arbudācala	Left nostril
lṛ	*lṛṁ āmrātakeśvarāya namaḥ*	Āmrātakeśvara	Right cheek
lṝ	*lṝṁ ekāmrāya namaḥ*	Ekāmra	Left cheek
e	*eṁ tristrotase namaḥ*	Tristrotasa	Upper lip
ai	*aiṁ kāmakoṭaye namaḥ*	Kāmkoṭa	Lower lip
o	*oṁ kailāsāya namaḥ*	Kailiasa	Upper teeth
au	*auṁ bhṛgunagarāya namaḥ*	Bhṛgunagar	Lower teeth
am	*aṁ kedārāya namaḥ*	Kedāra	Tip of tongue
ḥ	*hṁ candrapuṣkariṇyai namaḥ*	Candra Puṣkariṇī	Neck
ka	*kaṁ śrīpurāya namaḥ*	Śrīpura	Right underarm
kha	*khaṁ oṅkārāya namaḥ*	Oṅkāra	Right elbow
ga	*gaṁ jālandharāya namaḥ*	Jālanddhara	Right wrist
gha	*ghaṁ mālavāya namaḥ*	Mālava	Base of right fingers
ṅ	*ṅaṁ kulāntakāya namaḥ*	Kulāntaka	Tips of right fingers
ca	*caṁ devīkoṭāya namaḥ*	Devīkoṭa	Left underarm
cha	*chaṁ gokarṇāya namaḥ*	Gokarṇa	Left elbow
ja	*jaṁ mālarūteśvarāya namaḥ*	Māruteśvara	Left wrist
jha	*jhaṁ aṭṭhāsāya namaḥ*	Aṭṭahāsa	Base of left fingers
ñ	*ñaṁ virajāyai namaḥ*	Virajā	Tips of left fingers
ṭa	*ṭaṁ rājagehāya namaḥ*	Rājageha	Base of left thigh
ṭha	*ṭhaṁ mahāpathaya namaḥ*	Mahāpatha	Right knee
ḍa	*ḍaṁ kolāpurāya namaḥ*	Kolapura	Right ankle
ḍha	*ḍhaṁ elāpurāya namaḥ*	Elapura	Base of right toes
ṇ	*ṇaṁ kāleśvarāya namaḥ*	Kāleśvara	Tips of right toes
ta	*taṁ jayantikāyai namaḥ*	Jayantika	Base of left thigh
tha	*thaṁ ujjayinyai namaḥ*	Ujjain	Left knee
da	*daṁ citrāyai namaḥ*	Citrā	Left ankle
dha	*dhaṁ kṣīrikāyai namaḥ*	Kṣīrikā	Base of left toes
n	*naṁ hastināpurāya namaḥ*	Hastināpura	Tips of left toes
pa	*paṁ uḍḍīśāya namaḥ*	Uḍḍīśa	Right side of body
pha	*phaṁ prayāgāya namaḥ*	Prayāga	Left side of body
ba	*baṁ ṣaṣṭhīśāya namaḥ*	Ṣaṣṭhīśa	Buttocks
bha	*bhaṁ māyāpuryai namaḥ*	Māyāpuri	Navel
ma	*maṁ jaleśāya namaḥ*	Jaleśa	Stomach
ya	*yaṁ malayāya namaḥ*	Malaya	Heart
ra	*raṁ śrīśailāya namaḥ*	Śrīśaila	Right shoulder
la	*laṁ merave namaḥ*	Meru	Back of neck
va	*vaṁ girivarāya namaḥ*	Girivar	Left shoulder
śa	*śaṁ mahendrāya namaḥ*	Mahendra	From the heart to the right finger tips
ṣa	*ṣaṁ vāmanāya namaḥ*	Vāmana	From the heart to the left finger tips
sa	*saṁ hiraṇyapurāya namaḥ*	Hiraṇyapura	From the heart to the tips of right toes
ha	*haṁ mahālakṣmīpurāya namaḥ*	Mahālakṣmāpura	From the heart to the tips of left toes
ḷa	*ḷaṁ oḍyāṇāya namaḥ*	Oḍyāna	From the heart to the genitals
kṣa	*kṣaṁ chāyācchatrāya namaḥ*	Chāyāchatra	From the heart to the head

Source: Kaviraj (1963:211–212, 213), Padoux and Jeanty (2013:102–103).

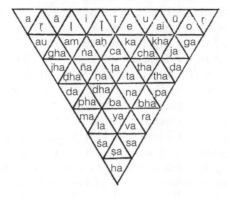

Figure 7.4 The Mātṛkā Yantra.
Source: Modified from Bühnemann (1991:299). Reprinted with Permission.

Figure 7.5 Mātṛkā Cakra.
Source: Hasanthi (2011).

A search for 'sacred geometry' or 'yantra' at Pinterest shows hundreds of geometric images related to Tantra. This includes 7.4, the downward-pointing *mātṛkā-yantra* (mother-diagram) triangle, which represents the *yonī* (the symbolic vagina as the source of manifestation). Bühnemann (1991:299) says it is mentioned in the Paramānanda Tantra. This interlaced network of 49 smaller triangles contains the entire Sanskrit alphabet. Yet, even with a basic knowledge of the alphabet, the Tantra-lite practitioner would not know how to proceed with the 'necessary adjuncts to the manipulation of alchemical substances'. This includes 'ritual worship, and the use of *maṇḍalas* [diagrams], *mantras*, etc.' (White 1996:145). What is lacking from Pinterest is a thorough explanation of *mantra-śāstra* (rules pertaining to *mantra*); and, most importantly, how to succeed in *mantra siddhi* (mantra realisation). Figure 7.5 also represents the *mātṛkā as* it is visualised in the *maṇḍala* form of the Śrī Yantra or Śrī Cakra. The difference between a *yantra* and a *maṇḍala* is that the former may or may not have a central point. The aspirant symbolically enters the central point where the entire cosmos is represented in miniature. However, this technology is more than just an aesthetically pleasing object to adorn one's back as a tattoo or a wall in a yoga studio. For the serious aspirant, they are employed within a ritual context to either: (1) pacify (*śāntika*), (2) expel antagonistic forces (*ucchātana*) or (3) to eliminate diabolical possession (*bhūta-ucchātana*) (Rao 1988:22).

In Figure 7.5, the spokes of the *cakra* contain the vowels while each of the eight petals contain the consonants and some extra ritual-related letters. To the uninitiated, who does not know the esoteric contents of the Vātula Tantra, the parsing of the letters into various: genders (masculine, feminine, neuter), elements (earth, water, fire, air, ether) and *guṇa-s* (active, sluggish, bright) is lost (Rao 1988:32–33). However, that might not matter, particularly if one would prefer to simply listen to MC Yogi beatbox the *bīja* (seed) *mantra*-s of the *cakra*-s (2010).

Conclusion

This chapter invited us to be tourists on a journey within Yogaland that began with the physical and ended with the metaphysical. It focused on how the myth-related but literally physical *śakti-pīṭha*-s are used by advanced tantric practitioners to create an internal map, which is based on combining ritual, creative visualisation, sound, diagram and breath. This was compared with the Tantra-lite versions of the same practice that are more popularly consumed in Yogaland, and the pilgrimage tourist packages.

Comparing these different options challenged us to consider that there are more ways to understand what it means to be a tourist and pilgrim; and, how there are many ways to embody, not only the tantric goddess but also different ways of embodiment related to being a *yogin-tantrika*, tourist and pilgrim. This involved demonstrating how 'tourism' within Yogaland can be both an internal and external journey, which, of course, depends on the individual's goals and level of experience. Furthermore, within the frame of the anthropology of tourism, we were invited to consider a broader definition of both 'movement' and 'journey', as the internal pilgrimage does not require a physical journey through time and space, but, rather, a metaphysical journey within. This urges us to reconsider what physically embodying being a tourist constitutes in its entirety.

While there are several entry-level ways in which Tantra-lite variants of more advanced practices creatively internalise and embody the goddess, the dominant forms consumed within an exceptionally commodified and commercialised Yogaland are generally a New Age, culturally appropriated bricolage. This leads to possibly different subjective experiences of embodiment that some advanced *tantrika*-s assert can potentially lead to dangerous consequences for the untrained. One wonders, finally, if there is a palpable difference between physically travelling to the 51 *śakti-pīṭha*-s, compared with the one-stop-temple where they are micro-cosmically represented; the meso-level representation of the shorter circuit; the internal, imagined pilgrimage; or any of the Tantra-lite versions available at countless New Age-inflected yoga studios or festivals? Regrettably, the highly subjective nature of this journey and the concomitant non-arbitrary epistemically relative truth claims that result, restricts us to qualitative methods of inquiry.

Acknowledgement

The author would like to thank McComas Taylor and Borayin Larios for reading drafts of this chapter and offering constructive feedback. Somadeva Vasudeva, Ian Reader, Rana Singh and Gudrun Bühnemann for kindly sharing their perspectives on this topic, making certain texts available and granting permission to reprint images. And, Dagmar Wujastyk for helping with a reference.

References

51 Shaktipeeth Circuit. (2017) *Vision: 51 Shaktipeeth Circuit.* Available at: http://www.51shaktipeethcircuit.com/51shaktipeethcircuit.aspx [accessed 25 September 2017].
Adieu Holidays. (2017) *Nav Shakti Peeth yatra.* Available at: http://www.adieuholidays.com/nav-shakti-peeth-yatra.html#tab17 [accessed 25 September 2017].
AimHealthyU. (2017) *Goddess yoga with Sianna Sherman.* Available at: http://www.aimhealthyu.com/courses/goddess-yoga-with-sianna-sherman-reg [accessed 12 September 2017].
Atarax42. (2014) Vishuddha Chakra. *Wikimedia.* Available at: https://commons.wikimedia.org/wiki/File:Chakra5.svg [accessed 07 June 2018].
Black, S. (2015) *From India, with Love: Cultural Appropriation and 50 Years of Light on Yoga.* Available at: https://theconversation.com/from-india-with-love-cultural-appropriation-and-50-years-of-light-on-yoga-51186 [accessed 06 September 2016].

Bowman, M. (2008) Going with the flow: Contemporary pilgrimage in Glastonbury, in P. J. Margry (ed.) *Shrines and Pilgrimages in the Modern World: New Itineraries into the Sacred.* Amsterdam: Amsterdam University Press, pp. 241–281.

Brown, C. (2015) *Why Make a Yoga Pilgrimage to India?* Available at: https://www. yogajournal.com/lifestyle/make-yoga-pilgrimage-india [accessed 19 September 2017].

Bühnemann, G. (1991) Selecting and perfecting mantras in Hindu tantrism. *Bulletin of the School of Oriental and African Studies,* 54: 292–306.

CleaningWings. (2014) *Chakra Removal: A Next Step in Removing Our Limitations and Manifesting Our Greater Presence.* http://chakraremoval.com/ [accessed 07 May 2018].

Copeman, J. and Ikegame, A. (2012) Guru logics. *HAU: Journal of Ethnographic Theory,* 2: 289–336.

Dey, S. (2017) *Must Visit Shakti Peethas in India: The Divine Seats of Cosmic Power.* Available at: https://www.tourmyindia.com/blog/must-visit-shakti-peethas-in-india/ [accessed 25 September 2017].

DoYouYoga (2017) *Top 15 Yoga Festivals in the USA.* Available at: https://www. doyouyoga.com/top-15-yoga-festivals-in-the-usa-15796/[accessed 26 September 2017].

Dyczkowski, M. (2001) The inner pilgrimage of the Tantras: The sacred geography of the Kubjikā Tantras with reference to the Bhairava and Kaula Tantras. *Journal of the Nepal Research Centre,* 7: 43–83.

Eck, D. L. (1985) *Darśan: Seeing the Divine Image in India.* Chambersburg, PA: Anima Books.

Eichenseher, T. (2017) *How to Use Yantras to Bring the Power of the Gods & Goddesses into Your Daily Life. Yoga Journal.* Available at: https://www.yogajournal. com/yoga-101/what-are-yantra-and-how-to-harness-their-energies [accessed 12 September 2017].

Feldhaus, A. (2003) *Connected Places: Region, Pilgrimage, and Geographical Imagination in India.* New York: Palgrave Macmillan.

Geil, I. (2005) *Chakras.* Wikimedia. Available at: https://commons.wikimedia. org/w/index.php?curid=178993 [accessed 07 June 2018].

Giridhar, M. (2013) *Śrī Lalitā Sahasranāma Stotram.* Available at: https:// sanskritdocuments.org/doc_devii/lalita.pdf [accessed 07 May 2019].

Goodall, D. and Rastelli, M. (Eds.) (2013) *Tāntrikābhidhānakośa.* Vienna: VÖAW.

Gooptu, N. (2016) New spirituality, politics of self-empowerment, citizenship, and democracy in contemporary India. *Modern Asian Studies,* 50: 934–974.

Goudriaan, T. and Schoterman, J. A. (1988) *The Kubjikāmatatantra.* Leiden: Brill.

Hasanthi. (2011). Matrika Chakra. Wikimedia. Available at: https://commons. wikimedia.org/wiki/File:Matrika_Chakra.jpg [accessed 06 June 2019].

Heilijgers-Seelen, D. (1994) *The System of the Five Cakras in Kubjikāmatatantra 14–16.* Groningen: Egbert Forsten.

Holiday Travel. (2017) *52 Shaktipeeths of India: Tourist and Pilgrimage Guide.* Available at: https://www.holidaytravel.co/destination-dtl/52_shaktipeeths_ tour_guide.htm [accessed 25 September 2017].

Javaid, F. (2017) *Three Divine Feminine Workshops with Yoga, Essential Oils & Ceremony.* Available at: https://www.eventbrite.com/e/3-divine-feminine-workshops-with-yoga-essential-oils-ceremony-tickets-38077682373?aff=erelexpmlt [accessed 26 September 2017].

Jain, K. (2007) *Gods in the Bazaar: The Economies of Indian Calendar Art*. Durham, NC: Duke University Press.

Kaur, J. (1985) *Himalayan Pilgrimages and the New Tourism*. New Delhi: Himalayan Books.

Kaviraj, G. (1963) Yoginī Hṛdaya: With Commentaries Dīpikā of Amṛtānanda and Setubandha of Bhāskara Rāya. 2nd ed. Varanasi: Varanaseya Sanskrit Vishwavidyalaya.

Kitada, M. (2012) *The Body of the Musician: An Annotated Translation and Study of the Piṇḍotpatti-Prakaraṇa of Śārṅgadeva's Saṅgītaratnākara*. Berlin: Peter Lang.

Lauren. (2015) *Your Vibe Attracts Your Tribe: A Cool Ass Yoga Experience*. Available at: http://thesisterprojectblog.com/2015/11/11/your-vibe-attracts-your-tribe-a-cool-ass-yoga-experience/ [accessed 09 September 2017].

Law, A. (2011) *Key Concepts in Classical Social Theory*. London: Sage Publications.

Lindholm, C. (2002) Authenticity, anthropology and the sacred. *Anthropological Quarterly*, 75 (2): 331–338.

Lochtefeld, J. G. (2010) *God's Gateway: Identity and Meaning in a Hindu Pilgrimage Place*. New York: Oxford.

Lucia, A. (2018) Saving Yogis: Spiritual nationalism and the proselytizing missions of global yoga, in B. E. Brown and B. S. A. Yeoh (eds.) *Asian Migrants and Religious Experience: From Missionary Journeys to Labor Mobility* Amsterdam: Amsterdam University Press, pp. 35–70.

Maier, F. G. (1985) Factoids in ancient history: The case of fifth-century Cyprus. *The Journal of Hellenic Studies*, 105(November): 32–39.

Mailer, N. (1973) *Marilyn*. New York: Grosset and Dunlap.

Mallison, J. and Singleton, M. (2017) *Roots of Yoga*. London: Penguin.

Margry, P. J. (2008) Secular Pilgrimage: A Contradiction in Terms? in P. J. Margry (ed.) *Shrines and Pilgrimage in the Modern World: New Itineraries into the Sacred*. Amsterdam: Amsterdam University Press, pp. 13–48.

McCartney, P. (2016) Utopian symmetries: Reflections on future worlds and trans-global yoga. *The Journal of the International Society for the Interdisciplinary Study of Symmetry*, 1: 86–89.

McCartney, P. (2017) Politics beyond the Yoga mat: Yoga fundamentalism and the 'Vedic Way of Life'. *Global Ethnographic*, May. Available at: http://oicd.net/ge/index.php/politics-beyond-yoga-mat-yoga-fundamentalism-vedic-way-life/ [accessed 26 September 2017].

Mishler, A. (2017) *Practice to Inspire Connection*. Available at: https://tv.wanderlust.com/programs/practice-to-inspire-connection [accessed 09 September 2017].

Morinis, A. (1992) *Sacred Journeys: The Anthropology of Pilgrimage*. Westport, CT: Greenwood.

Mukhopadhyay, A. (2018). *The Goddess in Hindu-Tantric Traditions: Devi as Corpse*. London: Routledge.

NaturalYoga. (2016) *Mystical India: A Sacred Journey to the Birthplace of Yoga*. Available at: http://naturalyoga.nl/event/mystical-india-autumn/#. WcSGI0qCyCU [accessed 22 September 2017].

Padoux, A. and Jeanty, R. O. (2013) *The Heart of the Yoginī: The Yoginīhṛdaya, a Sanskrit Tantric Treatise*. New York: Oxford University Press.

Palihawadana, M. (1968) Yoga and Kṣema: The significance of their usage in the Ṛgveda. *Vidyodaya*, 1: 185–190.

Rao, S. K. R. (1988) *The Yantras*. Delhi: Sri Satguru Publications.

Reader, Ian. (1993) Introduction, in I. Reader and T. Walter (eds.) *Pilgrimage in Popular Culture.* London: Macmillan, pp. 1–29.

Rostron, Allen. (2012) *Factoids.* Available at: http://papers.ssrn.com/sol3/papers. cfm?abstract_id=2302353 [accessed 18 November 2015].

Sanzaro, F.J. (2008) Darshanas, Mode and Critique of Perception: Hinduism's Liberatory Model of Visuality. *Axis Mundi:* 1–24.

Sastry, R. A. (1951) *Lalitā–Sahasranāman with Bhāskarāya's Commentary Translated into English.* Madras: The Theosophical Publishing House.

Shaktipeethas. (2017) *51 Shakti Peethas: Exact Location and Travel Information.* Available at: http://www.shaktipeethas.org/panchasat/topic191.html [accessed 25 September 2017].

Sherman, S. (2017) *Sianna Sherman's Hope for Humanity Rests with Our 'Collective Heart Tribe'.* Available at: https://www.yogajournal.com/lifestyle/the-future-of-yoga-sianna-sherman-collective-heart-tribe [accessed 12 September 2017].

Singh, R. P. B. (1995) Towards deeper understanding, sacredscape and faithscape: An exploration in pilgrimage studies. *National Geographical Journal of India,* 41: 89–111.

Singh, R. P. B. (2013) *Pilgrimage in the Hindu Tradition: Sacred Space and System.* New Delhi: Dev Publishers.

Singh, S. (2002) Managing the Impacts of Tourist and Pilgrim Mobility in the Indian Himalayas. *Revue de géographie alpine,* 90(1): 25–36.

Sircar, D. C. (1948) *The Śakta Pīṭhas.* New Delhi: Motilal Banarsidas.

Spinney, J. (2006) A place of sense: A kinaesthetic ethnography of cyclists on Mont Ventoux. *Environment and Planning D,* 24: 709–732.

Stebbins, R. A. (2014) *Careers in Serious Leisure: From Dabbler to Devotee in Search of Fulfilllment.* New York: Palgrave McMillan.

ThunderWizarddotcom. (2016) *Kundalini and the Reptilian Conspiracy: How They Control You?* Available at: https://www.youtube.com/watch?v=6nYCc3BojZI [accessed 07 May 2018].

Tribes. (2017) *Sister Chakra Workshop.* Available at: https://www.facebook.com/events/256699731506275/?acontext=%7B%22ref%22%3A%223%22%2C%22ref_newsfeed_story_type%22%3A%22regular%22%2C%22action_history%22%3A%22null%22%7D [accessed 26 September 2017].

Turner, V. (1986) *The Anthropology of Performance.* New York: PAJ Publications.

Urry, J. (2002) Mobility and proximity. *Sociology,* 36(2): 255–274.

Vidyāratna, T. and Avalon, A. (1913) *Shatchakranirupana and Padukapanchaka.* Calcutta: Sanskrit Press Repository.

Wanderlust. (2017) *Festivals.* Available at: https://wanderlust.com/festivals/ [accessed 09 September 2017].

White, D. G. (1996) *The Alchemical Body: Siddha Traditions in Medieval India.* Chicago, IL: University of Chicago Press.

Yoga, T. (2017) *Welcome to Tribe.* Available at: http://thesisterprojectblog.com/2015/11/11/your-vibe-attracts-your-tribe-a-cool-ass-yoga-experience/ [accessed 09 September 2017].

Yogi, M. C. (2010) Chakra Beatbox. *Youtube.* Available at: https://www.youtube.com/watch?v=Ph1cff2AITc&feature=youtu.be [accessed 07 June 2018].

Zangpo, N. (2001) *Sacred Ground: Jamgon Kontrul on 'Pilgrimage and Sacred Geography'.* Ithaca, NY: Snow Lion Publications.

8 Embodying dyke on bike

Motorcycling, travel and the politics of belonging on-the-move

Anna de Jong

Introduction

Belonging is what works to connect subjects, aligning them as either 'like' or 'unlike' – shaping subjectivities and expressions of identity. Thus, in deconstructing embodied experiences of belonging, we can begin to make sense of how certain identities, collectivities and performances of travel are constructed. Attending to the politics of belonging on-the-move, this chapter takes the Queensland Chapter of the Dykes on Bikes as its focus, examining their one thousand eight hundred kilometres return journey from Brisbane to the 2013 Sydney Gay and Lesbian Mardi Gras Parade. The concept of belonging is conceived as embodied, political and mobile through examination of the experiences of six women claiming non-normative sexualities, who rode their bikes to Mardi Gras, as part of a larger group of twenty riders. In doing so, the chapter examines the ways understandings of belonging, the self and body are experienced through travel to, and performance within, the Dykes on Bikes. Particular attention is granted to the ways members prepared, planned, attuned and regulated riding bodies, all of which worked to identify the Dyke on Bike identity.

It is helpful to first consider the history of the Dykes on Bikes in order to understand the role of travel to Mardi Gras for the Queensland Dykes on Bikes. The Dykes on Bikes is a chartered motorcycle group, with twenty-two chapters internationally; it is a group for individuals identifying as women and with a non-normative sexuality. The Dykes on Bikes challenge gendered understandings of motorcycling as masculine by enabling alternative subjectivities that rethink cultural expectations of what a woman is, and what a woman can do. Rather than rendering motorcycle riding as competitive, fast and risky, the Dykes on Bikes value complex entanglements of endurance, collectivity, care and strength. Central to the Dyke on Bike identity are the group's collective riding performances – where requirements relating to planning, preparing, attunement and regulation are constantly negotiated to ensure belonging is experienced during group rides.

Formal structuring of the Dykes on Bikes as a collective evolved through involvement in Pride parades; the first recognised mention of 'Dykes on

Bikes' being at the 1976 San Francisco Pride Parade, where a small group of women motorcycle riders came together informally to ride as part of the parade. It is here that one of the riders is said to have coined the epithet 'Dykes on Bikes' (San Francisco Dykes on Bikes 2013). Receiving traction in the media, the group rode with the name. It was not until the mid-1980s that the Dykes on Bikes became formally structured as a result of growing numbers. Traditionally, the Dykes on Bikes lead Pride parades – the revving of engines and blasting of horns signifying beginnings. The reasons for this are pragmatic; motorcycles have a tendency to overheat when kept stationary for too long (often a requirement when waiting, sometimes hours, for parades to begin). Placing motorcycles first also limits the possibility of accidents with other marchers and for the riders themselves, who rather than wearing helmets and protective clothing as they do during group rides, dress in a range of political, sexualised and flamboyant outfits. While pragmatic in origin, over time the Dykes on Bikes' leading role has rendered certain expectations and anticipations:

> The Dykes on Bikes *are* Mardi Gras Parade. It's our job to hype-up the crowd of 300,000 plus and get them ready for the parade. Dykes on Bikes pretty much starts the whole parade off, so you want them [the motorcycles] to be as loud as you can. The crowds [have] been out for hours waiting, so it's our job to get them started.
>
> Cam: Dykes on Bikes

The 1988 Mardi Gras Parade saw the arrival of the first Australian Dykes on Bikes, with fifteen bikes taking part (Carbery 1995). Two Sydney-based female motorcyclists had been inspired by the Dyke on Bike riders at the New York Pride the previous year (Dykes on Bikes Sydney 2015). Numbers steadily grew, and by the tenth anniversary, two hundred and fifty bikes were riding as part of Sydney Mardi Gras. The Queensland Dykes on Bikes formed as a subsidiary of the Sydney Chapter in 1995 (Dykes on Bikes Melbourne 2015). All of the international chapters are governed by the San Francisco Chapter, with a strict hierarchy ensuring the Queensland Dykes on Bikes follow the guidance of the Sydney Chapter while the San Francisco Chapter holds ultimate control. Travel to Mardi Gras, for the Queensland Dykes on Bikes, is so much a part of their identity that it is actually a requirement of becoming a patch holder, which is the signifier of full membership within the Chapter.

Return travel from Brisbane to Sydney consisted of four days riding. The Chapter left Brisbane Thursday morning, staying overnight halfway, and arrived in Sydney Friday evening. Mardi Gras Parade occurred on the Saturday evening while Sunday served as a rest day. Riders began the return journey Monday morning, again staying overnight halfway, before arriving back in Brisbane on the Tuesday night. The Sydney Gay and Lesbian Mardi Gras festival, itself, is Australia's largest queer Pride event, attracting hundreds of thousands of national and international tourists to Sydney each year. Mardi Gras Parade, the pinnacle event of the festival, is an elaborate spectacle of ten thousand people marching alongside over one hundred humorous and satirical floats. Mardi Gras has dramatically shifted since its political origins in 1978. Today, Mardi Gras is conceived by many as a form of street theatre and satire, eager to comment on, yet not necessarily threaten, the politics of the day (Markwell 2002).

Limited scholarship, however, pertains to the Dykes on Bikes. Where it is in existence, it is often only in brief reference to their role in the parade, repeatedly reporting the linear narrative of the Chapter's history, as outlined above (Kreitler 2011). In such narratives, voice is not given to the qualitative experiences of members or the embodied experience of riding as a Dyke on Bike. Motorcycling has, however, received scholarly attention more generally. There is much to thank the mobilities turn for this (cf. Pinch and Reimer 2012, Terry et al. 2015, Hansen 2016). Yet, whilst highlighting the embodied experiences of motorcycling, mobilities scholarship tends to either focus on masculine understandings of riding (Jderu 2013, Sopranzetti 2013, Terry et al. 2015) or is limited in its discussion of the gendered and sexualised dimensions of the practice (Hansen 2016). Beyond work on mobilities, scholarship exploring the intersections of women and motorcycling includes, but is not confined by, the subservient and demeaning role of women within outlaw motorcycle clubs (Quinn and Kock 2003, Veno and Winterhalder 2009); the rise of middle- to upper-class female riders (Meyer 2009, Thompson 2012); and the empowerment and tensions that arise through the non-traditional gendered identity of women who ride for leisure (Auster 2001, Roster 2007). What remains missing from scholarship examining women who ride are the particular embodied experiences, and resulting political, social and cultural importance bound up in riding for leisure. Riding is a suggestively affective and emotional experience; it thus seems undeniable that examining the riding body would open up new dimensions in understanding travel, events and identity within tourist studies.

Moreover, focus on women riders is of interest because their numbers are increasing. In Australia, while recent official figures pertaining to the number of motorcycle licence holders by gender are not available, older figures from the Australian Transport Safety Bureau (2004) detail that the number of women motorcycle riders increased by 7.7 percent between 1999 and 2003 in New South Wales while overall licenced motorcycle riders only increased by 4.3 percent over the same period. The Sydney Morning Herald reported continued increases for the five years from 2003 to 2008, claiming the number of women licences in New South Wales increased by 31 percent (Munro 2009). Similarly, the percentage of women riders in the United States increased from 8 to 14 percent between 1998 and 2014 (LaPalme 2015). While understanding the increasing popularity of women motorcycle riders is crucial, it is important to also recognise the numbers of licensed male motorcycle riders remain significantly higher and are also steadily increasing.

Indeed, motorcycles experienced the largest growth rate (22.3 percent) for any vehicle type in Australia over the five years between 2010 and 2015 (Australian Bureau of Statistics 2015). Supporting statistics, news articles detailing the rise in all-women riding groups and women-only motorcycle training are a constant fixture in Australian media space (cf. Munro 2009, Low 2015, Pearce 2016).

Belonging as mobile, relational, negotiated: a note on theory and method

In understanding the embodied experiences of belonging to the Dykes on Bikes, I follow Probyn's *Outside Belongings* (1996). For Probyn, belonging is a mode that cannot be located in some authentic, static, pre-existing state. Belonging is rather an act of constantly becoming, a constant movement which is never fully achieved, never really obtained. Belonging, is a longing, a desire to fit in. It is the restless process between being and longing, that is, be-longing. Belonging emerges through a desire to belong to something, which for the individual does not exist elsewhere. Yearning to belong is a felt, embodied experience – an emotional and relational affiliation that exists, not only between individuals and places but also between individuals and collectives and individuals and things – an essence that emerges as a relationship between things. Belonging aligns allied things, constructing identities through what does and does not conform. To this end, belonging may be conceptualised as a felt experience providing meaning to individual subjectivities and collectives (Wright 2015). To understand belonging, Probyn (1996) foregrounds the body as a place of passage because the surface is where social forces are produced and become visible. Observing the body as it performs and seeks connections reveals desires for belonging, and slippages between moments of belonging and not belonging amid bodies, places and materialities.

There is a politics to embodied experiences of belonging. One does not ontologically, inherently, consistently belong to anyone group. Individuals may consequently need to negotiate or exclude particular subjectivities. By way of example, certain elements of one's religion may be downplayed or heightened in seeking national belonging in new migratory contexts. Belonging may introduce or reinforce boundaries, a move that renders essentialised understandings concerning what belongs and what does not. There is also unevenness to belonging; some belong more than others, while certain individuals possess the power to determine the requirements of belonging (Yuval-Davis 2011). Belonging may serve as restrictive rather than progressive, or concurrently both.

In determining methods, attention to the body and its performances was conceived as a useful way to explore how belonging is continually made, remade and performed in messy and material ways (Wright 2015). Initially, I had planned to use photos and video to explore the embodied dimensions of riding. While some photos and video were collected, it was largely 'curated' by participants before sharing. Participants were hesitant to share most of their data because it was considered boring, mundane and irrelevant. This was despite encouragements that everything was of interest. Participants preferred to talk about the journey. The semi-structured interviews that had taken place with each of the six participants before and after Mardi Gras Parade became the central way through which riding experiences were examined. Participant observation also took place when I was invited to stay with one of the participants, and through this, socialise with some of the Chapter's members over two separate periods before and after the journey.

Alert to the methodological challenges interviews and observation pose in terms of offering insight into bodily capacities, emotions and embodiment, I drew upon Hayes-Conroy's (2010) concept of 'imagined bodily empathies'. This concept attempts to focus on the power and motion of participants' emotions, affective intensities and unconscious bodily judgements. Hayes-Conroy contends that researchers cannot expect to fully know participants' bodily realities; yet, the researcher can recognise or 'imagine' what an encounter feels like through empathetic communication by being there with participants: thinking through where things were shared and listening to how things were shared. Bodily empathies were recorded as field notes and analysed in parallel with a narrative analysis of transcribed interviews. Utilisation of interviews, a heavily text intensive form of method, affected the sorts of information captured. Rather than gaining insight into specific moments of movement, or the emotion of motion (Sheller 2003), insights of the journey were more reflexive, focusing on the themes of planning, attunement, regulation and frictions. I now move to discuss each in turn.

Preparing and planning the riding body to belonging

Dykes on Bikes' members were aware of the particular demands layered on riding bodies to ensure they held the capacity to complete the long distance journey; thus, collective planning practices were administered in the lead up to the event. The experience of undertaking these practices together strengthened social and emotional bonds among members and heightened anticipations of the impending journey. Long distance rides, for example, were planned in the months leading to the trip, providing practice opportunities for new members, while a rest period was initiated in the days before leaving:

JAY: So we go the first Wednesday of the month and then the last Wednesday of the month. So pretty much two weeks in a row we have a ride, like on a Wednesday night. And then on the Sunday, the second weekend of each month we ride as well. But usually over Mardi Gras, because we have the massive Mardi Gras, we try to keep pretty much, we don't do any rides there and at the end of that month we might do something.

Even the route taken was meticulously planned to ensure excitement and challenge:

DANNY: Riding is so different to driving. You know you can drive ten hours and get out of the car but riding, some of the roads that we do, they've got to concentrate. That's why we do so much planning. Like even me just planning the ride is huge because I make sure we do some awesome roads, we don't just go straight down the highway, that would be really easy, if we went straight down the highway and straight back home. That would be boring. I make sure we sort of get a motorbike trip as much as it is about Mardi Gras.

Limited luggage was carried on the bike requiring parade and weekend outfits to be carefully planned before leaving. On the nights before riding, adequate sleep was essential and limited alcohol could be consumed (with intake monitored by other members). For some choosing which bike to ride resulted in apprehension, with tensions between the aesthetics of the parade (which conventionally calls for a loud and eye catching bike, such as a Harley) and the practicalities of long distance riding (where certain bikes force the body to bend, causing the neck to bend up, a position difficult and tiring to sustain). Following a difficult ride the previous year Andy, by way of example, was excited for the possibilities her new bike afforded for the long journey:

ANDY: So I've got a 650 and the bike that I took down last year was a little ninja, so it was like a sports bike, so this one's going to be a sports touring bike, so it's more sitting up straight, whereas the other one was leaning over so I got a bit of a sore back, shoulders, lower back and neck. Whereas this time I'm pretty much going to be sitting up. More than likely it's going to work.

To ensure harmonious movement on the road, it was also essential for members to learn the Chapter's strict rules and practices before leaving Brisbane. This regulatory structure had evolved over time, through both the broader Dyke on Bike culture and the longer-term input of members of the Queensland Chapter (specifically the Queensland Dyke on Bike president, Danny). Danny shared how these requirements became embodied through practice rides:

ANNA: Do you try to stay at your own pace or do you try to keep together as a group?
DANNY: We try and stay together. I say to them [Dykes on Bikes members]: 'You know what, if you want to ride like a fuck wit, you go and ride on your own, don't do it on a club ride'. And all the girls respect that. We've got some girls who are pretty quick riders and they know that when they

come on a ride they baton off [back down] and they do what everybody else does. We have an experienced rider up the back. And when we go out on big rides the ones of us who are really experienced riders we keep an eye on the newer ones; young being riders, not young as in age. I mean part of the club is to teach people and prepare them for Mardi Gras so every now and then I'll go and ride behind someone and then afterwards go and pull them aside and go: 'This is what you need to do, just keep a little eye on that. You know technically wise, you need to do this'. And you just go: 'Mate, follow me for a little bit and just see, just watch the lines. I'm going slow and I just want you to follow, just watch, technically when we are on the road'.

There is a politics to the experience of belonging. While the spaces and temporalities of the ride from Brisbane to Sydney are open ended, fluid and generative, familiarity rendered through specific repetitive practices and rules is crucial to the construction of flow and seamlessness once on the road. For the Dykes on Bikes, it is essential to become attuned to the speed, formation and flow required to ride with, and belong to, the Chapter. Butcher (2011:246) suggests, in a discussion of metro use in Delhi, that 'knowing the "rules" of appropriate space use on the metro is linked to knowing how to use, and thus belong to the space of a modern cosmopolitan city'. Similarly, for the Dykes on Bikes, respecting and performing the rules was imperative to experiencing, and prioritising, belonging between riding bodies. There was, however, unevenness to belonging within the Dykes on Bikes. Danny's role as president granted her, as well as some of the 'older' riders, the power to determine, and to certain extents enforce the requirements of what belongs and what does not.

Regulating the Dyke on Bike identity: negotiating sexualities

The political dimensions of belonging to, and becoming, a Dyke on Bike were also reliant on characterising technologies of the bike and embodied riding performances as gendered, with the Dykes on Bikes as collective, non-competitive and non-aggressive considered feminine. In contrast masculine, male motorcycle collectives are understood to be driven by competition and speed. The construction and reproduction of these regulatory discourses and spatialised performances introduced clear boundaries regarding what belongs and what does not within the Chapter. As Danny detailed at length:

DANNY: We've got a girl in our club now, Jo…as soon as she turned up…she said to me 'I can tell who taught you how to ride'. And I said 'Oh? Who do you think taught me how to ride?' And she said 'You ride with guys'. And I said 'Yes, so did you'. And she said 'Yep'. And we've both learnt from guys and both of us independently are very aggressive riders. Whereas girls who have ridden only ever with girls are very timid, very timid.

ANNA: What do you mean?

DANNY: Just throwing the bike around a lot more, a lot harder…I suppose having more control but are more likely to really throttle, so get a lot of speed going out of the corners and break a lot harder into the corners. Whereas if I watch Andy [Dyke on Bike member] ride, who's obviously never ridden with guys on an ongoing basis, it's just very different, because guys they literally throw a motorbike around. Andy will allow the motorbike to ride around a corner…Andy's got a bike that's very easy to maneuver ….I describe it as, if Andy wants to go around a corner like that she just points her bike and the bike goes 'Oh, ok I'll go around the corner, cool'. My bike, if I want to just go around a corner, I'd get to about there and the bike would go, 'Get fucked'. And so I have to do one of two things, I either have to accelerate and really dump it down or I'll just come off. And that comes with riding with guys. The fact that you see guys and they will throw the bikes into the corners…when they are going around a corner they will dump, physically throw, physically move the bike. If I put Andy on a bike to do that, physically if she rode for two hours riding like that she'd be exhausted, exhausted… I'm the only one in our club with a big powered sports bike. There's no one else that has a bike like mine in our club and that's because women generally don't ride them because they are male dominated and they need a lot more aggression. The Harley is just difficult to maneuver because it's really heavy, you've got a two hundred kilogram bike and physically you just have to move it… Whereas my sports bike is lighter than my [other] bike but it's not about the weight of the bike, it's about the ability and the aerodynamics of the bike that force you to physically move it. And you find a lot of women don't ride the type of bike that I've got. And so you find that the women who have ridden with male riders are very much into testing each other.

The requirements of attuning the riding body to belong to the Dykes on Bikes both trouble and reconfirm normative understandings around motorcycle riding as a masculine performance. At one level, the feminine performance of the Dykes on Bikes is characterised through relational ethics, collectivity, non-aggressive and non-competitive embodied movements, and the preference for certain motorcycles deemed 'feminine'. Such characteristics threaten masculinised constructions of motorcycling as aggressive, competitive, speed oriented and daring. Further to this, Danny's riding performances trouble normative assumptions that appoint masculine performances as necessarily male. Yet, at another level, the Dykes on Bikes' reliance on essentialised comparisons between female and male riders and motorcycles – that recognise Danny and Jo's performances as out of place – serves to reinforce facile constructions positioning females as softer, non-aggressive and weaker, and males as dangerous, aggressive and strong.

Flow, attunement and the role of technology

To illustrate how belonging was able to emerge during the journey to Mardi Gras, it is useful to draw on conceptualisations of assemblage. Assemblages cut through dualistic understandings of body and thing, as bodies and materialities come together and scramble into shifting combinations (Waitt 2014). Following assemblage thinking belonging is emergent, through the coming together of various elements into socio-spatial formations that make sense as a coherent whole. 'Things' are not disparate, rather they coalesce in relational ways, confining and configuring what it means to belong and not belong whilst also configuring what they themselves are. For instance, riding bodies do not merely govern bikes, riders are also affected by the agency of the bike, road, other riders and vehicles, technologies and so on – where all these things begin and end is not always clear. Moreover, for the Dykes on Bikes, as bikes, bodies, technologies and regulated performances came together at certain moments during the journey, a seamlessness, or flow, was established – heightening the experience of belonging:

CAM: We have a Bluetooth. So we can talk to each other. It's pretty good because you can talk to the last person, you can talk to the middle person. That's how we kept everybody really close. Going down to Sydney was really handy, we had all of our members, every single one of us had mics on the bikes. This was the first year that I'd ridden with those in a big group. Usually we've gone away and we don't have them and it gets really hard. You've really got to concentrate on whose where and counting all the bikes. Those [Bluetooth and microphones] make it so much easier on long rides because I can lead and if Andy's at the end, Andy can go, 'Oh we just need to stay there and we've broken up a little bit, just slow down a little bit'. And those [microphones] go about a K [kilometre] and a half. Because you might be doing a hundred but us up the back might be doing eighty. Yeah you can get spread out pretty quick, like Thunderbolt because it's basically one big road, there's not really anywhere where you turn off...no cars are going to overtake you anyway. You're pretty much in one big set. That road is so bumpy but it's really really good. It's considered, they nicknamed it the roller coaster. So it's just big wide corners, big hills. So with the mic and Bluetooth you just don't worry, everyone just gets a really good rhythm on, and spreads across the road.

Edensor (2010:14) suggests the metaphor of flow is useful in conceiving 'the sequential process through which imminent experience is replete with successive moments of regular attunement to the familiar, and the surprising and contingent'. The experience of flow, Edensor further claims, holds the potential to escape feelings of alienation. The Chapter's moving material assemblage, conditional here on the role of communication technologies, enabled the group to remain as one, and brought forth a rhythmic flow – rendering belonging. Whilst technology was crucial to the experience of flow, it was reliant on knowledge of the group's regulated riding performances established through the extensive planning and preparation.

The absence of other vehicles was positively conceived because it enabled the group to remain seamless, during particular segments of the journey. The pleasures of belonging on-the-move to a larger 'gay' collective were heightened as other vehicles and symbols of gay Pride became incorporated into the mobile assemblage:

MEL: You'll have coming from Brisbane, or sort of Brisbane, Sunshine Coast, Gold Coast there's a, without knowing the numbers, there's a huge amount of gay people go down to Mardi Gras. It's like their annual travel. It's quite funny because when we ride, we'll ride from here down with our own flags and everything, you'll go past cars with big gay flags on the windows and it's like 'Woo, woo'.

Sexual politics for the Dykes on Bikes is illustrated through the pleasures of belonging, where the enjoyment of identifying with 'gay' symbols on the road functions as a form of entitlement and reclaiming that works against normative assumptions of a compulsory heterosexuality. Pleasure would not arise without the capacities to not only establish flow but also inhabit the road with ease (Ahmed 2004). The incorporation of others into the mobile assemblage, identified through their use of rainbow flags and queer symbols, extended the boundaries of belonging beyond the group, working to heighten the pleasures of identifying with a non-normative sexuality and as Dyke on Bike. In this sense, the pleasures of belonging to the Dykes on Bikes are not only felt personally but such pleasures also become highly visible political acts.

Moments of friction, moments of not belonging

The Dykes on Bikes flow was ruptured at particular moments as frictions cut through the assemblage. Negativity among the Chapter culminated as the Dykes on Bikes encountered traffic, rain and night upon entering Sydney, after riding nine hundred kilometres on the outward journey. Mel, Jay and Danny all shared how various elements worked against feelings of anticipated euphoria:

JAY: We were really tired because it took us ages to get to the hotel from Hornsby basically, and it was raining. So we were all really wet and really tired. It was just like 'Oh my god'. It got dark really quickly and then it started to sort of rain. And we were counting headlights because we couldn't really see which of us, because it was dark, and we couldn't distinguish between bikes. I was second last at the back and one of the girls was behind me. So we were counting headlights and we ended up with a group of people from somewhere else in the middle of our group. So we went through a set of headlights and she got stuck at a set of lights.

MEL: I enjoyed the ride down because I always enjoy endurance kind of rides. I was a little bit tired towards the end there, when it just started raining and it was cold. Towards the end, just about Hornsby; it just always seems to rain in that one particular spot and it just rained the whole way through, and I was just like, 'I'm freezing, I'm cold, I just want to get there'.

DANNY: Pretty much fifteen k's [kilometres] north of Sydney, as we're heading down to Sydney, it rained and it didn't stop raining. On top of that you have wet clothes because, for example, my wet weather pants had a little hole in the right. So they were soaking wet and I couldn't dry them. And my gloves were wet, so pretty much the next morning you wake up and put your hands back in the gloves, for the whole day it's wet. Just over it. And that's really different for the girls because if you think about it, our monthly rides and everything, we cancel if it's pissing down rain. So they never ride in it.

Frictions encountered upon entering the city pulled the group apart, scattering and rupturing the assemblage. As riding bodies separated, they became vulnerable and uncomfortable. Becoming lone riders they were forced to increase sensory awareness of certain materialities (such as clothing and the headlights of other traffic). Through this fracturing of the assemblage, the riders became aware of their bodies as a surface that was separate to that of the group's. The cold rain felt on skin, for example, forcing reflections of tiredness and irritation. Danny's final two sentences are telling. The unfamiliarity of riding in such conditions emphasised the shortcomings of planning and preparation. Shorter, casual monthly rides had not prepared riders for the frictions encountered during the long road to Mardi Gras. The flow of the group's riding assemblage was again fractured on the first day of the return journey, when heavy rain over the weekend closed several roads of the planned return route:

DANNY: The weather was looking like it was going to be shit. We said 'It's probably going to rain, get your wet weather gear on'. I think some of them were quite worried that they might have to ride in really really bad conditions. And that's sort of in your own head that's a bit of a challenge as well. The roads that we wanted to do were closed.

ANNA: Was Thunderbolts closed?

DANNY: Yeah, Cessnock was shut, Thunderbolt. Everything was cut off.

ANNA: So did you just go up the Pacific Highway?

DANNY: No we went Pacific and then New England, out to New England. And then because we were staying at Walcha, which is at the end of Thunderbolt, or you know up the top, so we actually had to go out to

Tamworth, out through Tamworth and then back track because we would have come this way and then up through Thunderbolt. So it was a pain riding all day in the wet, then doing night riding in the freezing cold.

Frictions threaten potentials of belonging to the Dykes on Bikes. Despite the immense planning and preparation undertaken by the group, the introduction of rain, detours and darkness, fractured the mobile assemblage during the return journey. Through the abandonment of the seamless mobile assemblage, riders were forced to individualise the journey; in certain circumstances, reconceiving the ride as challenging and painful, no longer desired, and thus no longer enabling the formation of mobile belonging. Exploring frictions reinforces the importance of flow and belonging in enabling riding bodies to not only undertake the journey but also experience it as pleasurable and undemanding.

Conclusion

This chapter contributes to scholarship on tourism and the body, in examining the embodied experiences of belonging on-the-move as a Dyke on Bike. It was argued that attention to the body is crucial in addressing the ways belonging during travel can be experienced as mobile, political and becoming. Riding is a suggestively affective and emotional experience, examining the riding body opens up new dimensions in understanding travel, identity and the body within tourist studies. Despite this, scholarship examining the embodied experiences of riding bodies, and resulting political, social and cultural importance bound up in riding for leisure, remains peripheral within this area of study. The objective of this chapter was to bring attention to the importance in attending to the scale of the body, in understanding the politics of belonging during travel.

The first empirical section focused on the ways Dyke on Bike members planned for the impending travel to ensure their bodies were prepared to undertake the journey's demands. Planning and preparing the body were shown to be integral in establishing the requirements of belonging to the Dykes on Bikes. In further discussing the requirements of belonging, the ways through which the Dyke on Bike identity both troubles and reconfirms normative understanding of motorcycle riding as masculine was examined. The 'Dyke on Bike' performance was illustrated to render an identity reliant on collectivity and absence of competition, troubling normative notions of riding as necessarily dangerous, fast and masculine. Moreover, the ways through which certain members negotiated masculine and feminine riding performances contested notions concerning gender and sexuality as necessarily dichotomous, essentialised and static. Yet, at the same time, the practice of constructing the Dyke on Bike was dependent on a form of strategic essentialism – with clear identification outlined regarding what it is (non-competitive, non-aggressive and timid), and what it is not (male, aggressive and competitive). Through this demarcation, feminine performances were preferenced while alternative riding styles were discouraged during group rides. Such distinctions are crucial because the identity of 'Dyke on Bike' is brought into existence through the alignment of things as either 'like' or 'unlike'.

The chapter next examined the ways Dyke on Bike belonging was able to emerge on-the-move, through an assemblage of bodies, materialities, rules and technologies, facilitating the experience of flow and togetherness. The pleasures of belonging to the Dykes on Bikes were shown to enable riders to inhabit the road with ease – a political act working against normative assumptions of a compulsory heterosexuality. In the final section discussion turned to flows and friction. Frictions brought attention to the fragility and limits of belonging on-the-move. It was illustrated how elements, such as rain, night, traffic and detours ruptured the group's assemblage, forcing the surfaces of bodies into existence. Examining moments of fracture highlighted the capacities belonging affords in enabling members to not only prepare for, undertake and finish the demanding one thousand eight hundred kilometres return journey but also experience it as pleasurable.

References

Ahmed, S. (2004) *The Cultural Politics of Emotion*. Edinburgh: Edinburgh University Press Ltd.

Auster, C. (2001) Transcending potential antecedent leisure constraints: The case of women motorcycle operators. *Journal of Leisure Research*, 33(3): 272–298.

Australian Bureau of Statistics. (2015) *Motor Vehicle Census*. Available at www.abs. gov.au/ausstats/abs@.nsf/mf/9309.0 [accessed 20 July 2017].

Australian Transport Safety Bureau. (2004) *Annual Review*. Available at: www.atsb. gov.au/media/36528/annual_review_2004.pdf [accessed 20 July 2017].

Butcher, M. (2011) Cultures of commuting: The mobile negotiation of space and subjectivity on Delhi's Metro. *Mobilities*, 6(2): 237–254.

Carbery, G. (1995) *A History of the Sydney Gay and Lesbian Mardi Gras*. Parkville: Australian Gay and Lesbian Archives.

Dykes on Bikes Melbourne. (2015) *About Us: Fun – Freedom – Friendship*. Available at: http://dykesonbikesmelbourne.org.au/index.php/about-us/ [accessed 20 July 2017].

Dykes on Bikes Sydney. (2015) *About Dykes on Bikes: How It All Began*. Available at: www.dykesonbikessydney.org.au/about/ [accessed 20 July 2017].

Edensor, T. (2010) Introduction, in Edensor, T. (ed.), *Geographies of Rhythm: Nature, Place, Mobilities and Bodies*. Farnham: Ashgate, pp. 1–20.

Hansen, A. (2016) Hanoi on wheels: Emerging automobility in the land of the motorbike. *Mobilities*. Online first, doi:10.1080/17450101.2016.1156425

Hayes-Conroy, J. and Hayes-Conroy, A. (2010) Visceral geographies: Mattering, relating and defying. *Geography Compass*, 4(9): 1273–1283.

Jderu, G. (2013) Motorcycles, body and risk: The motorcyclists' social career. *Journal of Sociology*, 51(2): 417–430.

Kreitler, K. (2011) Dykes on bikes, In Zeiss Strange, M. and Oyster, C. (eds.) *Encyclopedia of Women in Today's World*, 1st ed. Los Angeles, CA: Sage.

Pinch, P. and Reimer, S. (2012) Moto-mobilities: Geographies of the motorcycle and motorcyclists. *Mobilities*, 7(3): 439–457.

Probyn, E. (1996). *Outside Belongings*. New York: Routledge.

LaPalme, J. (2015) *Motorcycle Industry Council Survey Reveals Number of Female Motorcycle Owners on the Rise*. Available at: www.motorcyclistonline.com/motorcycle-industry-council-survey-reveals-number-female-motorcycle-owners-on-rise [accessed 20 July 2017].

Low, C. (2015) *Motorcycle Riders on Track to Hit Million Mark*. Available at: www.smh.com.au/business/motorcycle-riders-on-track-to-hit-million-mark-20150724-giju6u.html [accessed 20 July 2017].

Markwell, K. (2002) Mardi Gras tourism and the construction of Sydney as an international gay and lesbian city. *GLQ: A Journal of Lesbian and Gay Studies*, 8(1–2): 81–99.

Meyer, P. (2009) *We're Just Women Who Like to Ride: An Ethnographic Journey on a Woman's Motorcycle*, unpublished PhD dissertation. Carbondale: Southern Illinois University.

Munro, C. (2009) 'Ladies, start your motorbike engines'. *The Sydney Morning Herald*. Available at: www.smh.com.au/news/national/ladies-start-your-motorbike-engines/2009/01/17/1231609053584.html [accessed 20 July 2017].

Pearce, M. (2016) *Big Girls on Big Bikes and the Roaring Relationships of Women on Wheels*. Available at: www.abc.net.au/news/2016-03-15/big-birls-on-bike-bikes-and-the-roaring-relationships-of-women/7248346 [accessed 20 July 2017].

Roster, C. (2007) "Girl power" and participation in macho recreation: The case of female Harley riders'. *Leisure Sciences*, 29(5): 443–461.

Quinn, J. and Koch, S. (2003) The nature of criminality within one-percent motorcycle clubs. *Deviant Behaviour*, 24(3): 281–305.

San Francisco Dykes on Bikes. (2013) *History*. Available at: www.dykesonbikes.org/history [accessed 20 July 2017].

Sheller, M. (2003) Automotive emotions: Feeling the car. *Theory, Culture & Society*, 21(4–5): 221–242.

Sopranzetti, C. (2013) *The Owners of the Map: Motorcycle Taxi Drivers, Mobility and Politics in Bangkok*, unpublished PhD dissertation. Cambridge, MA: University of Harvard.

Terry, A., Maddrell, A., Gale, T. and Arlidge, S. (2015) Spectators' negotiations of risk, masculinity and performative mobilities at the TT Races. *Mobilities*, 10(4): 628–648.

Thompson, W. (2012) Don't call me "biker chick": Women motorcyclists redefining deviant identity. *Deviant Behavior*, 33(1): 58–71.

Veno, A. and Winterhalder, E. (2009) *Biker Chicks: The Magnetic Attraction of Women to Bad Boys*. Sydney: Allen & Unwin.

Waitt, G. (2014) Bodies that sweat: The affective responses of young women in Wollongong, New South Wales, Australia. *Gender, Place and Culture*, 21(6): 666–682.

Wright, S. (2015) More-than-human, emergent belongings: a weak theory approach. *Progress in Human Geography*, 39(4): 391–411.

Yuval-Davies, N. (2011) *The Politics of Belonging: Intersectional Contestations*. London: Sage.

9 A matter of life and death

Tourism as sensual remembrance

*Geoffrey R. Bird, Hilary Leighton
and Ann-Kathrin McLean*

Introduction

> A man sits down adjacent to a stone wall of engraved names at Lone
> Pine Cemetery, Gallipoli. He sits relaxed, his hand running over one
> particular name with a certainty and care. It is his grandfather's name.
> (Bird, personal journal entry 2015)

Each year, millions of tourists travel to sites of war memory around the
world. From the city of Ypres in Belgium, to Gettysburg National Park in
the United States, the Cu Chi tunnels of Vietnam, to the hills of Kokoda in
Papua New Guinea, travellers go to connect with the past in these places.
While watching a documentary, or reading a history book can be instructive, to learn by literally standing as close as one can to where battle, violence and death occurred can be a far more powerful and embodied act of
remembrance. From this vantage point, gazing upon, listening to, breathing
in, and making contact with the world through touch and movement, tourists seek to understand what happened, pay tribute and make meaning.

At work are what we call the sensual elements of remembrance perception, a larger theoretical, phenomenological framework of the experience
of being and dwelling in the world (Heidegger 1927[1962], Merleau-Ponty
1962) where, as Palmer writes, it is 'the intimacy of being that results from
the dwelling relationship between the senses and the body, a relationship
encapsulated in the concept of embodiment' (2018:27). A departure from
remembrance as an abstract, or disembodied activity at arm's length to
one in which the senses mediate between the mind and the body, informs
a kind of visceral intelligence with its locus of meaning-making found in
the body.

By exploring the relationship of the tourist body and its performance
at sites of war memory, we have an opportunity to better understand the
human condition and how touring these sites plays a role in defining our
mortality and perhaps too, our very aliveness. Setting aside valid concerns
about commodifying war and the dead (see McKenzie 2018), the tourist experience of visiting a landscape of war stands as the most resonant form

of remembrance (see Bird 2015). It is at these sites and with the sobering and palpable power of place that tourists can explore 'notions of memory: past-present, death-life, soul-shadows' (Hellier-Tinoco 2009:120). Specifically, 'the [prevailing meaning of the] flesh-and-blood bodies of living people interface with phantasmagorical bodies and souls of the past' (ibid:120–121). In this way, remembrance tourism can provide an unmediated and direct experience, emotional point of connection with war and the dead. Touring battlefields becomes a meditation on our mortality as well as our identity: what is important in life, what is worth dying for, our contribution to the world.

It is our aim to unpack battlefield tourism, or remembrance tourism, from the perspective of a more embodied and sensual way of knowing with the hope of deepening our interdisciplinary understanding of this particular and under-represented aspect of tourism. For many years, scholars of thana- or 'dark tourism' have noted a gap in terms of understanding the visitor experience (see Seaton 2009, Sharpley and Stone 2009). Works by Bird (2011, 2013, 2015), Winter (2006), Scates (2006, 2013) and others provide evidence of the emotional impact and connection that sites of war memory can have not only on veterans, their next of kin, but on post-war generations as well. Drawing primarily from field research on the visitor experience in the D-Day landscape of war in Normandy, France (Bird 2011, 2013, 2016), we will apply the conceptual lens of phenomenological embodiment. Within the context of warfare, this begs discernment between what might be called just and unjust wars as it is understood that aggressive action necessitates response in the service of life, as in the case of the Third Reich. Specifically, our intention is to describe the lived experience of the relationship between death, the body, and tourist performance as inextricably linked through the senses. In addition to thana- or dark tourism, war remembrance and the anthropology of embodiment, we found it helpful to expand our interdisciplinary reach by embracing concepts related to phenomenology as well as eco- and depth psychology. Due to the scope of this exploration, we have limited our research to four themes within an embodied perspective: attirement, movement, touch and sound.

Before continuing, it is important to respond to why battlefield tourism warrants its own specific attention through the lens of embodiment. Seaton (2009) argues that thanatourism, defined as visiting sites associated with death, is a unique form of tourism in that it encompasses a common element we all share as humans. While fatality in the collective sense may be at the crux of battlefield tourism, paradox it seems holds up either end of the spectrum of the experience. A tour itinerary over the course of a day exposes us to a relentless set of juxtapositions and ironies involved with travels to battlefields. For example, tourism is often viewed as an escape from our daily lives, yet visiting a battlefield puts us squarely face to face with our own inescapable mortality.

Often found at the historical confluence of people visiting places of war memory, a series of surreal contrasts rooted in perceptions of remembrance occur such as life-death, past-present, violence-peace, remembering-forgetting, tangible-intangible, grief-love, etc. It is not lost on us that the intact tourist body, in a stance of peacetime leisure, is standing on the ground that witnessed flesh blown to pieces, and in a place where at one time, some of the most dire human emotions, were faced. Touring battlefields also summons us into the liminal, non-linear position of the in-between of things – the oddness that is not *this* or *that*, neither *here* nor *there* (Aoki 1993); where secrets are revealed and concealed and reflection is stimulated, and where the process itself of moving towards the experience *out there* allows for the unpredictable, quiet workmanship of transformation and meaning-making to happen *in here*.

Embodiment summons a sensual form of knowing as the senses gather and metabolise information through the body that includes of course the more disciplined, rational mind (yet does not allow it hegemony). This presents us with a new way to understand war remembrance in situ. While science tells us that our memories reside in clusters of neurons in our brains, it is through the senses they are retrieved. As Ackerman states, 'the mind doesn't really dwell in the brain, but travels the whole body on caravans of hormone and enzymes, busily making sense of the compound wonders we catalogue as touch, taste, smell, hearing and vision' (1990:xix). As we live through our senses – touching, tasting, smelling and hearing the world – a fully human way to sustain our emotional engagement with death, and practice war remembrance is possible. But, if we are willing to go *feelingly* through the experience, it is not without risk.

This risk involves dredging up the past, countermanding myths and beliefs, and can evoke deep, often buried or unconscious intergenerational emotion. In speaking to a daughter of a D-Day veteran who visited Omaha Beach, she revealed,

> There was absolutely no one there the day that I went there. I had images in my brain...those Capa photographs with the guy coming out of - what do you call them, Higgin's boats – the images of the people, the men sitting in the water around the barbed wire and ... of course that was reinforced by Spielberg's movie and seeing the water red. And you're seeing things, what my father meant, and understanding what he saw [crying] and understanding about, that there's no way a person could see that and not be changed inexorably. And to understand that my dad saw it, I felt that God, how come I didn't know, how come I didn't understand?
>
> (Ilene American female interview, Bird 2011:285)

Standing on a battlefield, one is literally standing among the dead. This gruesome reality is difficult, if not impossible to contemplate. While many of us have not experienced war ourselves, the quote above reflects an effort to feel, and to start to penetrate the barriers of truly imagining the horrors of war.

From an ecopsychological perspective, for most of Western culture, we have become disembodied from the earth and from our own bodies. Many people have forgotten that we are earth incarnate and that we are from earth, are part of, not apart from, this living world system (see Roszak, Gomes and Kanner 1995, Fisher 1996, Roszak 2001). Ever since the Enlightenment (and likely a bit before that), some scholars believe we have suffered a crisis of perception in the belief we are dominant and superior by separating ourselves from and attempting to rule over all other life forms (see Macy and Brown 1998) but also in terms of separating ourselves from the inevitability of death and the preciousness of life.

Today, in a world accelerated by constantly evolving technologies (Virillio 2008), we risk forgetting even more. We are literally losing touch, becoming more and more disembodied. For example, other than the sanitised version of the funeral, we have few ways to interact with death in Western culture save the exception of television programming, cinema and video games that leave little to the imagination and dangerously ask nothing of us in return. Jay Winter, in his work, *Remembering War* (2006), notes that post-veteran generations rely on war documentaries as an agent of remembrance. In contrast, remembrance tourism, embodied as it is, is often laden with rituals, traditions and ceremonies to commemorate and connect with wartime and the dead as well as the natural spaces where battles took place.

In the following section, we examine the notion of attirement, taking here to mean 'dressing the part', and what this means in terms of the embodiment of experience.

Attirement

3:30 pm, June 6. Arromanches

Arromanches is abuzz with people and a celebratory atmosphere. A pipe band plays as beer-drinking veterans and visitors spill out of the cafés. The veterans generate attention of tourists and locals alike, often asked for autographs, a handshake or a photograph. I make my way to the town square, noting how many people are wearing World War II uniforms. I hear French and English voices as I pass by a group dressed as American GIs. What catches my eye are shoulder flashes on a Canadian uniform: Lincoln and Welland Regiment, from Southern Ontario. I make eye contact with them. I ask why they are wearing Canadian uniforms? They turn out to be Dutch, explaining their town was liberated by this regiment in October 1944. They wear Canadian uniforms 'out of respect and to honour the veterans'. I tell them that I am Canadian, resulting in warm handshakes and smiles. As fellow tourists, we share a cultural memory about the war, that Canadians liberated a large part of Holland. We exchange pleasantries, take a photo (Figure 9.1) and promise to keep in touch.

(Bird 2011:45)

Figure 9.1 Dutch re-enactors wearing Canadian military uniforms, Arromanches, June 6, 2008.
Source and copyright: Bird (2011).

The interaction with the Dutch represents the life-affirming symbolism of the commemoration at Arromanches. The short discussion was heartfelt, reflecting a shared heritage but also putting a face to each nation. The tourist interaction reflects an act of remembering shaped by a shared war memory.

Wearing military attire can be seen as tourist performance *in* remembering. The Dutch group reflect what Bagnall (2003:87) referred to as an 'emotional and imaginary relationship' with heritage, in this case with the Dutch war memory as well as the legend of D-Day. Gazed upon, they may be viewed as re-enactors, caught up in the nostalgia of an era and the commodification of war, but their reasons seem more complex than that, and much more personal. Their emotional tie to Canada is embodied in the felt sense of wearing the uniforms of the Lincoln and Welland Regiment, literally enrobing themselves in the powerful symbolism of what it meant to be freed by wearing the dress of the liberator.

This example helps to illustrate the extent to which clothes act as a mediator to bridge the time gap across and between generations and cultures. Like the brand of magic found in fairy tales, in the imaginal sense, uniforms, hats, helmets, shoes, cloaks, badges and shields can act as transportive devices enabling the physical body to time travel or to feel an exaggerated sense of strength or superiority (Pinkola-Estes 1992), as feeling literally *materialises* through the fabric of the costume. From Connerton, we learn that 'even ephemeral codes of fashion can function as vehicles for cultural remembering' (cited in Counsell 2009:6). But what he really wanted to emphasise with this argument is that 'cultural memory is not simply passed on [...], it is made afresh, bodies enacting new visions of a collective past' (ibid) each time the clothes of a certain person and era are put on. The uniform may also be seen as a costume that re-enactors embody as part of their 'toolkit' of props to partially perform a specific historic occurrence. According to Daugbjerg, 'in re-enactment, material and bodily elements work together with already existing knowledge and imaginations to co-produce entire atmospheric assemblages speaking to many senses at once' (2014:730).

However, we argue that there is a deeper, aesthetic connection between the uniform and the re-enactor. The uniform is also a metaphor for the wearing of an identity – a collective identity if you wish (see Daugbjerg 2014). This form of identity can also be associated with movement, as enacted through performance. Given that individuals construct their own realities through collective interaction with other human beings (Andrews et al. 2011) and the world, it is essential to acknowledge variations of embodiment over time. What is worn, as described in this section, is an attribute visible amongst post-veteran generations. In a way, 'the body has been constructed as an ideological apparatus via which ritualized social customs, shared histories and institutionalized cultural memories are carried and transmitted through generations' (Mitra 2009:41). In particular, social customs such as re-enactment offer an opportunity to 'move around in a world' that is re-imagined by those who did not experience it first hand, yet have now created 'a world of which they are an immanent part' (Küpers 2017:234).

Another example, in Canada, is that of wearing a red poppy over the heart during the weeks leading up to Remembrance Day observed in November each year. Originally, the tradition of the poppy was started to help raise funds for veterans coming home from war (Iles 2008). Wearing a poppy annually in Canada has become an accessible act of embodiment nationwide and across generations. Iles explained that, 'the poppy embodies a collage of stories and memories' (2008:218). This collage encompasses both society as a whole and the connection to the individual. Therefore, even younger generations are able to create personal connections through family stories by wearing a red plastic lapel flower. Over time, the poppy's symbolism has shifted as we now look beyond the initial, yet still vital idea of raising funds, towards a deeper self-reflexive practice evolving within the cultural memory of a family, generation and nation. Today, the poppy implies peace conveying the hope of 'never repeating' as well as 'not forgetting' (see Iles 2008).

Movement

> Feel the sand under foot. Just feel the contact. Look up and see the German placements. Try to time it that the tide is out, you see the distance to sprint.
>
> (Interview Ian male Canadian 30, in Bird 2011:298)

Most memorable part of visit: Running up the beach as the soldiers would have.

(Online 209, in Bird 2011:298)

I think there is something that's visceral about actually getting to touch the earth and walk on the beach and the soil where all of that actually happened... it is a different level of understanding.

(Interview Julia Canadian, in Bird 2011:305)

As the above quotes indicate, the sites themselves can also foster a sense of embodiment as the surrounding environment helps fire the imagination and stimulate the senses. The sheer power of being-in-place and the aura of the atmosphere it exudes open the imagination towards a time not personally experienced. In this sense, 'being' is concerned with interpretation and understanding of the experience in and of itself and as such, seeks a metaphysical, timeless truth (Merleau-Ponty 1962). A deeper connection to the past seems to be more challenging to achieve the further we move away from the event itself. As such, we argue that embodiment conveys a sense of spatiality that assists the visitor to create understanding through an intimacy of affective orientation (see Whitney 2012).

Jacks notes that walking stands in contrast to technological progress and efforts to eliminate exertion, thus becoming 'a rebellious and subversive act' (2004:5) towards enlivenment. The practice of walking can be viewed as realisation in action, a slow visceral improvisation where our imaginations take their cues from the landscapes and as we generate rhythm, we generate thought. With each next step, we learn by *going* (Thoreau 1982). Walking can be a form of moving meditation, contemplation of the here and now widening our focus by shifting our intelligence from the hegemony of the head into the whole body, expanding into and more easily connecting with the world.

Edensor reasoned that 'where there are opportunities for visitors to construct their own improvisational trails, a potential escape from dominant narratives and practices is enabled' (1998:106; see also Edensor 2009). Exploring how we move, specifically walking through or situating ourselves in a landscape of war letting the primacy of experience to flow in and through us, enlarging our personal as well as social sense of attachment to place (Manzo and Devine-Wright 2014). Walking, along with the more robust effort associated with trekking, offers a unique sense of connection to the earth, helping individuals break free of the 'supremacy of abstraction' (Yack cited in Jacks 2004:5) that characterises travel by car or motor coach.

Visits to the location of significant battles, whether as pilgrimage or mere curiosity, have existed since before the end of the World War I with the Belgian battlefield of Waterloo being seen as the start of what might be referred to as mass battlefield tourism (Lloyd 1998, Seaton 1999). The so-called war memory boom, which has occurred over the past thirty years, is marked by a range of World War II anniversaries that offer the image of returning veterans and their families (see Evans and Lunn 1997, Winter 2006, Scates 2013). Many veterans are fit and able, but collectively bus transportation takes them from place to place as they engage in their commemorative work. Special battlefield events have occurred where, for example, a regiment will trek or 'yomp', as in the case of the British Royal Marines Falklands battle (see Royal Navy 2014). Trekking the Kokoda Trail in Papua New Guinea, where fighting between Japanese and Australian forces in the World War II took place, may be viewed as one of the most extreme battlefield pilgrimage experiences. Between 2005 and 2010, approximately 4,000 trekkers per year have taken on this arduous ninety-six-kilometre trail (Scates 2013:232). For many, the trek is a unique bonding experience to this historical terrain as they take on the physical challenge to push their own limits and feel some of the pain that soldiers endured (ibid:244, 247).

In *Anzac Journeys* (2013), Scates discusses World War II battlefield pilgrimages relevant to veteran and non-veteran Australians. Collectively, they provide a case study of the importance of travel to sites of war memory as an act of remembrance. A closer look reveals how the battlefield pilgrimage takes place: it can involve an itinerary of sites, from memorials and cemeteries, to walking trails and car routes. In Belgium, bike and walking trails to the various war cemeteries and battlefields provide a more active and invigorating involvement with the landscape.

Place attachment research demonstrates that people walk to feel better as the positive effects of walking help to mitigate negative feelings (Johansson et al. 2011). Movement is nourishing and generative, faithful to both the means and ends, so when we walk to remember, we are in essence, walking in their footsteps, feeling what it was like, walking with them still (see O'Shea 1998; Solnit 2000). With each footfall, metaphors erupt, associations are made, so much accompanies the walker making real the path of remembrance.

But ambulation alone is not all that is happening when we walk. While there is an acceptance now that vision is not the primary sense (see Palmer 2018), it still has a central function: 'seventy percent of the body's sense receptors cluster in the eyes, and it is mainly through seeing the world we appraise and understand it' (Ackerman 1990:230). Rhythmic movement transfers active energy from left logic to right artist brain hemisphere where the discovery of new external perspectives arrives through saturated sense receptors. In essence, when we go out, we also travel inwardly in an active and thick discourse of back and forth (Abram 1996) beyond a pedestrian understanding. In this way, we understand our body in relationship to the world that is (and was) (Husserl 1962) with the body as expression of 'here' in motion moving towards and through various 'there's' (Solnit 2000) as the body walking *becomes* a remembrance site of its own where meaning is made.

As Scates (2006) notes in relation to a visit by a tourist to Gallipoli, a World War I battlefield involving Australian and New Zealand troops (ANZAC):

> It was a journey to what many call 'a sacred place' and, as Jenny's [an Australian tourist] experience suggests, involved an emotional ordeal that led ultimately to personal enrichment. [...] There is a sense of a 'quest', a journey 'out of the normal parameters of life [and] entry into a different other world', a visit to a landscape saturated with meaning....
>
> (Reader and Walker, 1993:3, 63, cited in Scates 2006:xix)

Linenthal (1991) characterises battlefields that evoke such emotion as hallowed ground, possessing a secular sacredness owing to their significance in the national memory. Like many visitors to battlefields, Jenny engages in what Chronis and Hampton (2008) refer to as the co-construction of meaning, involving the battlefield as a storyscape that evokes feelings of identity. Certainly, the embodied senses are central to this co-construction, as illustrated by Bastable:

> Even now, (the D-Day beaches) have a stillness about them, a solemn air that makes you inclined to tread softly and keep your voice to a whisper. You go mindfully when you explore the landing grounds, as if you were in a church. And it is not hard to tell where this sense comes from: it is the sanctity of spilt blood. You can still sense it, though the tides have washed over the beaches forty thousand times since the day of battle.
>
> (2004:8)

However, in some instances, too much movement can be viewed as disrespectful at a sacred site where memory is held sacrosanct and still. For example, at Omaha Beach, children noisily playing or sunbathers relaxing in the July sun can create angst and dissonance (see Diller and Scofidio 1994, Edwards 2009). Yet, some veterans view life-affirming play in these places as joyful, healing and an embodiment of freedom and liberty (Bird 2011).

The more subversive element of walking through a cemetery, in a trench, or across a battlefield, is that it allows visitors to come close to death. Motility can loosen the grip that emotional and psychological pain binds us to. Walking a battlefield can be viewed as a kind of truth process, an antidote to suppressed feelings and the pain carried from war memories. Psychiatrist Robert Jay Lifton coined the term 'psychic numbing' relating to the survival strategy of those who had lived through the bombings of Hiroshima and Nagasaki (see Solnit 2013:109). He found that a diminished capacity or desire to feel derived from disassociations and trauma, and burdened survivors with dehumanising effect (Solnit 2013). Situating ourselves in the field of the fallen, searching for fragments of the past, may open us up, expand rather than diminish our remembrances and bring solace through empathy with others.

Hallam and Hockey considered that 'the movement of the bodies of the living and the dead, in space, allows access to the sensual, imaginative and emotive aspects of death and memory in the twentieth century' (cited in De Nardi 2014:446). As such, Howes (2005) described embodiment as a paradigm that explores the intersection between the body, mind and environment.

Touch

> A man sits down adjacent to a stone wall of engraved names at Lone Pine Cemetery, Gallipoli. He sits relaxed, his hand running over one particular name with a certainty and care. It is his grandfather's name.
>
> (Bird, personal journal entry, 2015)

White argues 'history in these sites is an embodied, participatory history' (2016:184). The bodily act of the man running his hand over the memorial specifically describes a physical form of embodiment where there is a mysterious reciprocity revealed within the act of touching the stone. The man touches and, in turn, is *being touched* both emotionally and physically. Abram (1996) describes how our perceptions in the field are actually sensual exchanges taking place between sentient beings, even with what might appear to be an inanimate object such as the stone. He goes on to suggest that in fact, we may not have as much of a hand in all of this as we may think we do, and are in fact the vessels through which the world comes to know itself in terms of human consciousness because we *are* world, embodied. As Abram writes,

> ...to touch the coarse skin of a tree is thus, at the same time to experience one's own tactility, to feel oneself touched by the tree. And to see the world is also, at the same time, to experience oneself as visible, to feel oneself seen. We can perceive things at all only because we ourselves are entirely part of the sensible world that we perceive! We might as well say that we are organs of this world, flesh of its flesh, and that the world is perceiving itself through us.
>
> (1996:68)

Participatory acts such as this one are referred to as performance (see Edensor 1998, 2009) and describe how tourists create personal meaning *incarnate*. From the quote above, we understand that the man performed this ritual due to his personal connection with the name on the stone. Through touch, human beings envision a closer connection to a specific part of their heritage. Küpers mentioned that 'the living 'reflexive' body functions as a medium of crossing, where mind and matter; culture and nature, self and world, as well as meanings and forces, meet and unfold' (2017:235).

In essence, 'remembering involves investing in producing a presence for the deceased' (Parrott 2010:134) as when, for example, a woman visiting

Omaha Beach carefully selected a rock from the site to keep as a souvenir. This act reflects the assigning of meaning to a natural or found object (Love and Sheldon 1998), perhaps as a way to present closure to the visitor's pilgrimage, or simply as a way to remember her time there and to evoke feelings associated with Omaha Beach. In this context, taking the rock is part of the visitor performance of remembering with, the rock symbolising a mineralised metaphor of time travel occupying a physical place in her day-to-day life.

And finally, on a cautionary note, the embodied experience at a battlefield may indeed be defined by the motives and outcomes of a particular war, perhaps even by the weapons used. Would we, for instance, be comfortable to touch places that have been contaminated by Sarin gas or planted with land mines? Likely not. The residuals of war in some places may go beyond phantasmagorical memories, and may be quite literally found in the ground, possibly posing a continued risk to life and limb.

Sound

4:00 pm, June 6. Arromanches

The veterans' parade and service is an informal affair (see Figure 9.2). First, a brief march past by veterans, followed by a parade of military vehicles. Speeches are made and 'Last Post' played followed by a moment of silence. French re-enactors in British uniforms stand by their jeeps chatting during the service, and motorbikes and cars roll by during the

Figure 9.2 Sound: Auld Lang Syne sing-along, Arromanches, June 6, 2008.
Source and copyright: Bird (2011).

moment of silence. The language barrier and a poor sound system limit any sense of order. It all seems perfectly acceptable, the mixing of remembrance and the French Fete de la victoire. Hats are replaced; the formalities of remembrance are over. The Master of Ceremonies invites the audience to come in front of the grandstand, to join hands and sing Auld Lang Syne. French, British, Dutch and other nationalities start stepping forward to form a circle. It is a sudden and collective outpouring of friendship and joy, strangers hand in hand, sharing song and an uncommon and spontaneous bond. The circle, maybe 500 strong sways in unison.

(Bird 2011:246)

Even though we have focused on how the individual tourist embodies war remembrance in place, Tuan (1977) identified the environment to be both physical and social, providing us with an opportunity to explore social interactions amongst visitors (Howes 2005). Mitra noted that the individual body has become an 'ideological apparatus via which ritualised social customs, shared histories and institutionalised cultural memories are carried and transmitted through generations' (2009:41). Sound can be defined in several forms such as footfalls of marching (see Marshall 2004), storytelling and even silence. Our focus here is on the ritual of singing, as a whole-body expression, as one more form of sensual remembrance.

We describe singing in terms of embodiment in which the body acts as a physical mediator between the past and present, even transgressing culture through the expression of traditional song. The popularity in Western cultures of *Auld Lang Syne* (Burns 1788[1947]), for instance, connects nationalities through a bittersweet nostalgic song that asks a question and tells a story, as a collective act of remembrance (see Figure 9.2). Singing is unlike any other commemoration, quite separate from the sensory solemnity that Marshall (2004) identifies. Rather, singing together evokes a sense of being heard, of singing your heart out, and not least of all, it makes us feel good (see Mas-Herrero et al. 2018).

The lyrics of this famous Scottish folk song, written by Robert Burns (1788[1947] original italic), pose the difficult question:

> Should auld acquaintance be forgot,
> and never brought to mind?

Sung in unison, this song can act as a poultice to personal, war-torn memories, 'for the sake of old times' as we bid farewell but never forget. For the veteran generation, the tradition of singing this particular song has been infused with an emotional charge fuelled by a life of friendships and memories, ripened by age, as revealed in the English translation of some of the lesser-known verses:

> We two have paddled in the stream,
> *from* morning sun till dine;

> But seas between us *broad have roared*
> *since* auld lang syne.
> And there's a hand my trusty *friend!*
> And *give me* a hand o' thine!
> And we'll take a right good-will draught,
> for auld lang syne.

For the post-veteran generations participating in this kind of event, a fictive kinship can develop, a euphoric bond shared by an act of remembrance shaped by memory, place, sound and silence.

Conclusion

While many of us have not experienced war ourselves, a more embodied experience may pierce the barrier to truly imagining the horror of war. In terms of sensual remembrance, the relationship between the mind, the senses and the body is by no means a static construct. Rather, for sentient beings it is more of a fluid, emergent opening out from within (Abram 1996) that can best be perceived through walking or moving where mind, body and world are aligned for a time and we come to know the world through the body. A more embodied approach to visitation, enabled by the senses, congregates our mindscape and the landscape in a consonance between interior and exteriority, where situating ourselves goes far beyond mere location. And as Melville (1891[2001]) reminds us, all mythic reaches are '...not down on any map, true places never are' (1891[2001]:53).

In following this line of thinking, one can't help but wonder what is happening in a graveyard when a shiver runs up the spine? Or when in an open field, our most familiar touch receptor hair (Ackerman 1990) stands on end? The sense of a presence in a seemingly empty cemetery or a field defies explanation however, as Haswell writes, 'it is said that when the clouds are low and the wind is in a certain quarter you can hear the sound of battle on Omaha Beach; but many battlefields ... have their legends of haunting' (1979:9). What is interesting here is that the physical space encourages such experiences and reactions, and, in turn, we are shaped by it. For example, Wittman declared that

> ...trauma is repeated, its monstrosity is magnified or made spectacular, so that we can finally touch it, embody it, and dwell with it - so that it too, can descend into the human, becoming itself humanized, instead of haunting us from an impalpable beyond.
>
> (2011:197)

This reveals some realisations as we return to the life-death relationship in embodied remembrance. First, as McCarthy and Prokhovnik note, death is 'the absence of presence, with the loss of the living embodied other as the hard inescapable truth to be faced' (2014:23). For example, in the context of palliative care, '[t]he prevailing social imaginary suggest that, when the other is removed from the needs of corporeal being, the notion of 'caring after death' is rendered meaningless at best and pathological at worst (ibid:24). Yet often, battlefield visitors are actively engaging, walking even talking, with the dead, at least in a spiritual sort of way. And this can be viewed as healthy or even healing.

Second, Western societies honour the war dead as an expression of respect, not only in burial but also in regular commemoration. The dead body is central to this relationship, identified and buried with a grave marker, or as 'the Unknown Solider as a modern mystical body' (Wittman 2011:11). Wittman argues the 'Unknown Soldier Memorial' is an expression of the 'sacredness of the flesh' and an acknowledgement of the shared experience of mortality (ibid:12). Many of those killed in war have no known grave because their bodies were torn beyond recognition or blown to pieces. Standing on a battlefield, one is therefore literally standing among the dead: life and death at its intersection. And for a time, one gets the sense that we are all in this together, one human chain.

Can a renewed membership with life be made through a more sensual and embodied remembrance of death? What we have come to understand through this research, are the ways individuals and society interact with shadows of the past. Through the application of sensual embodied practices, we argue that profound connections can be made and healing can occur with what no longer exists on this earthly plane. Each time we acknowledge, name, enact and feel in war remembrance, we shine a bit of light on the darknesses of the past, and in so doing are granted the chance to release what has been trapped or repressed, held 'underneath', and bring life-furthering energy to the surface of consciousness (Jung 1952[1978]). And just like after a good cry, we can begin to 'see with new eyes' (Macy and Brown 1998:113), alleviating the unconsciously repressed material that strangles life, holds us hostage emotionally, and in essence, we are returned to our fuller energies and potential for wholeness. To avoid looking into the dark (due to its obviously disagreeable nature) ensures we continue to project our own demons and fears onto others, the precise requirements for feeding and fuelling war (Jung 1952[1978], Neumann 1973, Richo 1999).

Despite these barriers to a full embodiment of remembrance, we are obligated to try to face the inescapable truths about the matters of life and death. Somewhere in between what is and isn't said, what can be seen or remains unseen, what is made conscious or left to the unconscious realms, we can be moved towards a deeper and often life-serving understanding of own lives through authentically inclined, mystical relationships with our ancestors and what they fought and died for. Whereas there is no common outcome as a consequence of touring a battlefield – indeed, subjective experience is interpreted to align with one's own ideologies and belief systems. Yet there is enough in the literature to conclude that something is happening.

However, what role embodiment plays in how that something happens to un-fold is still somewhat intangible and mysterious. In this conclusion, we have stepped towards an understanding of embodiment as an extension of the efforts of the mind, body and soul to grapple with war and death in all of its juxtapositions and, as such is not an end in and of itself. As we have provided literal examples of sensual remembrance – where touching also means being touched, where movement in turn moves us, and where attirement transports us to another place in time – the full implications of developing a deep sensual connection, as a bridge between the past and the present, the living and the dead still needs to be more fully fleshed out through further research.

If we are to really learn from our embodied experiences, then it behoves us to take a closer look into Jung's (1921[1971]) work into the psychology of typography (the innate preferences we arrive with at birth), where he surmised that what at first appears to be a paradox of opposites for the human soul, in the end proves to be a continuum of complements with each end of the spectrum comprised of a bit of the other. Perhaps his most profound contribution to modern psychology was his recognition that the work of the adult is to take up a *both-and* proposition of each dichotomy towards a more complete and mature way of being (Jung 1921[1971]). It would follow then that an integration of the seeming dualisms found in remembrance tourism in the absences and presences, successes and failures, shadow and light, wounds and healing, life and death (as experienced in the felt sense and realised through the sensual body) as: awareness, movement, touch, song and ritual to name a few may hold the necessary ingredients for our wholeness and could in fact hold the personal and cultural keys to us never forgetting again. As Jung found, 'in the final analysis, we count for something only because of the essential we embody, and if we do not embody that, life is wasted' (as cited in Hillman 1996:x).

In the twenty-first century, we are no longer with the veteran's generation, their voice, their presence and their stories. We are left to connect with the past in more imaginative ways. By visiting fields, beaches, cemeteries and other places where battles occurred, powerful stories can be felt just by simply being there, where a site of memory is also a site of sensing and feeling if we bring our whole selves to the experience. In the more subtle embodied sense, where the sacredness of the flesh and the shared experience of mortality bind us all might we find our own meaning of life and death? With the passage of time and with it the loss of veterans and witnesses of the world wars, embodiment becomes a means by which we might sustain contact with the past in our present but fleeting existence and come to our senses as we fulfil Binyon's (1914) call, 'we will remember them'.

References

Abram, D. (1996) *The Spell of the Sensuous. Perception and Language in a More-than-Human World*. New York: Random House.

Ackerman, D. (1990) *A Natural History of the Senses*. New York: Random House.

Andrews, M., Bagot-Jewitt, C. and Hunt, N. (2011) Introduction: National memory and war. *Journal of War & Culture Studies*, 4(3): 283–288.

Aoki, T. (1993) Legitimating lived curriculum: Toward a curricular landscape of multiplicity, in W. Pinar and R. Irwin (eds.) *Curriculum in a New Key: The Collected Works of Ted T. Aoki*. Mahwah, NJ: Lawrence Erlbaum Associates, pp. 199–215.

Bagnall, G. (2003) Performance and performativity at heritage sites. *Musuem and Society*, 1(2): 87–103.

Bastable, J. (2004) *Voices from D-Day*. Newton Abbot: David and Charles.

Binyon, L. (1914) *For the Fallen*. Retrieved from The London Times 1914. Available at: www.poetryfoundation.org/poems/57322/for-the-fallen.

Bird, G. R. (2011) Tourism, remembrance and the landscape of war, PhD thesis. University of Brighton, UK. Available at: http://eprints.brighton.ac.uk/12252/.

Bird, G. R. (2013) Place identities in the Normandy landscape of war: Touring the Canadian sites of memory, in L. White and E. Frew (eds.) *Dark Tourism and Place Identity: Managing and Interpreting Dark places*. Oxon, New York: Routledge, pp. 167–185.

Bird, G. R. (2015) Landscape, soundscape and youth: Memorable moments at the 90th commemoration of the Battle of Vimy Ridge, 2007, in K. Reeves, G. R. Bird, L. James, B. Stichelbaut and J. Bourgeois (eds.) *Battlefield Events*. Oxon, New York: Routledge, pp. 68–83.

Bird, G. R. (2016) *Managing and Interpreting D-Day's Sites of Memory. Guardians of Remembrance*. Oxon, New York: Routledge.

Burns, R. (1788/1947) Auld Lang Syne, in G. F. Maine, (ed.) *Songs from Robert Burns 1759–1796*. Glasgow: Collins Clear-Type Press, pp. 47–48.

Chronis, A. and Hampton, R. (2008) Consuming the authentic Gettysburg: How a tourist landscape becomes an authentic experience. *Journal of Consumer Behaviour*, 7(2): 111–126.

Counsell, C. (2009) Introduction, in C. Counsell and R. Mock (eds.) *Performance, Embodiment and Cultural Memory*. Newcastle: Cambridge Scholars Publishing, pp. 1–15.

Daugbjerg, M. (2014) Patchworking the past: Materiality, touch and the assembling of 'experience' in American Civil War re-enactment. *International Journal of Heritage Studies*, 20(8): 724–741.

De Nardi, S. (2014) An embodied approach to second world war storytelling mementoes: Probing beyond the archival into the corporeality of memories of the resistance. *Journal of Material Culture*, 19(4): 443–464.

Diller, E. and Scofidio, R. (1994) *Back to the Front: Tourisms of War*. New York: Princeton Architectural Press.

Edensor, T. (1998) *Tourists at the Taj*. New York: Routledge.

Edensor, T. (2009) Tourism and performance, in T. Jamal and M. Robinson (eds.) *The SAGE Handbook of Tourism Studies*. Thousand Oaks, CA: Sage, pp. 543–557.

Edwards, S. (2009) Commemoration and consumption in Normandy, 1945–1994, in M. Keren and H. H. Herwig (eds.) *War Memory and Popular Culture: Essays on Modes of Remembrance and Commemoration*. London: McFarland & Company Inc., pp. 76–89.

Evans, M. and Lunn, K. (Eds.) (1997) *War and Memory in the Twentieth Century*. Oxford, Oxfordshire, New York: Berg.

Fisher, A. (1996) Toward a more radical ecopyschology. *Alternatives Journal*, 22(3): 20–26.

Haswell, J. (1979) *D-Day. Intelligence and Deception*. New York: Times Books.

Heidegger, M. (1927/1962) *Being and Time*. New York: Harper and Row.

Hellier-Tinoco, R. (2009) Dead bodies/live bodies: Myths, memory and resurrection in contemporary Mexican performance, in C. Counsell and R. Mock (eds.) *Performance, Embodiment and Cultural Memory*. Newcastle: Cambridge Scholars Publishing, pp. 114–139.

Hillman, J. (1996) *The Soul's Code. In Search of Character and Calling*. New York: Random House.

Howes, D. (2005) *Empire of the Senses: The Sensual Culture Reader*. New York: Berg.

Husserl, E. (1962) *Ideas. General Introduction to Pure Phenomenology*. New York: Collier.

Iles, J. (2008) In remembrance: The Flanders poppy. *Mortality*, 13(3): 201–221.

Jacks, B. (2004) Reimagining walking. Four practices. *Journal of Architectural Education*, 57(3): 5–9.

Johansson, M., Hartig, T. and Staats, H. (2011) Psychological benefits of walking: Moderation by company and outdoor environment. *Applied Psychology: Health and Well-Being*, 3(3): 261–280.

Jung, C. G. (1921/1971) *Psychological Types: Collected Works*. Vol. 6. (R.F.C. Hull, Trans.) Bollingen Series XX. Princeton, NJ: Princeton University Press.

Jung, C. G. (1952/1978) *Anion: Researches into the Phenomenology of the Self. Collected Works*. Vol. 9, Part 2, Edition 2. (R.F.C. Hull, Trans.), Bollingen Series XX. Princeton, NJ: Princeton University Press.

Küpers, W. (2017) The embodied inter-be(com)ing of spirituality: The in-between as spiritual sphere in practically wise organizations, in S. Nandram and P. Bindlish (eds.) *Managing VUCA Through Integrative Self-Management*. Cham: Management for Professionals, Springer, pp. 229–247.

Linenthal, E. T. (1991) *Sacred Ground: Americans and Their Battlefields*. Urbana: University of Illinois Press.

Lloyd, D. W. (1998) *Battlefield Tourism: Pilgrimage and the Commemoration of the Great War in Britain, Australia and Canada, 1919–1939*. New York: Berg.

Love, L. L. and Sheldon, P. S. (1998) Souvenirs: Messengers of meaning. *Advances in Consumer Research*, 25(1): 170–175.

Macy, J. and Brown, M. (1998) *Coming Back to Life. Practices to Reconnect Our Lives, Our World*. Gabriola Island, BC: New Society Publishers.

Manzo, L. C. and Devine-Wright, P. (2014) *Place Attachment: Advances in Theory, Methods and Applications*. New York: Routledge.

Marshall, D. (2004) Making sense of remembrance. *Social & Cultural Geography*, 5(1): 37–54.

Mas-Herrero, E., Dagher, A. and Zatorre, R. J. (2018) Modulating musical reward sensitivity up and down with transcranial magnetic stimulation. *Nature Human Behaviour*, 2: 27–32.

McCarthy, R. and Prokhovnik, R. (2014) Embodied relationality and caring after death. *Body & Society*, 20(2): 18–43.

McKenzie, B. (2018) Death as a commodity: The retailing of dark tourism, in P. R. Stone, R. Hartmann, T. Seaton, R. Sharpley and L. White (eds.) *The Palgrave Handbook of Dark Tourism Studies*. London: Palgrave Macmillan, pp. 667–691.

Melville, H. (1891/2001) *Moby Dick*. New York: Penguin/Signet Classics.

Merleau-Ponty, M. (1962) *Phenomenology of Perception*. (C. Smith, Trans.) New York: Humanities Press.

Mitra, R. (2009) Embodiment of memory and the diasporic agent in Akram Khan company's Bahok, in C. Counsell and R. Mock (eds.) *Performance, Embodiment and Cultural Memory*. New Castle: Cambridge Scholars Publishing, pp. 45–58.

Neumann, E. (1973) *Depth Psychology and the New Ethic*. New York: Harper & Row.

O'Shea, S. (1998) *Back to the Front: An Accidental Historian Walks the Trenches of World War I*. New York: Harper Perennial.

Palmer, C. (2018) *Being and Dwelling Through Tourism: An Anthropological Perspective*. Abingdon, Oxon, Milton Park: Routledge.

Parrott, F. R. (2010) Bringing home the dead: Photographs, family imaginaries and moral remains, in M. Bille, F. Hastrup and T. Sørensen (eds.) *An Anthropology of Absence: Materializations of Transcendence and Loss*. New York: Springer, pp. 131–146. Available at: https://link-springer-com.ezproxy.royalroads.ca/book/10.1007%2F978-1-4419-5529-6 [accessed 2018].

Pinkola-Estes, C. (1992) *Women Who Run with the Wolves. Myths and Stories of the Wild Woman Archetype*. New York: Ballantine Books.

Richo, D. (1999) *Shadow Dance. Liberating the Power and Creativity of Your Dark Side*. Boston, MA: Shambhala.

Roszak, T. (2001) *The Voice of the Earth. An Exploration of Ecopsychology*. Grand Rapids, MI: Phanes Press.

Roszak, T., Gomes, M. E. and Kanner, A. D. (1995) *Ecopsychology. Restoring the Earth and Healing the Mind*. San Fransico, CA: Sierra Club Books.

Royal Navy (2014) *HMS Protector's Royal Marines Recreate Epic Falklands Yomp*. Retrieved 30 June 2018 from www.royalnavy.mod.uk/news-and-latest-activity/news/2014/march/26/140326-protector-rm-yomp.

Scates, B. (2006) *Return to Gallipoli: Walking the Battlefields of the Great War*. Cambridge: Cambridge University Press.

Scates, B. (2013) *ANZAC Journeys. Returning to the Battlefields of World War Two*. Cambridge: Cambridge University Press.

Seaton, T. (1999) War and thanatourism: Waterloo 1815–1914. *Annals of Tourism Research*, 26(1): 130–158.

Seaton, T. (2009) Purposeful otherness: Approaches to the management of thanatourism, in R. Sharpley and P. Stone (eds.) *The Darker Side of Travel: The Theory and Practice of Dark Tourism*. Bristol: Channel View Publications, pp. 75–108.

Sharpley, R. and Stone, P. (Eds.) (2009) *The Darker Side of Travel: The Theory and Practice of Dark Tourism*. Bristol: Channel View Publications.

Solnit, R. (2000) *Wanderlust. A History of Walking*. New York: Penguin Books.

Solnit, R. (2013) *The Faraway Nearby*. New York: Penguin Books.

Thoreau, H. D. (1982) *The Great Short Works of Henry David Thoreau*. (W. Glick, ed.) New York: Harper & Row Publishers Inc.

Tuan, Y-F. (1977) *Space and Place: The Perspective of Experience*. Minneapolis: University of Minnesota Press.

Virillio, P. (2008) *Negative Horizon*. London: New Continuum.

White, G. (2016) *Memorializing Pearl Harbor: Unfinished Histories and the Work of Remembrance*. Durham, NC: Duke University Press.

Whitney, S. (2012) Affective orientation, difference, and "overwhelming prox-imity" in Merleau-Ponty's account of pure depth. *Chiasmi International*, 14: 415–438.

Winter, J. (2006) *Remembering War: The Great War between Memory and History in the Twentieth Century.* New Haven, CT: Yale University Press.

Wittman, L. (2011) *The Tomb of the Unknown Soldier, Modern Mourning, and the Reinvention of the Mystical Body.* Toronto, ON: University of Toronto Press.

10 Bodies at sea

'Water' as interface in Viking
heritage communication

Michael Haldrup

Introduction

There are numerous signs and markers at museums and heritage sites instructing bodies to 'stop, look and listen' (Ingold 2000:243). Screens to be
watched, gadgets and touch sensitive switches to be activated, films to be
gazed at in silent or interactive spectacles to participate in are but a few
examples of the many artefacts and devices museums work through in order
to involve and engage the bodies of visitors. Yet, this dense embodied choreography, this profound *corporeality* (Massumi 2014:56) of the museum/
heritage encounter, has been strangely absent from current museology and
heritage studies (Candlin 2004), reflecting a more profound 'blind spot' regarding bodies in social theory (Crossley 2006).

While tourism studies, following Veijola and Jokinen's (1994) article on
the absence of bodies in tourist studies, have seen an upsurge in interest
in theories and approaches relating to embodiment, these have to a large
extent been reserved for particular ways of sensing and performing tourism. Hence, there is still a need to develop more systematically a repertoire
of vocabularies and methods directed at the various 'affective materialities' (Anderson and Wylie 2009) at play in tourism. Drawing in particular on performance-based readings of heritage consumption and tourism
(Haldrup and Larsen 2010, Waterton and Watson 2014, Haldrup and Bærenholdt 2015) as well as developments in non-representational theory and
affect theory (Anderson and Harrison 2010a, Massumi 2014, Timm Knudsen and Stage 2015, Vannini 2015a), this chapter explores more broadly the
role (and interplay) of embodied sensations in heritage communication. It
does so by considering the role of sailing and rowing as a way of exploring,
enacting and experiencing Viking culture and lifeworlds at the Viking Ship
Museum, Roskilde, Denmark, conceiving of these 'as active interventions in
the co-fabrication of worlds' (Anderson and Harrison 2010b:14).

By viewing the sea and its surface as 'a space that is not so much known
than experienced' (Steinberg in Anderson and Peters 2014:xiv), this chapter
focuses on how the corporeal and ludic performances of bodies at/on the sea
presents the world of the Vikings to visitors. This chapter aims to explore

this profoundly embodied experience of 'becoming-Vikings' through the performance of sailing – and learning to sail – a Viking Ship. It does so primarily through a methodological experiment. During the summer season of 2016, I participated in twenty sailing trips with varying types of participants and over varying time spans (from one to four hours). In addition to this, I engaged in discussions and various other forms of participant observation with sailing instructors and assistants with the purpose of producing a visual (auto)ethnography of the experience of 'becoming-Vikings'. In this chapter, I want to use the material generated as an exploration of not only how we may re-present this experience but also where the borders for re-presenting such embodied knowledge occur.

The Viking Ship Museum

The Viking Ship Museum in Denmark is one of the central heritage sites in Scandinavia. Both with regard to Nordic maritime heritage and its modernist exhibition hall overlooking Roskilde fiord which is part of the Danish state authorised canon of national heritage. As a museum and heritage institution, it is also an excellent example of how heritage sites have expanded the way they want to engage the public. Established in 1969 as an exhibition site for five shipwrecks from the eleventh century found in the fiord, in the late 1970s and early 1980s, the museum appeared in popular historical TV programmes about historical crafts in shipbuilding and was a pioneer in using experimental archaeology as a way of engaging with the public.

Since the first reconstructions of a Viking ship (Roar Ege) in 1984, the museum has continued to use these as ways of engaging the public, both in relation to spectacular highly mediatised events such as 'The Return of the Sea Stallion' (the sailing of the largest Viking ship reconstruction so far from Roskilde Denmark to Dublin, Ireland in 2008) but also by providing a physical harbour environment where people can watch traditional crafts related to shipbuilding and try to sail a replica of a Nordic boat themselves (see Bærenholdt and Haldrup 2004, 2006, Haldrup and Bærenholdt 2010, 2015). Reconstructions, re-enactment and participation are of course widespread strategies in contemporary museum and heritage management. The diversity of different strategies enable various configurations of embodiment and materiality to be brought into being through the use of original objects (the wrecks of five ships), visual material, posters, video's, film screening in the adjoining exhibition rooms, costumes enabling visitors to dress up as, for example, merchants or warriors and posing with replica boats equipped with ropes and sails as well as barrels, bundles of hide and other forms of supposedly typical 'Viking' deck cargo.

While theatrical elements are widely used in contemporary heritage communication, the role of the embodied experience of 'trying out' is particularly intriguing. One of the striking things in relation to this is how these different configurations relate to how visitors conceive of 'dead' and 'living' objects and materials at the museum. For example, at the Viking Ship Museum, both staff and visitors will refer to the exhibition hall as 'the crypt' or 'the sarcophagus' and the ships displayed there as 'dead' (or even 'unreal') as opposed to the 'living' (or 'real') that you can 'see on the fiord' or even 'try out there in the harbour'. Hence, in this chapter, I am interested in exploring how embodied experiences of sailing, and of the fiord as an experiential space that opens up new ways of sensing and perceiving 'Viking-ness'. In other words, how do the moving waters of the fiord work as a communicative interface in the encounter between boats and bodies at sea and what kind of body-material configurations make the 'experience of the Viking ship' come alive.

In geography, posthumanism has been criticised for degrading human agency to a 'residual' (Simonsen 2012:13), for '...an embracing of the tools of deadening matter', 'killing the vitality of objects, things, artefacts', and as a result producing only 'surface geographies' (Tolia-Kelly 2011:157). My purpose here is to explore the particular 'affective materialism' (Anderson and Wylie 2009:319) at play while sailing Viking Ships on the fiord as part of the museum visit in terms of how this may offer ways for engaging and animating lived experience. In other words, to develop an account of 'how both self and world and other perpetually devolve from their co-constitutive being-with each other' (Ash and Simpson 2016:58).

In the context of this chapter, in order to explore the sensations and situations that, when assembled into 'the experience of sailing', are apparently able to animate and resurrect the ships and relics on display in the exhibition hall, requires an experimental approach. How are such 'affective materialities' researched? How do we develop a repertoire of affective methodologies (Timm Knudsen and Stage 2015) or non-representational ethnographies (Corsínjiménez 2003, Vannini 2015a, 2015b)? In other words, research and represent what, in a sense is beyond cognition and representation, the corporeal sensing and learning in and through our bodies as they feel their way in the world. In doing this, the experiment is of course doomed to fail. As Dewsbury observes,

> Researching ... has always been and is always about ever trying and ever failing: the difference of a performative approach is that it relishes this failure, 'no matter', and uses it to mount a serious political critique of the restrictions that methodological protocols might impose on what can count as knowledge. It therefore advocates resolute experimentalism – 'try again, fail again, fail better'.
>
> (2010:321)

The chosen path for this study was to combine a visual ethnography with a focus on capturing the space produced in the encounter between, or assemblage of, water, boats and bodies by using video and photography as ways of holding on to the nauseating space of the sailing trip. This combination produced an auto-ethnographic registration of the embodied sensation of as well as the thoughts triggered by the experience. In this sense, this study is bound to fail, based as it is on faith in the written word and visual re-presentations. However, in failing I hope to demonstrate the limitations when speaking of and re-presenting embodied visitor performances and experiences in a museum/ heritage context and also to point to the place where new potentials for experience and transformation emerge and becoming begins.

In what follows I use my visual, as well as auto-ethnographic, notes (in italics) to stage a discussion between embodied experience and theory as a way to trace out the role of embodiment in producing the experience of 'becoming-Vikings'.

Absent bodies

Sitting at the railing being gently rocked and pushed by the movements of the boat, the waves, the currents of the fiord as we gently shoot through the water, skating over the surface of the fiord I watch the ever-shifting topography of the sea surface I wonder what has become of embodied experience in the literature I have read of museum and heritage.

Bodies seem to be largely absent from studies of visitor behaviour in museums. While recent years have seen a material turn towards engaging with objects, artefacts and materialities in museum and heritage studies, notably propelled by collections such as Dudley (2010), Dudley, Barnes and Binnie (2011), this interest in 'materialising' the museum experience, however, has not led to an increased focus on the 'material' living and breathing bodies of visitors within the museum halls. As Dudley posits '...it is a commonplace to think of museum objects as not only decontextualized – because of their movement from their original contexts – but also 'dead'" (2011:1).

Only when objects have been cut off from their 'real life' as cups, chairs, boats can they enjoy their prolonged afterlife as museum objects. Dead objects. Like the ships placed in the exhibition hall, the crypt, the sarcophagus overlooking the fiord where real, living, Nordic boats, descendants of their ancestral Viking Ships, rock in the waves. Apparently, the same can be said for human bodies. When bodies appear in museum and heritage studies, it is primarily as 'dead objects' to be put on display (or not), whether as testimonials of history (Cornish and Saunders 2014), or as objects of fear and fascination (Alberti 2009; Luckhurst 2012, McLeary and Toon 2012). Transformed bodies cut off 'from their original contexts' (as Dudley 2010 writes). Bodies stripped of their skin, or dressed up in costumes to step in as media for some past craftsmanship.

An exception to this is perhaps the literature on disablement and museum visitors. Here, the bodies of museum visitors suddenly emerge as living, physical, sensuous bodies engaging with the materialities of the museum (Hetherington 2002, Candlin, 2004, Larkin 2012). Ironically, it seems that it is only when visitor bodies diverge from what Manning and Massumi call 'neurotypical' models of embodied cognition and perception (2014:19) that bodies emerge as an object of study. Paradoxically, for as Candlin rightly observes in the opening lines of a study of blindness and museums:

> Watch the crowds in any museum and despite the prohibitive ropes and signs somebody will be touching something. Once the guards' backs are turned museum visitors touch precisely because it is forbidden; but they also use touch to investigate an object's surface, to verify what they have seen or in an attempt to make a connection with the past.
>
> (2004:71)

Is it only when we deviate in our bodily capabilities or behaviour that the body emerges? Could it be that the invisibility of bodies in museums mirrors what can be said generally to be a 'blind spot' in social and cultural studies more broadly. As Nick Crossley has argued from a phenomenological perspective, '...from the point of view of consciousness, culturally appropriate bodily action and coordination 'just happen' and, as such, fall below the threshold of perception and reflective knowledge' (2007:83).

Action and cognition are embodied, habitual and contextual. We act as we do because our bodies 'know' what to do in a particular context. We see, and hear as we do, because our bodies, 'know' what to look and listen for. Cognition and action are intentional. 'My embodied consciousness, which comprises a structure of lived sensations, intends a world beyond me' (Crossley 2007:82, see also Crossley 2006). But from my perspective, my position in the boat, my body uncomfortably sitting on the planks, facing backwards, tired of rowing, tired of trying to get the oar to work in tandem with the body in front of me, and constantly being surprised by the commands from the skipper (using words I do not know the meaning of) and the movements of the boat (which I can't interpret the significance of) I feel more bewilderment and confusion than intention and understanding of the world beyond me.

While phenomenology does provide a way of describing how experiences and perceptions are produced through bodily states and processes, it also reaches its limits when accounting for how transformations in perception and action emerge; how things and bodies 'become'. As noted by the philosopher Brian Massumi, phenomenology is simply not suited to capturing the emergence of new potentials – perceptions or actions – as its prevailing conception is that, '...the personal is prefigured or "prereflected" in the world, in a closed loop of "intentionality". The act of perception or cognition is a reflection of what is already "pre-"embedded in the world' (2001:191).

Trying to become part of the crew of the boat, this looks very different. We clearly have no understanding, no intention of what to make of and with the world of which we are suddenly part, yet we participate in its coming about, we handle the ropes and the oars our bodies on the boat, we need a vocabulary for speaking of this profound 'corporeality' of the situation

(Massumi 2014:56). A vocabulary that not only articulates embodiment but also corporeality; habitual practice but also affect; the potentiality of situation not only context.

The collective body

'Mummy, shall I die now', the little girl asks her mother as we wait for the skipper to begin his rowing instructions. 'No no no. Just relax. It's not dangerous at all', her mother answers grabbing the hand of her daughter. It is late in the afternoon. After 2 weeks of hot summer. Purple-black thunderclouds emerge over the fiord. You can feel the electricity in the air.

We have just finished the safety routine. The skipper has made clear that during thirty years of sailing with museum visitors no one has ever fallen in the water. So death is not an option. Entering the boat is the first major threshold in the transformation of museum visitors into a collective body of sailors. Even in good weather, the stumbling and fumbling of bodies unfamiliar with the boat and its unpredictable movements causes people to lose their foothold and needing a hand to find a place to sit without falling over.

Two teenage girls jokingly approach the same issue: 'Why is the bottom of the hull filled with stones?' And as the skipper is busy getting everyone on board the other girl dryly explains: 'It is so that we can be sure to get a quick and painless death when the ship goes down'. For most participants, entering the boat is a situation that dampens whatever excitement they are feeling. This is not so much because of the life jackets or the safety instructions, but rather a feeling that enters the group when standing in the line on the quay, looking down on the boat, listening to the rowing instructions. Having seen the museum in advance, some visitors might have prepared questions regarding the craftsmanship of the Vikings, others indulge in joyful incantations about *'blood, gold, naked women, ho ho ho'* but it is as if the anticipation of finding a foothold in this unknown world dampens such moods.

And it is a hazardous experience. Not being able to anticipate that the boat will tip when twelve people enter at the same moment or for that matter not knowing how to move your body with four-metre-long oars around without getting stuck in the ropes, hitting the mast or seriously injuring someone puts a break on songs, talk and provides room for caution, anxiety and reluctance to enter in. Once on board, the final phase of the transformation into crew takes place, as the boat needs to be rowed out of the harbour. In the beginning, all we hear is the clacking of oars against each other. Some people might drop their oar in the water, or panic while pushing it deeper down in the water.

'Stretch your arms. Lean your body backwards. Watch the person in front of you to starboard side. Feel the rhythm'. Johannes patiently repeats. 'But I can't feel the rhythm' she says silently, and turning to me 'I'm just making this

worse for you' (referring to her oar being stuck in the water). 'Well, come on, try again, I say. Just remember...' and I repeat the instruction. 'But that's three things. I can't do that', she says and then asks the skipper if she can go to the bow of the ship, hence leaving her oar.

The challenge of becoming a collective body rather than your own in-dividual two-legged, two-armed organism seems to be to 'feel the rhythm' rather than 'follow the instruction'. On some of the trips, people would ask, 'But in reality, out on the North Sea, there would be someone counting the rhythm, beating a drum or singing, right?' people would ask. 'No. Don't think there's any evidence for that, the skipper might say. I guess you just had to feel the boat and the rhythm'.

At the meeting point, where people gather before the sailing trip the museum visitors are met with instructive grey posters containing dia-grams of the typical 'ship of the north', its geographical origin, typical rigging, and names for the various parts and devices that make up the 'machinery'. Here you can study it, rehearse the various names of the equipment and guess their roles in making the ship sail. Out on the fiord, this knowledge is now futile. At sea, even your orientations break down. Starboard turns left as you reach for the oars. Upwards leans dangerously to the right as the wind fills the sail. Here you have to 'feel the boat', re-acts to its movements, counterbalance its impulses. Become part of the collective multi-faced body facing the rear end of the boat: stretch, lean, watch, feel. Splash, splash, splash, splash. Become part of the machine (Figures 10.1–10.3).

Figure 10.1 Thunderstorm.
Source: Author.

Figure 10.2 Safety routine.
Source: Author.

Figure 10.3 Entering the boat.
Source: Author.

Rhythm, pulse and duration

'You have to treat them like children, I know this sounds arrogant, but the trick really is, to make them relax and do it without knowing it. You know like teaching a pre-school child to read or to ride a bike… That's why I joke and try

to distract them. I always try to get them away from staring at their own oar, *for that won't work'.*

We've just finished one trip and are having a short break and a coffee before the next. One of the things I find intriguing is the difference between rowing out and rowing in and Johannes explains to me that the 'tipping point' is well known among the instructors and on a later trip he grasps me on the arm, when we are on our way out. 'Michael, here it comes.... the tipping point.... did you notice it', when we arrive at the exact moment when the tense, atmosphere vaporise, the oars start moving slowly, rhythmically, and silence sets in as we slide through the water.

To the novice sailor, the boat at sea appears as a chaotic environment constantly in flux. Feeling the boat, sensing the water its currents and waves, the movement of other human bodies, we sense the rhythm; we become part of the rhythm. Or rather play our part in a polyrhythmic orchestral performance 'that builds a symphony from different instruments, each one playing its own tune to its own rhythm' (Edensor 2010:24. See also Lefebvre 2004).

But just as we cannot reduce a symphony to the rhythms and tunes played by each musician, the rhythm we feel is not necessarily the rhythm we make with our own individual instruments, hands, bodies, feet. Moreover, while the skipper certainly cries out commands from time to time, there is no baton to follow, no steady pulse beat, the rhythm seems to emerge out of nowhere. 'Rhythm is the milieus' answer to chaos', Deleuze and Guattari write, 'what chaos and rhythm have in common is the in-between-between two milieus, rhythm-chaos or chaosmos' (Deleuze and Guattari 1980:345). Like the birds' songs, or Hindu chants the rhythm which we all form is a territorial assemblage of water, waves, wind, bodies and boat.

Becoming part of the machinery, feeling it, performing its rhythms and silently manoeuvring your body around, keeping the pace, balancing the hull in response to pulses from the surface, waves, currents enables an episodically habitable space to emerge. My body connects itself to other bodies, the boat, the waters surface and its unpredictable play with the boat, through rhythm, hence becomes part of a 'machinic assemblage', a 'state of intermingling of bodies and society including all attractions and repulsions, sympathies and antipathies, alterations, amalgations, penetrations, and expansions that affect bodies of all kinds in their relations to one another' (Deleuze and Guattari 1980:99). In so doing, it not only propels the boat on the surface. It also becomes new, open to hitherto unknown sensibilities, affects and unconscious fantasms. The machinic assemblage of boat, water and bodies, enables refrains, 'catalysing', as Guattari argues, 'the emergence of incorporeal universes (...) crystallising the most deterritorialised existential territories' (1995:16), through a moment, a singularity, in which:

> time is not something to be endured; it is activated, orientated, the object of qualitative change (...) that make an immense

complexification of subjectivity possible – harmonies, polyphonies, counterpoints, rhythms and existential orchestrations, until now unheard and unknown.

(ibid:18–19)

Relax. Calm down. Sense the flocking birds, their cries, look out for seals or fish. Landmarks along the coastline. Sense the passing of water under the hull, the changes in the direction and strength of the wind, the movements of the boat as we move around or cross. Become part of the ship. Be the ship.

Whether we are on a trip lasting for forty-five minutes, barely leaving the harbour or a trip for four to five hours up along the coast of the fiord and around some of its islands the duration adds a further dimension. From the dampening of voices at the beginning, the struggle for 'feeling the rhythm' until it emerges (if it does), the silence and calmness that may occur when we silently drift through the water or the excitement, fear and joy of trying out more hazardous manoeuvres such as going back in the harbour with all sails set. All these episodes of 'sense-awareness' (Stengers 2011:53–54) of the boat, the pulse of the waves and our body responding to these are 'durations', that happen and pass in tune with the particular assemblage that we are part of: the assemblage of water, waves, wind, bodies and boat; rhythm, pulse, duration, sensation (Figures 10.4–10.6).

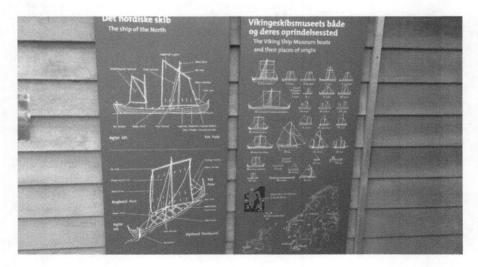

Figure 10.4 The ship of the North.
Source: Author.

Figure 10.5 Oars in the water.
Source: Author.

Figure 10.6 Night sky.
Source: Author.

Sensing the surface

In Tim Ingold's version of landscape phenomenology, rhythm and melody are central, as he argues:

> In music, a melodic phrase is not just a sequence of discrete tones; what counts is the rising and falling of pitch that gives rise to the phrase as a whole. Likewise in wayfinding, the path is specified not as a sequence of point-indexical images, but as the coming-into-sight and passing-out-of sight of variously contoured and textured surfaces.
>
> (Ingold 2000:238–239)

But at sea the coming-into-sight and out-of-sight of textures and surfaces takes a very different form than it does on land. Here, textures and surfaces are constantly in flux, constantly making their arrival in my consciousness through a hardly foreseeable series of physical and multi-sensual encounters:

> Landscape (is) perhaps best ... thought of as a series of tensions: tensions between distance and proximity, observing and inhabiting, eye and land, culture and nature; these tensions animate the landscape concept, make it cogent and productive.
>
> (Wylie 2007:216)

Recently, geographers have 'discovered' the sea and its surface as a terra incognita for landscape research. The seventy percent of our planet defined as 'beyond' geographical conceptualisation and theorisation, '...a space of nature to be fetishized, a space of alterity to be romanticized, or even a space beyond society to be forgotten' (Anderson and Peters 2014:xiv). What would a landscape topology of the sea look like, with its ever-shifting, pulsing affective materialities: seductive-aggressive, caring-brutal, aggressive-beautiful-terrifying, accommodating-repulsive?

At the shed where the safety instructions are handed out, several maps of the topography of the fiord are displayed. Apart from being visual signifiers of the fact that 'we are now going on a sailing trip', the practical use of these maps is to show how far out in the fiord in terms of distance and time, the ebb and flow of the currents will allow us to go. The corporeality of sailing this landscape is widely removed from the flat, two-dimensional world projected on the walls of the shed. On short trips, the instructors will set a course taking the boat to the east coast of the fiord. Apart from the visual impressions from cruising along the coast, this also takes us into the shallow parts of the fiord – where we will go so close to the shore that we can see the bottom and the stones reaching up from the seabed beneath.

This stratification of layers, the third dimension of the landscape, is significant in terms of the sailing experience and how we conceive of the seascape. This third dimensionality of the landscape is even more evident when at sea than on the land. Often the skipper will ground the boat (more or less by accident) and show how we are able to manoeuvre the boat simply by moving our bodies around the boat, to make it tilt and get free from the stones beneath. Likewise, on a day where the water is still, there is no wind and we have to put out our oars and row in the middle of the fiord. Here, the layer between seabed and surface becomes important as the currents might carry the boat out into the fiord if the pace of the rowing is not maintained.

But not only is the layer beneath the surface significant with its varying depths, stones, currents and so on, so too are the layers above the surface. One day we suddenly discover that the sail is not properly fastened around the top of the mast. Dylan, who is the skipper on this trip, and I talk about whether to return to the harbour (disappointing and possibly annoying the visitors) or pull the sail down and fix it in place (losing precious time as we have to be back within an hour). Dylan reflects a couple of seconds on this dilemma and then suddenly jumps to the railing, seizes the ropes and climbs to the top where he fixes the sail and slides down into the boat again, the visitors that hardly notice what happens stare in surprise at the mast as if they have just discovered its full extension. As hills and woods surround the fiord, and the fiord itself contains numerous islands and coves the wind is constantly changing in direction and strength. The mast, the boat and the shifting winds are just as important for our sailing as our ability to pass over rocks and shallow grounds.

Today was a tricky trip, I wrote in my diary one afternoon between two trips, moments with good wind alternated with sudden shifts where the surface would be absolutely still. On the way out with a good wind coming in from the south, Johannes, placed himself balancing on the railing, the visitors holding their breath in terror or surprise. We are having a good speed. The boat keels over in the wind. When he observes the reaction of his 'crew'. He jumps down rearranges the position of bodies in the boat and encourages two of the most expressive women to do the same. Balancing straight on the keeling ship, their bodies stretching out in a crooked angle in relation to us who are sitting and the mast tilting towards portside – they start to relax and smile: though everything looks crooked and lopsided as we shoot over the water from where I sit, everyone is at ease again. On the way back, the wind goes down. Only the appearance of 'cat paws', sudden depressions on an otherwise still sea surface indicates that there are wind gusts that might be caught by the sail setting us in motion despite the apparent lack of a breeze. Again, Johannes directs our bodies to make the boat keel over, hence enabling the otherwise insensible wind to fill our sails and carry us towards the harbour.

Perceiving of our bodies, as ballast activating and orientating the direction and position of the boat on and in the water, affords new sensations and perceptions of our own and other bodies. Becoming 'movable ballast' turning the boat to catch the breeze or tilting the hull to move free of the stones on the seabed enables me to sense the weight of bodies and the gravity of the earth in new ways. My body becomes rock-like urged to press vertically down towards the surface of the boat, the sea and the seabed. Balancing on the railing experiencing the weird angles where 'up' suddenly is perceived as a diagonal line vis-a-vis the horizon. My body becomes ship-like, topsy-turvy dancing over the surface of the waves (Figures 10.7–10.9).

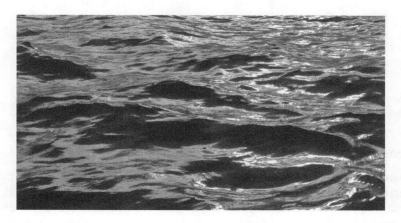

Figure 10.7 Surface.
Source: Author.

Figure 10.8 Bottom.
Source: Author.

Figure 10.9 Dylan climbing.
Source: Author.

Becoming-Vikings?

When I began this exercise in trying to bring out the various configurations of embodiment and materiality, which allow the museum visitors to speak of the sailing trips in replica ships as a 'living experience' or a 'real experience' as opposed to the objects displayed inside the museum or the various representations and re-enactments, I knew I was sailing dangerous waters: On the one hand, the introduction of various forms of posthumanism has been argued to make 'dead geographies' live (Thrift and Dewsbury 2000). As Anderson argues, '[t]he emergence and movement of affect, and its corporeal expression in bodily feelings, create the transpersonal sense of *life* that animates or dampens space-times of experience' (2006:737, original italic).

On the other hand, posthumanism has been accused of annihilating human experience and creativity by putting humans, things and matter on an equal footing. What I hope to have shown here is that there is plenty of scope for developing ethnographies and geographies of how lived experience is animated and 'comes to life' though affect, corporeality and matter rather than beyond, beside or above it. What produces the 'experience' of the Viking sailor is being part of, *becoming*, this assemblage.

So, what is it that emerges through this 'real' or 'living' experience? The expectation of the visitors when they line up before the trip is twofold. For some visitors, it is an extension of the educational posters and instructive demonstrations of craftsmanship seen in and around the museum: How did they *really* do it. These Vikings, what were the skills that enabled them to conquer their neighbouring territories and settle as far as Greenland and North America? There is clearly a curatorial/managerial intention to respond to this question, and the instructors are able to answer all types of questions relating to how sails and ropes were made, how ships were built and so on. For other visitors, the sailing trip is a welcome opportunity to 'play' after a tiresome museum visit. To be captains, kings, pirates, warriors, Vikings. But in the boat these intentions, intensities and inclinations melt away at the moment we sit by the oars and the process begins where bodies become the machine. So, what is the experience that 'comes to life' on the fiord?

On my way to the car park this evening I spot one of the families I have just been sailing together with. I draw closer to listen to what they say. Being silent on the whole trip, the guy – obviously the father – turns towards his daughter a girl in her late teens. 'Quite Scandinavian invention this...huh?' 'What do you mean?', his daughter replies. 'Well, having to do everything for yourself, collective responsibility cooperation and so on...typical Scandinavian isn't it'.

But such speculation about Scandinavian collectivism and its implications are not of interest here. The father was one of the people who before our trip was most excited about going, yelling 'I want to be a Viking', 'I want to conquer England', and now, as he silently leaves the scene, he seems to be more consumed by the experience of being forced into the collective, the 'assemblage' of the boat, than the experiential world of Viking heritage he has just been a part of co-creating. Something has happened. Something is transformed. Something new has emerged and been brought to life while we have passed through the various thresholds becoming-collective, becoming-rock, becoming-ship, becoming-Viking. What emerges is not easily grasped, and is soon forgotten. In that sense, my experiment has failed. But in failing it has pointed to the embodied engagement as enabling a transformative moment to occur. Not through theatrical staged authenticity or as awe provoked by the 'auratic' authenticity of 'dead objects', but through the embodied engagement and assembling that enables a feeling, a sense of 'the living', a feeling we may term – for want of a better word – affectual authenticity.

References

Alberti, S. (2009) Wax bodies: Art and anatomy in Victorian medical museums. *Museum History Journal*, 2(1): 7–36.

Anderson, B. (2006) Becoming and being hopeful: Towards a theory of affect. *Environment and Planning D*, 24(5): 73–52.

Anderson, B. and Harrison, P. (Eds.) (2010a) *Taking-Place: Non-Representational Theories and Geography*. Aldershot: Ashgate.

Anderson, B. and Harrison, P. (2010b) The promise of non-representational theories, in B. Anderson and P. Harrison (eds.) *Taking-Place: Non-Representational Theories and Geography*. Aldershot: Ashgate, pp. 1–34.

Anderson, J. and Peters, K. (2014) *Water Worlds: Human Geographies of the Ocean*. Aldershot: Ashgate.

Anderson, B. and Wylie, J. (2009) On geography and materiality. *Environment and Planning A*, 41: 3318–3335.

Ash, J. and Simpson, P. (2016) Geography and post-phenomenology. *Progress in Human Geography*, 40: 48–66.

Bærenholdt, J. O. and Haldrup, M. (2004) On the track of the Vikings, in M. Sheller and J. Urry (eds.) *Tourism Mobilities: Places to Play, Places in Play.* London: Routledge, pp. 78–89.

Bærenholdt, J. O. and Haldrup, M. (2006) Mobile networks and placemaking in cultural tourism. *European Urban and Regional Studies*, 13(3): 209–224.

Candlin, F. (2004) Don't touch! hands off! art, blindness and the conservation of expertise. *Body and Society*, 10(1): 71–90.

Cornish, P. and Saunders, M. (2014) *Bodies in Conflict.* London: Routledge.

Corsínjiménez, A. (2003) On space as capacity. *Journal of the Royal Anthropological Institute*, 9(1): 137–153.

Crossley, N. (2006) *Reflexive Embodiment in Contemporary Society.* Maidenhead: Open University Press.

Crossley, N. (2007) Researching embodiment by way of 'body techniques'. *The Sociological Review*, 55(1): 80–94.

Deleuze, G. and Guattari, F. (1980) *A Thousand Plateaus. Capitalism and Schizophrenia.* London: Continuum.

Dewsbury, J. D. (2010) Performative, non-representational, and affect-based research: Seven injunctions, in D. DeLyser, S. Herbert, S. Aitken, M. Crang and L. McDowell (eds.) *The Sage Handbook of Qualitative Geography.* London: Sage, pp. 321–334.

Dudley, S. (Ed.) (2010) *Museum Materialities.* London: Routledge.

Dudley, S. (2011) Museum and things, in S. Dudley, A. J. Barnes and J. Binnie (eds.) *The Thing about Museums.* London: Routledge, pp. 1–11.

Dudley, S., Barnes, A. J. and Binnie, J. (Eds.) (2011) The Thing about Museums. London: Routledge.

Edensor, T. (2010) *Geographies of Rhythm. Nature, Place, Mobilities and Bodies.* London: Routledge.

Guattari, F. (1995) *Chaosmosis. An Ethico-Aesthetic Paradigm.* Bloomington: Indiana University Press.

Haldrup, M. and Bærenholdt, J. O. (2010) Tourist experience design, in J. Simonsen, J. O. Bærenholdt, M. Büscher and J. D. Scheuer (eds.) *Design Research: Synergies from Interdisciplinary Perspectives.* London: Routledge, pp. 187–200.

Haldrup, M. and Bærendholdt, J. O. (2015) Heritage as performance, in E. Waterton and S. Watson (eds.) *A Companion to Contemporary Heritage Research.* Basingstoke: Palgrave MacMillan, pp. 52–68.

Hetherington, K. (2002) The Unsightly: touching the Parthenon Frieze. *Theory, Culture & Society*, 19(5/6): 187–205.

Ingold, T. (2000) *The Perception of the Environment.* London: Routledge.

Larkin, J. (2012) *The Body in the Museum.* Aldershot: Ashgate.

Lefebvre, H. (2004) *Rhythmanalysis.* London: Bloomsbury.

Luckhurst, R. (2012) Science versus rumour: Artefaction and counter-narrative in the Egyptian rooms of the British museum. *History and Anthropology*, 23(2): 257–269.

Manning, E. and Massumi, B. (2014) Coming alive in a world of texture, in E. Manning and B. Massumi (eds.) *Thought in the Act.* Minneapolis: University of Minnesota Press, pp. 3–22.

Massumi, B. (2001) *Parables of the Virtual. Movement, Affect, Sensation.* Durham, NC: Duke University Press.

Massumi, B. (2014) *What Animals Teach Us about Politics.* Durham, NC: Duke University Press.

McLeary, E. and Toon, E. (2012) "Here Man Learns About Himself" visual education and the rise and fall of the American museum of health. *American Journal of Public Health*, 102(7): 27–36.

Simonsen, K. (2012) In quest of a new humanism: Embodiment, experience and phenomenology as critical geography. *Progress in Human Geography*, 38: 1–17.

Stengers, I. (2011) *Thinking with Whitehead. A Free and Wild Creation of Concepts.* Cambridge, MA: Harvard University Press.

Thrift, N. and Dewsbury, J-D. (2000) Dead geographies – And how to make them live. *Environment and Planning D*, 18: 411–432.

Timm Knudsen, B. and Stage, C. (2015) *Affective Methodologies.* Basingstoke: Palgrave MacMillan.

Tolia-Kelly, D. (2011) The geographies of cultural geography III: Material geographies, vibrant matters and risking surface geographies. *Progress in Human Geography*, 37: 153–160.

Vannini, P. (2015a) *Non-representational Methodologies. Re-envisioning Research.* London: Routledge.

Vannini, P. (2015b) Non-representational ethnography: New ways of animating lifeworlds. *Cultural Geographies*, 22(2): 317–327.

Veijola, S. and Jokinen, E. (1994) The body in tourism. *Theory, Culture & Society*, 11(3): 125–151.

Waterton, E. and Watson, S. (2014) *The Semiotics of Heritage Tourism.* Bristol: Channel View Publications.

Wylie, J. (2007) *Landscape.* London: Routledge.

11 Daily female embodied experiences of slow food making in Halfeti Southeast Turkey

Anna Elisabeth Kuijpers

Introduction

Slowness is in fashion nowadays. There is an ever-growing need for people to escape their hectic stressful lives and turn back to the basics of calmness and simplicity. According to Parkins and Craig (2006), the increased popularity of pastimes like knitting or sewing shows an enhanced interest and need for a slower and more 'down to earth' way of life as counterbalance to our frantic modern society. In this context, slow food and slow tourism have found a ground for existence.

Slow tourism and slow food merge in the so-called *slow cities* (see www. cittaslow.net). Slow city is a quality label established by an Italian-based organisation called Cittaslow, an amalgamation from the words *citta*, Italian for city, and the English word *slow*. Slow refers here to time in its literal sense where a slower pace of life and more enjoyment are the aims (Radstrom 2011), going against the hastened stressful lifestyles of modern times. The organisation promotes and imagines slow cities as places where people still take time for each other, live stress free, follow the passing of the seasons, have respect for the authentic value of their local products, crafts and trades and, most importantly, enjoy slow and quiet living. The philosophy of slow food and the so-called 'Eco gastronomy' is closely connected to the ideology of slow living because slow foods play an important role in sustaining a romantic and authentic image of rural 'slow' life. Germov et al. claim that one of the major themes in the image creation on slow food is romanticism; the lifestyle of the countryside is seen as an idyllic antidote to the hectic urban life (2010:89). But is the countryside only idyllic, and does it stand in such a stark contrast to the city?

This chapter focuses on the slow city of Halfeti in the southeast of Turkey. Halfeti became a slow city in 2013. During my fieldwork in 2013–2014, I realised that the romantic image Cittaslow creates on slow food is not necessarily always in accordance with real-life performances. This chapter demonstrates, based on empirical material gathered during eight months of fieldwork, what happens in a slow city where local women are making slow foods for tourists to earn a living. I grasp an understanding of what it is like for women to produce slow foods for the sake of tourism and the effect this has on their bodies by looking at the interplay between the embodied experiences of women in relation to the making of slow food and the images created on slow food by Cittaslow. I argue that the daily-embodied experiences of women involved in making slow food in Halfeti, when compared with the romanticised images of slow food, reveal the influence of tourism on the female body.

Tourism and the female body

Tourism studies, like the social sciences more generally, were hesitant for a long time to integrate the body into their research (Pettman 1997), but nowadays in the study of tourism the body is seen as increasingly important (Veijola and Jokinen 1994), going against the dominant Cartesian-Kantian tradition where the mind and body are separated, and the status of the mind is given more importance (Wang 2000:66). To study the body and its behaviour gives access to important knowledge beyond the spoken word. According to Elisabeth Grosz, '...all the effects of subjectivity, all the significant facets and complexities of subjects, can be adequately explained using the subject's corporeality as a framework.... Bodies have all the explanatory power of minds' (1994:vii). Most cultural knowledge is preserved in behaviour rather than in words (Hastrup 1995). According to Richard Osborne, 'the body is no longer to be seen as a simple material reality, but as a complexly constructed object of social discourses' (2002:51). Williams and Bendelow (1998) claim that in theorising the body we have to study the dialectical relationship it has with other facets of society, like in this study the interplay between the body and the romantic images created for tourism.

Not only does the body have to be given more attention in the study of tourism, the female voice also needs to be heard more in tourism studies, since much research on tourism leaves out female perspectives or experiences (Pritchard et al. 2007:6). Although gender and embodiment are now being addressed more specifically (see Cole 2018), the study of tourism still tends to produce what Johnston referred to as 'hegemonic, disembodied and masculinist knowledge' (2000:181). In this chapter, female bodily actions will be the main subject of study and thus contributing to addressing the concerns raised by Johnston.

I conceptualise the bodily actions of the women involved in slow food making as daily-embodied experiences because the concept embodiment has the 'ability' to overcome the binary divide between nature and culture. Embodiment as a concept captures well the '"inflection" of mind into body and body into mind' (Williams and Bendelow 1998:3). For Thomas Csordas, 'embodiment is our fundamental existential condition, our corporeality or bodylines in relation to the world and other people' (2011:137). In addition, I approach these daily-embodied experiences as *performances* meaning here: 'everyday embodied modes of expressive enactment by which individuals "constitute and sustain their identities and collectively enact their worlds"'

(Conquergood 1983:27 in Coonfield and Huxford 2009:458). Like the study of the body, the study of human behaviour as performances gives access to 'ephemeral knowledge and meaning' (Conquergood 2002:146 in Coonfield and Huxford 2009:465) that goes beyond what people say. More specifically, I approach food making as a *gendered performance*. According to Adkins, 'when we see gender as an act and performance we acknowledge it as work: as flexible and fluid, performative in character; as a property that can be disentangled and abstracted from a person – instead of being an inherent property through authorship, biology or origin' (Adkins 2005 in Veijola and Valtonen 2007:19). Food making is here a gendered performance seen in relation to the romantic image Cittaslow tries to sustain about slow food.

In what follows, first the way Halfeti is imagined as a slow city and the importance of slow food regarding this image will be explained. In addition, based on empirical material, the factors that interplay with the image and the consequences this has on the daily-embodied gendered performances of women will be described. Since the focus lies on the female body, this chapter contributes to the study of female embodiment in tourism.

Slow food in the slow city

Halfeti is one of the nine Cittaslows of Turkey, and the first one in the southeast of the country. It used to be a lively small village next to the Euphrates at the centre of the province Sanliurfa. In 1999, two-thirds of Halfeti were submerged by water due to the completion of the Birecik dam that is part of the GAP[1] (Southeast Anatolian project). As a result of the flooding, most of the population lost their houses and their ways of living. Many people left and Halfeti as a town was on the verge of extinction. In 2007, GAP stepped in and revived Halfeti's socio-economic life by introducing tourism. GAP collaborated with international organisations like, for example, Cittaslow to develop tourism in Halfeti on a national and international level.

Cittaslow aims at re-establishing a *sense* of place. by supporting the unique assets of a region, like specific crafts and foods, and ways of life that traditionally formed the identity of a city. This is opposed to a feeling of alienation of place, in which it is argued that people do not know any more where their products for consumption are coming from (Conway and Timms 2010:333). Local production of foods and the development and use of independent businesses are key elements of a slow city; also, mass-tourism and commercialisation should be discouraged (Ekinci 2014:180). For a city to become a member of Cittaslow, it must accept the guidelines of slow food and it has to collaborate in the philosophy of 'conviviality' and the conservation or preservation of the local environment. In addition, a Cittaslow member agrees to establish goals that will improve the quality of life of both its citizens and visitors and to share ideas and knowledge with the wider Cittaslow network (Hoeschele 2010, Miele 2010 in Yurtseven and Kaya 2011, Heitmann, Robinson and Povey 2011).

As aforementioned, slow foods are an important facet of the slow city, and like slow cities slow food is surrounded by an image of romanticism and unspoiled pure traditions. According to Pratt, alternative food movements like slow food:

> Attempt to re-establish practical and discursive links between production and consumption, and in doing so they give these foods a history, one that is largely missing (and often for good reasons) in much of the food industry. This history is often constructed within a romantic discourse of the local, the traditional and the authentic.
>
> (2007:285)

These nostalgic and romantic images that long for a return of a past (that was perhaps not lived) also receive criticism for being fabricated based on idyllic notions where people and nature were one (Jonas et al. 2003, Laudan 2004, Panagia 2007 in Germov et al. 2010:102). In the context of tourism, these romantic notions can be taken home in the form of souvenirs like local (slow) food products. Slow foods are popular, especially among tourists, for various reasons: they symbolise place and culture, they can provide a moral 'feel good factor' connected to their consumption, or consumers feel an enhanced connection to their destination (Sims 2009:328). According to Bessiere (1998) and Urry (1990), local foods are popular among tourists because they are seen as 'iconic' products that capture the 'typical' nature of a particular place. 'There is a growing desire to obtain experiences and products that are original and the real thing, not contaminated by being fake or impure' (Yeoman et al. 2007:1128). The customer adds value to these products, a value that is based on direct contact with those who produce the food. Pratt said the following about slow food: 'This food is the product of a continuous and collective endeavour, it pre-dates industrialised food systems and its value derives from that opposition' (2007:294). Consumers (tourists) in Halfeti are often people from big Turkish cities who feel they may have lost connection with these authentic ways of living and food making. By buying slow foods, an image and experience of the slow city is bought that people can take home and consume.

In Halfeti, the production of slow foods for touristic purposes, next to the production for private consumption, is a relatively new phenomenon that originated with the rise of tourism. Due to the popularity of slow foods, there are a considerable number of women in Halfeti that respond to the demand and make more of these foods to sell to tourists, often in little improvised stands in the village, or in tourist shops their families own. But the developments around slow food production and consumption are not without consequences for the women involved. In the next section, the embodied daily performances of the food making for commercial goals, and the interplay between these performances and the image of the slow city will be discussed in more detail.

Consequences of slow food production on the female body and mind

In Halfeti, food making traditionally is for a large part concerned with the preservation of goods providing households with provisions throughout the year. The harvest season starts in September and that automatically entails the preparation of (slow) foods. I realised that the production of slow food demands a lot of the body when I was involved in the production process myself. Being part of the daily-embodied procedures made me part of a 'co-performative witnessing' that goes beyond sheer cognitive experiences (Conquergood 2002), also I integrate my own female body into the experience, since research on the body benefits from the 'researcher's embodied experiences' (Johnston 2000:196).

My work consisted of cleaning vegetables like bell peppers and hot peppers to make, amongst others, *pul biber* (dried red pepper flakes), a commonly used spice in Turkish and Kurdish cuisine. To make *pul biber*, hot and sweet peppers are cleaned and cut into little pieces to dry in the sun. When the peppers are dry enough, they are ground. Cleaning the spicy peppers makes your eyes and hands burn, especially when you clean peppers from 10 in the morning until 7 in the afternoon. Besides sore eyes and hands, women kneel for hours, sitting on their heels to get the work done. These repetitive movements over days cause considerable pressure on the body. My landlady, Deniz, confirmed this. At the time I stayed with her she was 64 years old and lived with her husband in the centre of town, where she had lived all her married life. Deniz's house was spared from the flooding of the town during the construction of the dam. She was socially very active and often involved in making slow foods, helping out her neighbours. One evening she came home from a gathering where she helped to make bread. She sat down on her sofa. I asked her how her day was. The first thing she mentioned was the pain she had in her arms and hands while she was rubbing them. She told me how she sometimes was tired of helping other people because she was an old lady. Elderly women frequently complained, they told me how tired they were in the evening because of the (extra) work they had to do, or how painful their hands and arms were from the work.

Besides the physical burden food making has on the body, there is also psychological stress involved that creates strain on the body. An important factor that causes stress is deadlines to have foods ready for customers. On more than one occasion, unexpected last minute additional orders were made. These orders can be big. In one case, a customer ordered enough *cevizli sucuk* (sweet sausage) for a whole year. This popular sweet snack in the shape of a sausage is a mixture of grape molasses *(üzüm pekmezi)* and pieces of walnut. One can find industrial versions of *cevizli sucuk* in supermarkets, souvenir shops and so on but these are nothing compared to the homemade variety. The production of these sweets is very cumbersome.[2] The woman who received the last minute order, which she had not be able to foresee, had to begin from scratch the whole extensive practice of making these sweets because she had nothing already prepared that could satisfy the request.

Besides unforeseen deadlines, another unstable factor that creates stress is the weather. Slow foods are usually made in the outdoors. In general, the weather is good in September in the southeast of Turkey, but unexpected weather conditions like rain can cause problems. It can prolong the production process, or when the foods are ruined new raw materials must be purchased and the process has to start again. The latter happened to one woman who was in the process of making *pul biber*. The peppers were spread out on the roof for several days and regularly turned so they could dry in the sun. Suddenly, it started to rain. The woman ran up to the roof, collected the food and stored it elsewhere, covered from the rain. But the damage was done; the rain affected the dried peppers. She decided, against the usual protocol, to grind the peppers the next day because she wanted to sell the flakes in her shop. Because the peppers were not dry enough, the result was not to her satisfaction and therefore useless, and she had to start all over again. Dependence on unstable factors like the weather creates additional stress for women. This is especially so when extra financial investments are made related to tourism, the loss of products can have detrimental effects on the financial situation of families when they are dependent on the income of food production.

Due to the increased popularity of slow foods, the additional workload for women has also risen. In Halfeti, the workload increased because more foods have to be made, and simultaneously women are still expected to take care of the household and raise the children. According to Allen (1999), there are alternative food movements that add to both the workload of women working in agriculture and to the workload of food procurement and preparation at home. The slow food movement, that strongly promotes the consumption of homemade meals, neglects the fact that women are often under time pressure (Allen and Sachs 2012:35).

Physical strain on the body and stress are elements that do not exist in the image of slow cities. Slow food promotes 'sustainable food systems, regional food traditions, the pleasures of the table and a slower and more harmonious rhythm of life' (Yurtseven and Kaya 2011:91). When slow food is commodified for tourism, the increased workload creates a heavy burden on the female bodies. In addition, when foods are being made on demand, additional factors that create stress, like, for example, unforeseen deadlines or circumstances beyond control, for example bad weather conditions, are involved. In these cases, slow living or slow food production are not necessarily romantic and relaxed, but cause strain on female bodies in the form of psychological stress. To live up to the ideal that is created about a slow city, Cittaslow does not show how the work is done 'behind the scenes' because that would detract from the romantic slow living and slow food-making image. Factors like stress or physical strains are hidden from the public because they are not seen as part of a romanticised image but rather as part of the problems of 'modern society' and thus not associated with slow city village life.

The social context of slow food production

Food brings people together at the table for daily social interaction (Mintz 2006), besides that, sharing a meal 'is a physical event' (Douglas 1984:12). Not only the consumption, but also the production of slow foods is a social process; rarely did I see women make slow foods completely on their own. Help is necessary because due to the long production process these foods are made in large quantities. Because of the growing popularity these foods have among outsiders new ways of gathering arise in which women from different socio-economic backgrounds meet each other. In this section, I describe the embodied aspect of slow food production in relation to its social aspect. Slow food production is not simply work, it is part of a social reality in which female bodies come together in private spaces sharing moments together.

Women of all ages produce slow food, and more importantly, since the production of slow foods has increased because of tourism, women depend on other women for help. These women can be friends, neighbours or family. Many times an appeal is made to people living in the same vicinity, but it is also possible that family or friends who do not live close by come to help. The economic relation between women that help each other is mostly based on a reciprocal exchange. This means that women who received help will return it later, and women who have been helping get some of the end products they helped to make. It is important to reciprocate the physical help, even if food has been given in return for assistance. I realised the importance of reciprocating help when one morning a friend of mine in Halfeti suddenly dashed off to a neighbouring town to aid a relative to make bread. She told me that it was important for her to go there because they helped her in the past. She made it clear to me that she absolutely needed to return the favour now. My friend underlines here the importance of reciprocating her help related to food making.

Since the workload has increased, contrary to the time following the flooding of the town, reciprocal ties have again become more important. Female bodies gather together and support each other physically and mentally, as Csordas notes, the body is not only an 'indeterminate methodological field' but also a 'discrete organic entity.... embodiment is a matter of shared, mutually implicating, and never completely anonymous flesh' (2011:137). As the female bodies come together to help each other with the physical work that must be done the women chat, gossip, make jokes and share their hardships with each other.

Women who know each other help one another make food. However, slow food production also causes women who do not know each other to come together. According to Appadurai in India, cookbooks bring together women from different parts of the country with different socio-economic backgrounds: 'Cookbooks allow women from one group to explore the tastes of another, just as cookbooks allow women from one group to be represented to another' (1988:6). In Halfeti, I witnessed women with different socio-economic backgrounds meeting each other via the preparation of slow foods. My neighbour Ayşe taught two women from 'the big city', Ankara, how to make certain local slow foods. Both women had bought an enormous pile of paprika to create their private stock of 'home-made' *salça* and *pul biber*. It was the first time they made these foods, and Ayşe, together with some other ladies from the village, assisted them. Ayşe was providing her knowledge and help but also her house to make the foods, letting the city women inside the intimacy of her private space. At the end of a few days' work, the ladies from Ankara paid Ayşe for her services with money. After the work was completed, Ayşe and I were reflecting on these past busy days. This talk led to a conversation about Ayşe's childhood. She told me that she lost her mother in her teenage years; she married when she was 18 and left the parental house to move in with her husband. Ayşe explained to me that the knowledge of food making traditionally is passed on from mother to daughter, but in Ayşe's case her older sisters helped her out; also, she learned many things concerning food making from her current neighbour. Here again Ayşe underlines the gendered aspect of traditional food making, in which knowledge is passed down from generation to generation from woman to woman.

Unlike Ayşe, the women from Ankara learned how to make slow food from women in the village they do not know very well. Here, the transmission of knowledge is based on an economic relationship of monetary exchange rather than on a reciprocal one of help. Knowledge is passed on to outsiders and turned into a commodity that can be bought. But there is more to it than simply providing a service and being paid. Women from different socio-economic backgrounds get to know each other through the representation of foods different from their own, and, also, by eating these foods, the other is symbolically incorporated.

Expected gendered performance related to slow food production

There is tension between the materiality of the body and the socialisation it undergoes, or as Turner puts it: 'the relationship between nature and culture concerning the body' (1996:1). According to Mary Douglas (1978), there are two bodies: the social and the physical. These two bodies are continuously interacting, but the social body restricts the physical body in the way it is seen in society. As Douglas argues, 'The physical experience of the body, always modified by the social categories through which it is known, sustains a particular view of society' (1978:70). The relationship between the two is complex as both aspects are entwined, which makes it hard to disentangle in practice (Holland et al. 1994:22). In this section, I approach food making as a gendered performance that is imagined as belonging to a female gender role.

Women in Halfeti are in charge of slow food making, this has been the case before the town was integrated in a tourist economy. Now that the foods are sold to tourists another dimension is added to it: for the sake of tourism, the wider public or tourists *expect* the performance of slow food making to be undertaken by women. Hazel Tucker remarks, in her study of tourism in Göreme Turkey, that 'women and elderly come to represent the 'traditional' to tourists because they mostly continue with the 'traditional village' activities of farming and food production' (2003:102). In the image creation of the slow city, women are imagined as close to a traditional life-style, meaning here amongst others taking care of food making. According to Charles and Kerr (1988:2), food practices can reproduce a social division of gender. According to Pietrykowski (2007:314), drawing on Fine et al. (1996) and de Certeau et al. (1998), criticism on slow food is that

> The pleasure of the table abstracts from the gendered division of house-hold labour; the quest for artisan-produced, regional foods and support for antique varieties of corn, apples, turkeys and other products can easily slip into a discourse of authenticity bent on preserving peasant traditions.
>
> (Fine et al. 1996, de Certeau et al. 1998 in Pietrykowski 2007:314)

In the context of the slow city, the gendered performance of slow food production as female is seen as necessary to maintain a credible image for the tourists. We should not underestimate the role images play in 'the cultural construction of places and people as gendered sites and sights' (Aitchison 2001:4). Besides that, bodies act, interact and react (Grosz 1994). Both the female food makers and the tourists need each other to create and preserve the gendered performance. Tourists are attracted by an 'authentic' lifestyle and come to watch the gendered performance. Women, in turn, execute the performance because the audience expect it. West and Zimmerman speak of *doing gender* that is executed by individuals but nevertheless 'is a situated do-ing carried out in the virtual or real presence of others who are presumed to be oriented towards its production' (1987:126). The performance of slow food making is expected to 'belong' to a certain gender. Judith Butler claims that gender is 'an identity instituted through a stylised repetition of acts… it is a performative accomplishment which the mundane social audience, including the actors themselves come to believe and to perform in the mode of belief' (1988:519–520). The expected behaviour can be explained within the concept *gender role* meaning: 'being a man or a woman means enacting a general role definitive of one's sex – "the sex role"' (Connell 1987:48). Here, Cittaslow creates images of slow cities in which the normative sex roles are reproduced. To be congruent with the image these roles have to be performed. Stereotyp-ical images created for tourism have the power for people to transform their appearance to be in line with tourists' expectations (Albers and James (1983).

This does not mean that what is normative is also the standard; the normative is rather the standard of what the socially powerful see as such (Connell 1987:51). The socially powerful are in this case Cittaslow and GAP. GAP claims to be a socio-economic developmental project with a strong focus on gender-balanced development.[3] Sariaslan claims about GAP and its gender balanced program that, 'Projects targeting "empowerment" of women via "alternative" education and employment opportunities maintain existing gender roles and therefore power relations' (2015:607). A danger concerning the tourism industry is that it can be a force 'objectifying indigenous women and female employees as part of the tourism "package" (ILO 2003), and perpetuating hetero-masculinist discourses which merge the feminine and the exotic' (Mackie 2000 in Pritchard et al. 2007:9). Although some women in Halfeti are gaining more financial independence by working in tourism, this does not necessarily lead to gender equality in life in general, several Turkish scholars claim that women in Turkey are emancipated but not liberated (Kandiyoti 1987, Arat 1989, Tekeli 1995).

Expected bodily performances based on normative ideologies of powerful stakeholders create a vicious circle in which gender roles need to stay traditional in order to earn money. The romantic message about life in the countryside Cittaslow and the slow food movement convey contributes to the reproduction and enhancement of traditional gender roles in which women make the foods and take care of the household and children. Images created of the slow city underline, confirm and reify performances and expectations of female bodies. Women comply with this stereotypical role because that is a way to earn a living.

Conclusion

In this chapter, the interplay between the image created on slow food making in the slow city Halfeti and the daily-embodied performances of women that take part in the process of slow food making is investigated, with the aim of revealing the influence of tourism on the female body.

The emergence of a new market concerning the production of slow food for tourists in the slow city of Halfeti has several consequences on the female body. Because women are integrated in the tourist economy, their workload has increased: not only are women making (more) slow foods they are also taking care of the household. The production of more slow foods causes a heavy burden on the body, especially for the elderly, due to sitting for hours in the same position cleaning vegetables, executing repetitive movements over several days. Besides the physical strain, there is psychological stress created by factors like deadlines, or unforeseen conditions, for example, bad weather that can ruin the production process. These aspects stay hidden from the public because the romantic image of a slow city and the performances that go with it has to be maintained.

Slow food making not only causes stress and strain on the body but also brings together women. On the one hand, slow food making gathers women who help each other make foods based on a reciprocal exchange, creating stronger social cohesion in the village. However, slow food making also brings together women from different socio-economic backgrounds to meet and share the knowledge of food making, and in the process get to know each other. In addition, by eating the food symbolic incorporation of the other takes place.

Finally, I state that the romantic image Cittaslow and slow food propagate has an effect on the female bodily performances. For the performance of slow food making to be credible or 'authentic' buyers *expect* local women to make the foods. Cittaslow produces images for tourism based on stereotypical sex roles that create a gendered performance in which the female body is (again) connected to the private domain and life in the countryside is romanticised and glorified. As a result, food making ties women to private spaces and creates expected performative behaviour based on gendered stereotypes that maintain the status quo between men and women. I argue that organisations like Cittaslow and slow food that create this romantic image also maintain a gendered division of labour in which women are expected to have certain roles. It is debatable as to how the gender-balanced program these organisations claim to provide is implemented into the tourism economy. By living up to the slow food or slow city ideology, it is almost impossible to simultaneously live up to a gender balanced society.

Notes

1 Güneydoğu Anadolu Projesi (GAP) is a hydroelectric power project executed by the Turkish government. The project is carried out in the provinces of Mardin, Gaziantep, Adıyaman, Diyarbakir, Şanlıurfa, Siirt, Batman and Şırnak, an area covering 75,000 km^2 or ninety-five percent of Turkey. 1.7 million acres are supposed to be irrigated by twenty-two dams in combination with nineteen power plants that will double the amount of electric power (Kolars and Mitchell 1991:24), to satisfy the national demand for energy in the country (Warner 2008).
2 Walnuts are peeled, put on a string and dried for a few days. In addition, a thick syrup of *pekmez,* flour and water is made, the walnut strings are dipped a few times inside the syrup and subsequently the sausages are dried in the sun. The whole process takes a few days.
3 GAP received the Millennium Award from the International Water Resources Association because of its exemplary work towards implementing, amongst others, women's participation (Ünver 2001).

References

Aitchison, C. (2001) Theorizing other discourses of tourism, gender and culture: Can the Subaltern Speak (in Tourism)? *Tourist Studies*, 1(2): 133–147.
Albers, P. C. and James, W. R. (1983) Tourism and the changing image of the great lakes Indian. *Annals of Tourism Research*, 10(1): 128–148.

Allen, P. (1999) Reweaving the food security safety net: Mediating entitlement and entrepreneurship. *Agriculture and Human Values*, 16(2): 117–129.

Allen, P. and Sachs, C. (2012) Women and food chains: The gendered politics of food, in P. Forth and C. Counihan (eds.) *Taking Food Public: Redefining Food Ways in a Changing World*. New York: Routledge, pp. 3–40.

Appadurai, A. (1988) How to make a national cuisine: Cookbooks in contemporary India. *Comparative Studies in Society and History*, 30(1): 3–24.

Arat, Y. (1989) *The Patriarchal Paradox: Women Politicians in Turkey*. London and Toronto: Associated University Presses.

Bell, V. (1999) *Performativity and Belonging*. London: Sage Publications.

Bessiere, J. (1998) Local development and heritage: Traditional food and cuisine as tourist attractions in rural areas. *Sociologia Ruralis*, 38: 21–34.

Butler, J. (1988) Performative acts and gender constitution: An essay in phenomenology and feminist theory. *Theatre Journal*, 40(4): 519–531.

Charles, N. and Kerr, M. (1988) *Women, Food and Families*. Manchester: Manchester University Press.

Cittaslow International. Available at: www.cittaslow.net/content/association [Accessed 27 September 2017].

Cole, S. (Ed.) (2018) *Gender Equality and Tourism. Beyond Empowerment*. Wallingford: CABI.

Connell, R. (1987) *Gender and Power: Society, the Person and Sexual Politics*. Cambridge: Polity Press.

Conquergood, D. (2002) Performance studies: Interventions and radical research. *The Drama Review*, 46(2): 145–156.

Conway, D. and Timms, B. (2010) Re-branding alternative tourism in the Caribbean: The case for 'Slow Tourism'. *Sage Journals*, 10(4): 329–344.

Coonfield, G. and Huxford, J. (2009) News images as lived images: Media ritual, cultural performance, and public trauma. *Critical Studies in Media Communication*, 26(5): 457–479.

Csordas, T. (2011) Cultural phenomenology, embodiment: Agency, sexual difference, and illness, in F. E. Mascia-Lees (eds.) *A Companion to the Anthropology of the Body and Embodiment*. Oxford: Blackwell Publishing, pp. 137–156.

Douglas, M. (1978) *Natural Symbols*. New York: Praeger.

Douglas, M. (1984) *Food in the Social Order: Studies in Food and Festivities in Three American Communities*. New York: Russell Sage Foundation.

Ekinci, M. (2014) The Cittaslow philosophy in the context of sustainable tourism development; the case of Turkey. *Tourism Management*, 41: 178–189.

Germov, J., Williams, L. and Freij, M. (2010) Portrayal of the slow food movement in the Australian print media conviviality, localism and Romanticism. *Journal of Sociology*, 47(1): 89–106.

Grosz, E. (1994) *Volatile Bodies*. Bloomington: Indiana University Press.

Hastrup, K. (1995) *A Passage to Anthropology: Between Experience and Theory*. New York: Routledge.

Heitmann, S., Robinson, P. and Povey, G. (2011) Slow food, slow cities and slow tourism, in P. Robinson, S. Heitmann and P. Dieke (eds.) *Research Themes for Tourism*. London: MPG Books Group, pp. 114–127.

Holland, J., Ramazanoğlu, C., Sharpe, S. and Thomson, R. (1994) Power and desire: The embodiment of female sexuality. *Feminist Review*, 46: 21–38.

Johnston, L. (2000) (Other) Bodies and tourism studies. *Annals of Tourism Research*, 28(1): 180–201.

Kandiyoti, D. (1987) Emancipated but unliberated? Reflections on the Turkish case. *Feminist Studies*, 13: 317–338.

Kolars, J. and Mitchell, W. (1991) The Euphrates river and the Southeast Anatolian development project. Carbondale: Southern Illinois University Press.

Mintz, S. (2006) Food at moderate speeds, in R. Wilk (ed.) *Fast Food/Slow Food: The Cultural Economy of the Global System*. Lanham, MD: Altamira Press, pp. 3–13.

Osborne, R. (2002) *Mega words: 200 Terms You Really Need to Know*. London: Sage.

Parkins, P. and Craig, W. (2006) *Slow Living*. Oxford: Berg.

Pettman, J. (1997) Body politics: International sex tourism. *Third World Quarterly*, 18(1): 93–108.

Pietrykowski, B. (2007) You are what you eat: The social economy of the slow food movement. *Review of Social Economy*, 62(3): 307–321.

Pratt, J. (2007) Food values. The local and the authentic. *Critique of Anthropology*, 27(3): 285–300.

Pritchard, A., Morgan, A., Ateljevic, C. and Harris, S. (2007) *Tourism & Gender. Embodiment, Sensuality and Experience*. Oxfordshire: CABI.

Radstrom, S. (2011) A place-sustaining framework for local urban identity: An introduction and history of Cittaslow. *International Journal of Italian Planning Practice*, 1(1): 90–113.

Sariaslan, K. (2015) Housewives 'in Progress': Stories of gender-balanced development in Southeast Anatolia. *Paper International Conference on Knowledge and Politics in Gender and Women's Studies*. October 9–11 ODTÜ Ankara, pp. 601–610.

Sims, R. (2009) Food, place and authenticity: Local food and the sustainable tourism experience. *Journal of Sustainable Tourism*, 17(3): 321–336.

Tekeli, S. (Ed.) (1995) *Women in Modern Turkish Society*. London: Zed Books.

Tucker, H. (2003) *Living With Tourism. Negotiating Identities in a Turkish Village*. London: Routledge.

Turner, B. (1996) *The Body and Society: Explorations in Social Theory*, 2nd ed. London: Sage.

Ünver, O. (2001) Institutionalizing the sustainable development approach: Coordination across traditional boundaries. *International Journal of Water Resources Development*, 17(4): 511–520.

Urry, J. (1990) *The Tourist Gaze: Leisure and Travel in Contemporary Societies*. London: Sage.

Veijola, S. and Jokinen, E. (1994) The body in tourism. *Theory, Culture & Society*, 11(3): 125–151.

Veijola, S. and Valtonen, A. (2007) The body in tourism industry, in A. Pritchard, N. Morgan, I. Ateljevic and C. Harris (eds.) *Tourism & Gender. Embodiment, Sensuality and Experience*. Oxfordshire: CABI, pp. 13–30.

Yeoman, I., Brassb, D. and McMahon-Beattiec, U. (2007) Current issue in tourism: The authentic tourist. *Tourism Management*, 28(4): 1128–1138.

Yurtseven, H. R. and Kaya, O. (2011) Slow tourists: A comparative research based on Cittaslow principles. *American International Journal of Contemporary Research*, 1(2): 91–98.

Wang, N. (2000) *Tourism and Modernity: A Sociological Analysis*. Oxford: Pergamon Press.

Warner, J. (2008) Contested Hydro hegemony: Hydraulic control and security in Turkey. *Water Alternatives*, 1(2): 271–288.

West, C. and Zimmerman, D. (1987) Doing gender. *Gender and Society*, 1(2): 125–151.

Williams, S. and Bendelow, G. (1998) *The Lived Body: Sociological Themes, Embodied Issues*. London: Routledge.

12 Clay, glass and everyday life

Craft-artists' embodiment in the tourist landscape

Solène Prince

Introduction

Tourism can be seen as an exotic practice that puts travellers in contact with foreign cultures and extraordinary sights. This notion has been mostly perpetuated in academia through the pioneering work of Dean MacCannell (1976) and John Urry (1990) who have suggested in their own ways that the tourist was looking for something out of the ordinary while away from home. As the performance turn gained prominence in tourism scholarship, it became evident that there was something very ordinary about tourism. After all, visiting sites and encountering new cultures are primarily made possible through an array of unreflexive habits, everyday technologies and an understanding of tourism as a taken-for-granted activity (Edensor 2001, Franklin 2004, Larsen 2012). A scholarly focus on the performances behind tourism informs the researcher of its mundane, social and material character. Tourist places come to life through embodied movements where actions, such as doing, being, touching and gazing, performed by hosts and guests alike, engage human bodies with their physical surroundings in very real ways (Crouch 2000, Coleman and Crang 2002).

In this chapter, I explore bodies that are practically engaged in the formation of their world. More specifically, I seek to define how tourism's mundane character weaves itself in the cultural landscape through the embodied practices of local stakeholders. It is an examination of how tourism becomes a part of the everyday life of those who dwell within toured places, a focus that remains underexplored in tourism scholarship. Too often it is the movements of the tourist that catches the researcher's attention. Those of the host have been mostly studied in terms of internalising the tourist gaze or working on the tourist stage, making their encounters with these guests rather fleeting to their existence. To make the embodied practices of the host meaningful to a conceptualisation of tourist places as socially performed realms of everyday life, the work of anthropologist Tim Ingold (2011), who suggested framing the cultural landscape through a dwelling perspective, is useful. In my study of craft-artists from the popular summer destination of Bornholm in Denmark, I apply the dwelling perspective to give spatial and social meaning to the host's everyday practices (see also Prince 2018). I contend that the cultural landscape, when presented as a host's realm of mundane embodied practices, cannot be detached from the landscape that tourists encounter.

Place and performance in tourism

To explain tourism as a social phenomenon, scholars have early on relied on dichotomies between the authentic and the modern, and the exotic and the ordinary, coupling travel to a search for the pre-modern and extraordinary. MacCannell (1976) articulated this form of reasoning with his notion of staged-authenticity, where cultural groups suit the viewers' desire for exotic sights through staged cultural representations. This framework has been questioned to suggest a consideration for post-modern hyper realities and new purposes of travel not centred on exotic sights (Stephen 1990, Urry 1990, Wang 1999). Urry (1990), with the concept of the tourist gaze, associated the construction of tourist places to the fact that there were tourists who looked for sights, experiences and novelties they could not find at home. This search would influence the way places around the world were (re)built, seeking to please the tourist gaze. These structural theories have been criticised for their neglect of bodily sensations and human consciousness (Larsen and Urry 2011). Some scholars deplored their lack of consideration for the meaning of social interaction and other senses, such as touching and playing, while on holiday (Johnston 2001, Perkins and Thorns 2001, Obrador-Pons 2003, 2007, 2009, Edensor 2006). Many scholars have espoused the performance turn in their analysis of tourist places, ultimately recognising that these places emerge from corporeal movements, and not merely from the creation of a cultural or scenic backdrop (Edensor 2000, 2001, 2006, Larsen 2012).

In the social sciences, a shift towards a more performative conception of place emanated from the critique of deeply intellectual ways of thinking about the world in terms of signs, structures and symbols (Dewsbury 2000, Nash 2000, Thrift and Dewsbury 2000, Lorimer 2005, Thrift, 1996, 2001, 2004, 2008). Rather than seeing places as containers for social action, their formation is here conceived through the performances of social bodies. Early on, Edensor (2000, 2001) proposed seeing tourism as materially and symbolically staged through the theatrical work of key staff members who follow scripts and use props to guide tourists in their actions. In light of the performance turn, tourist places are conceived as made through the interrelated actions of tourists, tourist workers and local people, acting within bounded settings controlled by regulations and social codes of conduct (Edensor 2000, 2001, Baerenholdt et al. 2004, Larsen 2010, 2012). Doing tourism is a learnt behaviour for both host and guest as they rehearse their respective social roles (Edensor 2001). These tourist stages are dynamic realms; constantly enacted through the movements of these diverse individuals, encompassing various material elements, which are transformed each time they are acted out. In this sense, places are complex nexuses where hosts, guests and things of all sorts are continually brought together to perform their social role (Hannam et al. 2006).

With tourism scholarship embracing performativity, tourism scholars now apprehend the multisensory interactions occurring between humans, nonhumans and objects in the doing of tourism (Crouch 2002, Cloke and Perkins 2005, Waitt and Cook 2007, Gibson 2010, Grimwood 2014). Non-humans, such as mundane objects, technologies, plants and animals, are all elements that mediate the performances that interlink the body to an environment (Crouch 2000, Michael 2000, Whatmore 2002). Common equipment and tools, such as soil and shoes involve the human subject directly in the world by affording practices such as gardening and hiking. When it comes to tourism, it is objects such as cameras, guide books, scuba gear and bungie cords that actively involve the body at a destination (Bell and Lyall 2002, Haldrup and Larsen 2006). Bodies and things grant place a practical, as well as symbolic and expressive, form (Whatmore 2002). Tourism is a social performance related to material interrelations and embodied movements of doing, touching and being, which taken together generate tourist places (Coleman and Crang 2002).

Everyday life and tourism

These embodied movements performed in tourist places highlight the mundane character of tourism. The mundane relates to the unquestioned and unremarkable behaviours and ways of doing individuals adopt in their daily lives. By engaging with performativity, tourism scholars have called for the de-exoticisation of tourism (Coleman and Crang 2002, Baerenholdt et al. 2004, Larsen 2005, 2008). A close look at bodily movements outlines the mundane aspect of the practice of doing tourism. For instance, Stebbins (2002, 2007) writes that special interest tourism is simply the pursuit while on holiday of activities usually practised at home in order to accumulate cultural capital. Moreover, tourists engage in quotidian habits while on holiday which are similar to the routines they follow at home (Edensor 2000, 2001, 2006, Obrador 2012). With the inevitable help of tourism workers and pressure from social monitoring, tourists adopt familiar and prescribed coded patterns of behaviour while abroad (Baerenholdt et al. 2004). For instance, wake-up calls and bathroom breaks are often based on a schedule reminiscent of the one from a busy day at work. Bodies are groomed to fulfil the same beauty standards followed at home. The souvenir shops sell banal objects such as t-shirts and mugs.

The social character of tourism attests to the everydayness of its practice. Most tourism performances are done to derive pleasure from being with friends, family members and other individuals, rather than from experiencing extraordinary places and encountering primitive others (Obrador-Pons 2003, 2007, Haldrup and Larsen 2010). Both Tucker (2007) and Edensor (1998) observed that young participants on guided tours would pay more attention to each other than to their guides and the sites ahead. Furthermore, the everyday life of the host is consumed as a cultural product by tourists strolling around and enjoying cafés, boutiques and other sites of mundane local meaning (Ivanovic 2008). Social interactions between host and guest are part of the ordinary for the local producer, shop owner and resident as these individuals routinely encounter tourists at their work spaces and in public areas.

Even if the mundane is often scripted, there is room to uncover creativity and divergence while studying embodied movements in tourism. Tourism performances are often innovative and spontaneous for the actors involved in bringing them about (Edensor 2000, 2001, Larsen 2005, 2012). Human activities are fluid and spontaneous, rather than deterministic, and can give impulse to various unscripted and unexpected performances (Weaver 2005). Maoz (2006) demonstrated, in her study of Israeli backpackers in India, that Indians project the performances expected of them back at backpackers searching for spiritual gurus. This shows that power is not the property of any particular actor during the tourist encounter, but rather flows between the host and guest who gaze at each other, provoking unusual and unexpected performances (Maoz 2006). Performances between host and guest are not solely mediated by the socio-cultural expectations of a tourist gaze and its related symbolic discourses they can be the result of resistance, adaptation or confusion in response to this gaze (Larsen and Urry 2011).

A scholarly interest in embodied movements and performativity denotes an appreciation for the occurrence of everyday life in all its creative and repetitive forms. McCormack (2008) notes that certain activities find their meaning in tangible corporeality of individual expressions. Mundane activities such as gardening, touring and hiking are meaningful in and of themselves because they involve the human body in the world. It becomes important to pay attention to the material compositions and mundane human activities taking place in the world (Dewsbury et al. 2002). In this regard, non-representational ways of thinking have gained prominence in the social sciences where representation is to be given to manifestations of everyday life, rather than to cognitive processes aimed at deciphering text and imagery (Dewsbury 2000, Nash 2000, Thrift and Dewsbury 2000, Thrift 2008). Lorimer asserts that with the non-representational theoretical approach, '[t]he focus falls on how life takes shape and gains expression in shared experiences, everyday routines, fleeting encounters, embodied movements, precognitive triggers, practical skills, affective intensities, enduring urges, unexceptional interactions and sensuous dispositions' (2005:84). Everyday life is as such a significant matter of inquiry in social science research.

The dwelling perspective

Tourism scholars have been inspired, directly or indirectly, by the tenet of the dwelling perspective which links the physical elements of a cultural landscape to the practices of its inhabitants (see Palmer 2018). Narratives of inhabiting a world through mundane embodied movements while on holiday and the importance placed on banal tourist objects can arguably be traced down to the work of Tim Ingold (2011) in anthropology. Nigel Thrift (1996, 2001, 2004, 2008), the author of non-representational theory, was inspired by the work of Ingold on dwelling. So were other scholars interested in the relational production of everyday life such as Sarah Whatmore (1999, 2002). Ingold (2011) proposes the application of the dwelling perspective in the scientific conceptualisation of the cultural landscape to give substantial meaning to the practices of those who inhabit it. Traditionally, landscape implies a place has visual features that can be gazed at by an observer (Wylie 2007). This position has led many scholars to develop theories revolving around the symbolic meaning of landscape and the power dynamics behind these representations (see, for instance, Cosgrove 1984, Mitchell 1994, Duncan and Duncan 2001). Ingold (2011) disagrees that these sights should be defined through the analysis of attributes cognitively processed by a detached observer. Instead, he offers a perspective that makes the embodied practices of those involved in a place the key elements behind the formation of its landscape.

Central to the dwelling perspective is Maurice Merleau-Ponty's (1962) notion of a body that inhabits space and time. This is a body that does more than merely finds itself out there (Ingold 2011). This position is in opposition to the mind and body dichotomy, where Merleau-Ponty (1962) argues that the body is not to be seen as a simple object, but rather as the condition and context which enables one to have a relation with the substances of the world. In his work, Ingold (2011) was also influenced by Martin Heidegger's (1971) phenomenology. In this sense, humans are perceived to inhabit their world through their ongoing practices. It is by inhabiting a place that humans give significance to place. As Simonsen (2012) explains while speaking of dwelling, humans turn this world of theirs into a realm of daily involvement, where they both find their way and feel at home. Illustrating this position, Crouch (2003) speaks of gardens not as flowers and vegetables aligned on the ground, but as the materialisation of the art of sowing seeds, clipping twigs and weeding, which involves the gardener's body in the fabrics of the landscape. Ingold (2011) considers this process of incorporation to be embodiment, which differs from processes of inscription whereby a cultural template is used to give meaning to a landscape. People know their way through a landscape by engaging with its elements, not by processing texts and images.

Ingold (2011) proposes that landscape arises from the activities of those who dwell within it. The processes that give rise to human activity weave themselves in the environment, such that 'the landscape is constituted as an enduring record of – and testimony to – the lives and works of past generations who have dwelt within it, and in so doing, have left there something of themselves' (2011:189). Embodied practices contain transformative elements that fashion places in enduring ways. For instance, Cloke and Jones (2001) demonstrate that the fruit orchard is the result of pruning practices, simultaneously influencing and influenced by the character of the trees. Dwelling ultimately implies people extract resources over time through various mundane practices, build and refashion structures, form institutions and create bonds of a different nature and strength, with their material place and its other inhabitants, human and nonhuman alike. Importantly, Ingold (2011) sees a temporality to landscape as it is formed through chains of interrelated and embodied actions unfolding into space through time. Landscape is always in the making, and as such critics of the dwelling perspective argue that the latter should not be conceived as rooted in essences and pre-modern times. Rather, landscape should be seen as dynamic and hybrid because it is physically impacted by the various ways humans make sense of their mobilities, technologies and global modes of production (Cloke and Jones 2001, Wylie 2003). Cloke and Jones (2001) mention the technologies, new tree species and marketing strategies meshed in the history of the orchard, presenting it as a modern and hybrid realm of dwelling.

Franklin (2004), Obrador-Pons (2003) and Larsen (2008) encourage applying such non-representational frameworks to tourism analysis to give it more materiality and performativity. Speaking of dwelling, Obrador-Pons (2003) argues for making the corporeal involvement of tourists in their place of holiday, such as the beach, matter in the social conceptualisation of tourism. In such a case, it is the movements of the tourist that catches the researcher's attention. In this chapter, I want to envision dwelling in terms that place the host's embodied practices during tourism at the centre of the formation of an enlivened cultural landscape of everyday life. The movements of the host within the performance turn have mostly been studied in terms of internalising the tourist gaze or working on the tourist stage, making encounters with guests rather fleeting to the former's existence, and insignificant for matters beyond tourism. Materiality, everyday life and practice, as I have described here, are not usually associated with the host's bodily experience and role in producing tourist landscapes. As I described in earlier work, hosts partake in tourism in the light of multiple personal, economic, professional and social aspirations, which interlink them to diverse local and extra-local processes (Prince 2017). Tourism is a part of the complexity of inhabiting the world. The theoretical arguments brought about by the application of the performance turn and non-representational approaches in tourism scholarship are critical to understanding the mundane, material, social and performative character of tourism. It is upon these frames of thinking that I locate my own point of scientific departure to speak of tourism, where encounters with guests are more than fleeting moments of theatrical performance to the existence of the host. To make the everyday practices of the host meaningful to a conceptualisation of tourism as in itself a mundane practice, I use the dwelling perspective as it was intended: to explain the formation of the cultural landscape.

Clay, glass and tourism on Bornholm

The case I present is about the craft-artists of Bornholm and their everyday relation to tourism. Bornholm is a Danish island in the Baltic Sea, accessible primarily by plane from Copenhagen, Denmark and by ferry from Ystad, Sweden. With its 39, 632 permanent residents (Statistics Denmark 2018), Bornholm receives annually around seven hundred and fifty thousand tourists, mostly Danes and Germans, who come from the beginning of June to late September (Larsen and Rømer 2013). Tourism is generally hotel and camping-based, consisting mostly of regular visitors returning to a favourite spot on the island. Families and retirees represent the largest tourist segments. Larsen (2006) holds that Bornholm epitomises for many of its visitors a place for memorable family vacations in idyllic rural settings.

Over the past decades, many craft-artists have established art-studios on the island in response to the studio-art movement gaining traction in the world. Pottery was a part of Bornholm's economy since the middle-ages, until clay factories vanished from the island's trade scene in the nineteen sixties. As potters and ceramists left the local fabrics as early as the nineteen thirties, redefining their aspirations to work with clay as artists, they contributed to the tradition of studio-art on the island. More recently, glass – and other craft-art also became elements of local studio-art. The presence of glass artists on Bornholm stems from an attempt by a Danish businessman to contribute to the island's economic development in the nineteen seventies. The traditions of glass and ceramic both culminated in 1997 in the foundation of the School for Ceramics and Glass in Nexø, which was affiliated in 2010 to the Danish School of Design in Copenhagen and became the School of Design Bornholm.

Most of the craft-artists take advantage of the tourist season by advertising their creative spaces on tourism websites and opening up to tourists during the summer time. Craft-art has become a brand for Bornholm with the practice being widely advertised in the island's touristic promotional material as a significant aspect of the local culture. Bornholm underwent economic restructuring when its fishing industry started collapsing in the seventies and completely halted in the nineties (Ioannides and Peterson 2003). The case of Bornholm reflects wider discourses of tourism development in European regions. With the decline of traditional agrarian activities, tourism is often expected by local and national authorities to fill an economic void in peripheral regions (Saarinen 2007, Lane 2009). Bornholm now relies heavily on tourism during its summer months to bring foreign currency to its businesses. The shift to tourism came with the development of many micro-businesses involved generally with specialised foods, hospitality and handcrafts, which now define the island's cultural landscape (Manniche and Larsen 2013) (Figure 12.1).

In the early 2000s, the development of the arts and craft cluster garnered attention from local politicians seeking to brand Bornholm's municipalities

Figure 12.1 A view of Gudhjem, a popular tourist destination on Bornholm where many craft-artists sell their creations in local boutiques.
(Photo by Prince, 2013).

to encourage tourism growth. This strategy included branding the Hasle municipality as a centre for craft-art. The interest from local politicians encouraged the grassroots formation in 2002 of the Arts and Crafts Association Bornholm (ACAB). The ACAB was founded to provide a competitive advantage to the local craft-artists on the international craft-art scene and during the island's tourist season. Membership in the ACAB is based on a selection process meant to up keep high-quality standards within the group. It is exclusively reserved to craft-artists established permanently on Bornholm. The ACAB proved to be a good forum to secure funds from the European Union promote a competitive brand for Bornholm and strengthen the administrative competences of its members. The ACAB began with twenty-eight members and expanded to its current sixty-four members. It is a cornerstone for professional artists who establish themselves on Bornholm to apply for membership in the ACAB, attesting to the development of the association into a local symbol for quality and professionalism.

Craft-art practices and tourist encounters

I have encountered the craft-artists of Bornholm through two sets of qualitative fieldwork on the island, undertaking nineteen in-depth interviews with the artists. Of particular interest here are narratives from the interviews with the one potter, ten ceramists and five glass designers. As I sought to understand these actors' relationship to the island's intensive tourist season, it became apparent that their mundane embodied practices are meaningful to a conceptualisation of tourist places. In this case, an attention to their movements reveals that the properties of the material these craft-artists work with interweave themselves in the landscape that tourists encounter. Simultaneously, the presence of tourists influences the relationship the craft-artists have with their chosen craft. This influence is evident when the practices of the ceramists and the potter are compared to those of the glass-artists.

Clay is sticky and wet as the ceramist or potter manipulates it. It is a material that is fashioned into art by hand, and these hands inevitably become dirty during the process. Ceramists enjoy the corporeal feeling of working with this substance, often describing having their hands submerged in clay as a significant factor behind their choice of craft. Tourists are welcomed to Bornholm as customers of arts and crafts, and clay has its own way of defining the type of relationship the potters and ceramists will have with the tourists. As Michael (2000) argues in relation to walking boots materials have their own agentic properties and affordances that may 'disturb' the wearer as, for example, when boots cause blisters to the foot. In this case, because of the stickiness of clay, ceramists usually find it easier to separate the production process from customer interactions because their dirty hands make sales transactions awkward to negotiate. They thus chiefly prefer to sell outside of their homes in local boutiques. Even ceramists who display their production process to tourists in their workshops, believing it will add to their sales, realise that sticky clay on fingers gets in the way of finalising sales. One ceramist, who displays and sells his creations in the workshop next to his house, lets tourists watch him work. Often, though, when the tourists see that he is busy working, with his fingers full of clay, they prefer to come back later to buy. This demonstrates that it is through their involvement with clay that these ceramists experience the tourist season. But also, that it is through their involvement with the tourist season that these individuals experience the materiality of their craft. Ingold's (2011) proposition that a landscape takes shape through various embodied practices is apparent here.

It is not only dirty hands that mediate encounters with tourists but also that clay as a substance requires immediate attention so that it does not dry too soon. Ceramists corporeally engage with a material that needs attention to become a piece of art. One ceramist, who sells her creation in local boutiques, even describes clay as a little child:

> You have to be around it all the time. Feel it; is it now or is it not? It takes a long time. If I sat down there and threw clay [to entertain tourists], for example, I couldn't work to sell anything. I can't go out and dry my hands all the time.

Making a ceramic piece is a long process. When the piece of clay is finally moulded into the desired shape, it needs to dry. It then goes into a kiln for a certain duration to get its glossy coat. Then it needs to cool. This re-quires patience and attention. It is a long process that is not conducive to entertaining an audience. As the quote attests, attending to tourists draws the craft-artist's focus away from his or her creation. Similarly, the potter believes that the only thing that interests curious tourists is to see the clay spun on the wheel. This eventually convinced him that he did not want his workshop to be open to tourists. Regardless of the material property of their craft, the tourist season is beneficial to every craft-artist on Bornholm. The tourists who come to the island represent a good pool of customers in search for place-based products for these craft-artists who seek to sell their creations (Prince 2017). There is, nonetheless, more than economic and pro-fessional strategies at the root of their engagement with tourists. It is not just cultural norms over what a tourist experience implies that guide the movements of people who dwell in toured landscapes; material substances guide actions too (Bell and Lyall 2002, Obrador-Pons 2003, Franklin 2004, Haldrup and Larsen 2006).

The ceramists embody the slow processes associated with their craft's materiality by building creative spaces adapted to their preferred type of engagement with tourists. One ceramist who defined herself as particularly reserved explains her decision to locate her workshop outside the town as being due to not wanting to be flooded with tourists dropping by in her cre-ative space out of curiosity that would be too stressful for her, she clarifies. This embodiment leads to a resistance to the socio-cultural expectations of the tourist gaze, where agency flows to the host (Maoz 2006). However, unlike the reserved ceramists, glass-artists are more extroverted in their practice, embracing the gaze of tourists upon their performative work much more easily. Glass goes through a molten state as it is fashioned into art. This process is visually pleasing for the observer as it creates a spectacle involving heat and colours, all twirling around a pole handled skilfully by a glass-artist. The glass-artists using this technique were quick to say they did not mind having people watch them while they, or their employees, create. To one glass-designer, working in front of people was something she had always done throughout her career. This shows that the tourist landscape these craft-artists form is, as Larsen (2008) explains, not an exotic sight, but a landscape formed by the mundane work practices of those who dwell therein, though arranged to accommodate the presence of tourists. In this way, the craft-art scene on Bornholm can be described, as Cloke and Jones (2001) and Crouch (2003) hold, as a pattern of corporeal movements that reveal different kinds of creative practices done in relation to other beings and material entities.

Entertaining tourists is exactly what one couple of glass-artists is doing on Bornholm, where they have elevated their glass-artistry as a full-on show for an audience. Besides their scheduled daily appearances during the tourist season to showcase their skills, these two glass-artists also present weekly theatrical performances after their business hours where spectators can see them make pieces of glass to the sound of music and the effects of lighting. This is an incredible sign of material embodiment akin to the theatrical tourist stage, Edensor (2000, 2001) describes. It is a different corporeal engagement to that of the ceramists but it also highlights how individuals constantly interact with their social and material surroundings, giving them meaning in their everyday life (Ingold 2011). These theatrical representations symbolise for these glass-artists a fundamental part of their particular experience of evolving as professional artists and business entrepreneurs on an island branded as a hub for craft-art. With tourism a reality of everyday life on Bornholm, these craft-artists subsequently incorporate its dynamics in their daily movements in various ways that become mundane practice to them.

Conclusion

Bornholm's tourist brand of professional and handmade craft-art has developed over time through various human practices. This evolution is closely linked to the everyday involvement of craft-artists with their materials as they build their creative spaces, economic enterprises and professional careers. The craft-art scene on Bornholm is a very hybrid realm connected to extra-local processes such as the rise and fall of the clay industry, the propagation of the studio-art movement and urban migration to the countryside. Moreover, the materials these craft-artists work with are imported, designs are reproduced to increase sales and few craft-artists are originally from Bornholm. Nonetheless, the various corporeal movements described through this case study are all part of the mutually attentive ways in which people engage with each other within a landscape in space and time (Ingold 2011). The presence of tourists on the island is in itself the result of extra-local relations, but tourists inevitably become integral elements behind the everyday interactions of the craft-artists with their materials. This makes dwelling something that is dynamic, as Cloke and Jones (2001) implied. Tourism becomes a part of the mundane of being a craft-artist on Bornholm. It is apparent that the objects, technologies, spaces and skills making up the tourist landscape are tied to the cultural, material and social lives of the individuals who have built living spaces there over time. In this way, the cultural landscape, when presented as a host's realm of embodied practices, cannot be detached from the landscape that tourists encounter.

The story of the craft-artists of Bornholm is meant to outline that the embodied practices of the host are meaningful to a conceptualisation of tourist places as socially performed realms of everyday life. The craft-artists' encounters with tourists are more than fleeting performances occurring on a space akin to a theatrical stage; these encounters influence the formers' existence by mediating their interactions with their chosen craft. In turn, their interactions with tourists are largely defined by the way they dwell on their island as craft-artists, incorporating their embodied relations with their creative material in their experience of the tourist season.

Following the claims of Crouch (2000), Bell and Lyall (2002) and Haldrup and Larsen (2006) on tourism and materiality, I contend in this case that the material properties and techniques used to turn clay and glass into artistic creations are crucial for explaining the type of interactions the different craft-artists cultivate with tourists. Considering the diverse elements at the foundation of everyday life avoids reducing human involvement to behavioural models, scientific theories and intellectual critique, which ultimately risks severing science from the world of the living by disembedding its subjects from their realities (Dewsbury 2000, Nash 2000, Thrift 2008, Ingold 2011). The same can be said within tourism anthropology. With the dwelling perspective, the emphasis is put on the observations and sensations of practical activities, revealing how individuals shape their cultural environments by resisting, coping with and taking advantage of tourism through their mundane practices. Such intricacies have been revealed in case studies interested in investigating tourism as a performative phenomenon (for instance, Edensor 1998, Maoz 2006, Tucker 2007). There is nevertheless room to develop the study of everyday life and its materiality, through non-representational approaches like the dwelling perspective and anthropological methodologies such as in-depth interviews and ethnographic fieldwork, from the perspective of the host.

References

Baerenholdt, J., Framke, W., Larsen, J. and Urry, J. (2004) *Performing Tourist Places*. London: Ashgate.

Bell, C. and Lyall, J. (2002) The accelerated sublime: Thrill-seeking adventure heroes in the commodified landscape, in S. Coleman and M. Crang (eds.) *Tourism: Between place and performance*. Oxford: Berghahn, pp. 21–37.

Cloke, P. and Jones, O. (2001) Dwelling, place, and landscape: An orchard in somerset. *Environment and Planning A*, 33(4): 649–666.

Cloke, P. and Perkins, H. C. (2005) Cetacean performance and tourism in Kaikoura, New Zealand. *Environment and Planning D: Society and Space*, 23(6): 903–924.

Coleman, S. and Crang, M. (2002) *Tourism: Between Place and Performance*. Oxford: Berghahn.

Cosgrove, D. (1984) *Social Formation and Symbolic Landscape*. London: Croom Helm.

Crouch, D. (2000) Places around us: Embodied lay geographies in leisure and tourism. *Leisure Studies*, 19(2): 63–76.

Crouch, D. (2002) Surrounded by place: Embodied encounters, in M. Crang and S. Coleman (eds.) *Tourism. Between Place and Performance*. Oxford: Berghahn, pp. 207–218.

Crouch, D. (2003) Spacing, performing and becoming: Tangles in the mundane. *Environment and Planning A*, 35(1): 945–1960.

Dewsbury, J. D. (2000) Performativity and the event: Enacting a philosophy of difference. *Environment and Planning D: Society and Space*, 18(4): 473–496.

Dewsbury, J. D., Harrison, P., Rose, M. and Wylie, J. (2002) Enacting geographies. *Geoforum*, 33(4): 437–440.

Duncan, J. S. and Duncan, N. G. (2001) The aestheticization of the politics of landscape preservation. *Annals of the Association of American Geographers*, 91(2): 387–409.

Edensor, T. (1998) *Tourists at the Taj: Performance and Meaning at a Symbolic Site.* London: Routledge.

Edensor, T. (2000) Staging tourism: Tourists as performers. *Annals of Tourism Research*, 27(2): 322–344.

Edensor, T. (2001) Performing tourism: Staging tourism: (Re)producing tourist space and practice. *Tourist Studies*, 1(1): 59–81.

Edensor, T. (2006) Sensing tourist places, in C. Minca and T. Oaks (eds.) *Travels in Paradox: Remapping Tourism.* Lanham: Rowman and Littlefield, pp. 23–46.

Franklin, A. (2004) Tourism as an ordering: Towards a new ontology of tourism. *Tourist Studies*, 4(3): 277–301.

Gibson, C. (2010) Geographies of tourism: (Un)ethical encounters. *Progress in Human Geography*, 34(4): 521–527.

Grimwood, B. S. R. (2014) Advancing tourism's moral morphology: Relational metaphors for just and sustainable arctic tourism. *Tourist Studies*, 15(1): 3–26.

Haldrup, M. and Larsen, J. (2006) Material cultures of tourism. *Leisure Studies*, 25(3): 275–289.

Haldrup, M. and Larsen, J. (2010) *Tourism, Performance and the Everyday: Consuming the Orient.* London: Routledge.

Hannam, K., Sheller, M. and Urry, J. (2006) Editorial: Mobilities, immobilities, moorings. *Mobilities*, 1(1): 1–22.

Heidegger, M. (1971) *Poetry, Language, Thought*, A. Hofstadter (trans.) New York: Harper Colophon Books.

Ingold, T. (2011) *The Perception of the Environment: Essays on Livelihood, Dwelling and Skill*, 2nd ed. London: Routledge.

Ioannides, D. and Petersen, T. (2003) Tourism 'Non-Entrepreneurship' in peripheral destinations: A case study of small and medium tourism enterprises on Bornholm, Denmark. *Tourism Geographies*, 5(4): 408–435.

Ivanovic, M. (2008) *Cultural Tourism.* Cape Town: Juta and Company Ltd.

Johnston, L. (2001) (Other) Bodies and tourism studies. *Annals of Tourism Research*, 28: 180–201.

Lane, B. (2009) Rural tourism: An overview, in T. Jamal and M. Robinson (eds.) *The SAGE Handbook of Tourism Studies.* London: Sage Publications, pp. 354–370.

Larsen, J. (2006) Picturing Bornholm: Producing and consuming a tourist place through picturing practices. *Scandinavian Journal of Hospitality and Tourism*, 6(2): 75–94.

Larsen, J. (2005) Families seen sightseeing: performativity of tourist photography. Space and Culture, 8(4): 416–434.

Larsen, J. (2008) De-exoticizing tourist travel: Everyday life and sociality on the move. *Leisure Studies*, 27(1): 21–34.

Larsen, J. (2010) Goffman and the tourist gaze: A performative perspective on tourism mobilities, in M. H. Jacobsen (ed.) *The Contemporary Goffman.* New York: Routledge, pp. 313–332.

Larsen, J. (2012) Performance, space and tourism, in J. Wilson (ed.) *The Routledge Handbook of Tourism Geographies.* London: Routledge, pp. 67–73.

Larsen, J. and Urry, J. (2011) Gazing and performing. *Environment and Planning D: Society and Space*, 29(6): 1110–1125.

Larsen, K. T. and Rømer, L. (2013) *Creative Communities in Rural Areas: A Case from Bornholm.* Nexø: CRT.

Lorimer, H. (2005) Cultural geography: The busyness of being 'More-Than-Representational'. *Progress in Human Geography*, 29(1): 83–94.

MacCannell, D. (1976) *The Tourist: A New Theory of the Leisure Class.* Berkley: University of California Press.

Manniche, J. and K. Larsen (2013) Experience staging and symbolic knowledge: The case of Bornholm culinary products. *European Urban and Regional Studies*, 20(4): 401–416.

Maoz, D. (2006) The mutual gaze. *Annals of Tourism Research*, 33: 221–239.

McCormack, D. P. (2008) Geographies for moving bodies: Thinking, dancing, spaces. *Geography Compass*, 2(6): 1822–1836.

Merleau-Ponty, M. (1962) *The Phenomenology of Perception.* London: Routledge.

Michael, M. (2000) These boots are made for walking…: Mundane technology, the body and human-environment relations. *Body and Society*, 6(3–4): 107–126.

Mitchell, W. J. T. (Ed.) (1994) *Landscape and Power.* London: Routledge.

Nash, C. (2000) Performativity in practice: Some recent work in cultural geography. *Progress in Human Geography*, 24(4): 653–664.

Obrador-Pons, P. (2003) Being-on-holiday: Tourist dwelling, bodies and place. *Tourist Studies*, 3(1): 47–66.

Obrador-Pons, P. (2007) A haptic geography of the beach: Naked bodies, vision and touch. *Social and Cultural Geography*, 8: 123–141.

Obrador-Pons, P. (2009) Building castles in the sand: Repositioning touch on the beach. *The Senses and Society*, 4(2): 195–210.

Obrador-Pons, P. (2012) The place of the family in tourism research: Domesticity and thick sociality by the pool. *Annals of Tourism Research*, 39(1): 401–420.

Palmer, C. (2018) *Being and Dwelling Through Tourism: An Anthropological Perspective.* Abingdon, Oxon, Milton Park: Routledge.

Perkins, H. C. and Thorns, D. C. (2001) Gazing or performing? Reflections on Urry's tourist gaze in the context of contemporary experience in the antipodes. *International Sociology*, 16(2): 185–204.

Prince, S. (2017) Craft-art in the Danish countryside: Reconciling a lifestyle, livelihood and artistic career through rural tourism. *Journal of Tourism and Cultural Change*, 15(4): 339–358.

Prince, S. (2018) Dwelling in the tourist landscape: Embodiment and everyday life among the craft-artists of Bornholm. *Tourist Studies*, 18(1): 63–82.

Saarinen, J. (2007) Contradictions of rural tourism initiatives in rural development contexts: Finnish rural tourism strategy case study. *Current Issues in Tourism*, 10(1): 96–105.

Simonsen, K. (2012) In quest of a new humanism: Embodiment, experience and phenomenology as critical geography. *Progress in Human Geography*, 37(1): 10–26.

Statistics Denmark (2018) Folketal. Available at: www.dst.dk/en/Statistik/emner/befolkning-og-valg/befolkning-og-befolkningsfremskrivning/folketal [accessed 23 March 2018].

Stebbins, R. A. (2002) *Organizational Basis of Leisure Participation: A Motivational Exploration.* State College, PA: Venture Publishing.

Stebbins, R. A. (2007). *Serious Leisure: A Perspective of Our Time.* Piscataway, NJ: Transaction Publishers.

Stephen, C. (1990) The search for authenticity: Review essay of Dean MacCannell, the tourist. *Berkeley Journal of Sociology: A Critical Review*, 35: 151–156.

Thrift, N. (1996) *Spatial Formations*. London: Sage Publications.

Thrift, N. (2001) Afterwords. *Environment and Planning D: Society and Space*, 18: 213–255.

Thrift, N. (2004) Intensities of feeling: Towards a spatial politics of affect. *Geografiska Annaler*, 86(1): 57–78.

Thrift, N. (2008) *Non-Representational Theory: Space, Politics, Affect*. London: Routledge.

Thrift, N. and Dewsbury, J.-D. (2000) Dead geographies – and how to make them live. *Environment and Planning D: Society and Space*, 18: 411–432.

Tucker, H. (2007) Performing a young people's package tour of New Zealand: Negotiating appropriate performances of place. *Tourism Geographies*, 9(2): 139–159.

Urry, J. (1990) *The Tourist Gaze: Leisure and Travel in Contemporary Societies, Theory, Culture and Society*. London: Sage.

Waitt, G. and Cook, L. (2007) Leaving nothing but ripples on the water: Performing ecotourism natures. *Social and Cultural Geography*, 8(4): 535–550.

Wang, N. (1999) Rethinking authenticity in tourism experience. *Annals of Tourism Research*, 26(2): 349–370.

Weaver, A. (2005) Interactive service work and performative metaphors: The case of the cruise industry. *Tourist Studies*, 5(1): 5–27.

Whatmore, S. (1999) Hybrid geographies: Rethinking the 'human' in human geography, in D. Massey, J. Allen and P. Sarre (eds.) *Human Geography Today*. Cambridge: Polity Press, pp. 22–39.

Whatmore, S. (2002) *Hybrid Geographies: Natures, Cultures, Spaces*. London: Sage.

Wylie, J. (2003) Landscape, performance and dwelling: A Glastonbury case study, in P. Cloke (ed.) *Country Visions*. Harlow: Pearson Education Ltd, pp. 136–157.

Wylie, J. (2007) *Landscape*. New York: Routledge.

13 Material-bodily assemblages on a multi-day wilderness walk

Kaya Barry

Introduction

Walking in wilderness areas often conjures ideas of human conquest against wild terrain or the willingness to immerse oneself in pristine 'natural' environments. Tourists often approach these walking expeditions in national parks or conservation areas with the expectation that they will be immersed and connected to nature, with their body soaking up such experiences (Edensor 2000, Olafsdottir 2013). However, the marketing and imagery of outdoor activities such as overnight or multi-day walking (also known as hiking, trekking or tramping) is built around the way that the human body needs support from high-tech performance materials and equipment. Tourists undertaking walking, trekking, expeditions and other durational outdoors activities spend a significant amount of time and attention to planning what equipment and materials they will bring with them (Edensor 2000, Gyimóthy and Mykletun 2004), such as backpacks, boots, clothing, light-weight food and assorted walking 'essentials'.

Advice and guidelines for what equipment and clothing to bring listed on national park websites or in walking guidebooks describe distinct material types, compositions and properties that are required (Bain et al. 2006, Wearing and Whenman 2009). Items such as merino wool clothing layers, Gore-Tex-coated rain jackets and boots, ultra-light-weight titanium cookware or carbon fibre walking sticks are frequently listed as desirable or essential hiking materials. The Lonely Planet guide to *Walking in Australia* cautions that 'you need to think carefully about what you pack to ensure you are comfortable and prepared for an emergency' (Bain et al. 2006:389). While there are obvious practical applications for these materials, the point is that very particular material properties, compositions and capacities directly influence and mediate the walking experience. The materiality of the equipment that cocoons, supports, enables and mediates is integral to the experiences of tourists' bodies as they move through wilderness areas.

In this chapter, I explore how material objects reconfigure the tourist body within wilderness spaces, reshaping and co-producing tourist experiences. Drawing on ethnographic observations and interviews with tourists who were walking the Three Capes Track in Tasman National Park, Australia, I explore how tourist bodies are assembled into material-bodily configurations that give rise to new attentions and relationships between the moving body, the materials it carries and the environmental surrounds. The Three Capes Track is a four-day wilderness walk on the southern island state of Australia. Tasmania is well known for its extensive National Park areas and World Heritage Wilderness areas, and thrives on tourism to these places. Developed by Tasmania Parks and Wildlife Services over the past decade, the walk has received international attention since opening in late 2015. The methodology used is at the intersection of anthropological, ethnographic and actor-network inspired approaches. The fusion of disciplinary influences manifests in a practice-led approach that acknowledges that I was an active participant on the walk, undertaking the four-day trip, staying in communal huts and sharing living space. The interviews were carried out in April 2017 as part of a multi-sited project on walking and tourist experiences in Tasmanian parks (2017–2018). I draw from these entangled experiences as a tourist on this walk and part of the group of forty-eight people walking at the same pace, as well as an observer of the actions that unfolded. The value of this approach is in the attention to the myriad of actors that are assembled (Ingold 2011, Van der Duim et al. 2012, Beard et al. 2016), which includes myself, fellow tourists and the nonhuman materials brought with us that co-construct and co-produce the research and the tourism experience.

In three sections, this chapter will explore how materials and bodies assemble tourism experiences of wilderness walking. First, I examine how tourist bodies have been conceptualised in tourism and walking literature, with an increasing attention to the body in relation to the material objects and agencies. Next, I draw from interviews and observations with tourists walking the Three Capes Track on their preparations for the walk, and the way that the bags and the load they carried influenced their experience. The third section explores how the hiking bag mediates movements between the tourist body, the materials and equipment carried and the environmental surrounds, fusing material and bodily sensations together in an assemblage. I argue that these material-bodily assemblages reconfigure tourism expectations and experiences, fostering an awareness of the entanglement of human action within the nonhuman realm.

Material assemblages of walking experiences

Significant attention is paid to the objects that tourists carry with them for longer walking trips. In the planning stages and during the walk, the emphasis on what equipment is required and used efficiently tends to dominate conversations within huts and campgrounds as people socialise. Types of equipment is often the conversation icebreaker between tourists, as comparisons are made between different brands, sizes, and versions of boots, backpacks, walking sticks, and cookware that each person has brought. The overall emphasis and attention to materials on durational walks is significant. In the tourism literature, there has been an increase in attention to the role that material actors (human and nonhuman) play in enabling and supporting tourism. Objects such as bags, hiking boots, buckets and spades, rocks, cameras and postcards, to name a few, have been examined by scholars as playing an important role in the formation of tourist experiences (Lury 1997, Michael 2000, Walsh and Tucker 2009, Scarles 2010, Palsson 2013, Franklin 2014, Barry 2017). Because tourism experiences 'emerge as a fusion of fluid and dynamic mobilities and materialities, embodied and affective encounters' (Scarles 2010:905), attention to the intersections and assemblages of bodies and materials is critical in understanding tourism as a co-produced range of sensations and movements within and surrounding the body.

The idea of spending a few days 'off the grid', without regular internet access, sleeping in huts or tents, and walking in whatever weather conditions arise each day, are key motivations for these tourists doing wilderness walks. These tourist ideals contribute and inform the experiences of walking through remote landscapes with the absence of obvious traces of anthropogenic intervention. While there has been extensive writing on the way that tourists perceive their impact on earth systems and natural environments (Hillery et al. 2001, Gren and Huijbens 2016, Pietilä and Fagerholm 2016), these are often focused on the large tourist numbers causing impact, rather than an individual's reflection on their actions and consumption patterns. The materials that are consumed and discarded in wilderness areas is also a point of contention among tourists, where food scraps, evidence of toilet waste or littering has a negative impact on tourists' experiences (Dorwart et al. 2009, Pietilä and Fagerholm 2016, Edensor 2017). Actions of discarding anthropogenic materials and other 'unacceptable' tourist behaviours highlight the level of attention tourists give to materials that are 'out of place' (see Edensor 2017). Isolated landscapes that are void of any anthropogenic traces dominate much of the imaginaries of wilderness areas and what kinds of experiences tourists will have (Franklin 2006). This 'paradox' of desire for isolated experiences (Franklin 2006), yet a need for provisions of tourism infrastructures and materials raises important debates on how tourists negotiate fellow humans, materials and environmental conditions that co-constitute tourism sites and activities.

At the same time, increased attention to the relational and affective experiences between tourists and landscapes (Wylie 2005, Merriman et al. 2008, Benediktsson and Lund 2010, Ingold 2011, 2012, Lund 2013, Edensor 2017) explores how tourist bodies are positioned with-and-in particular environmental destinations. In particular, walking long distance or in remote wilderness areas is saturated with the ideas of a 'continuously solitary one-on-one communication with the natural world [that] gears the walking-body' into a heightened sensory immersion (Olafsdottir 2013:211).

However, as Mike Michael describes, the 'key intermediary in this process of alignment is technology' (2000:107). The walking tourist body and the equipment that clothes and supports it includes '[d]ifferent forms of cultural capital' that are 'transmitted via these products' (Edensor 2000:98). Having equipment that smoothens the passage through the environment, that 'mediate the sublime relationship' (Michael 2000:210), is critical in maintaining attention to the scenic landscapes around, rather than to the pain of a blister or the rubbing of a strap against the shoulders. In literature on backpacking tourists, the bag itself plays a crucial role in the identity and cultural category of these tourists, in addition to a practical tool to help navigate the journey (Richards and Wilson 2004, Hannam and Ateljevic 2007, Walsh and Tucker 2009, Barry 2017). Of course, the tourists who are undertaking multi-day wilderness walks are not necessarily 'backpackers' (although they do carry large backpacks), but the point is that a material object or piece of equipment plays a crucial role in how tourists' bodies are receptive to, and productive of, different kinds of socio-cultural symbols and identities through the materials that they carry with them.

The conceptualisation of tourist bodies in activities that involve certain types of physical competency (for example in adventure tourism, or nature-based tourist destinations) tends to focus on the abilities of the tourist bodies and the social experiences that are co-produced. Walking practices over long distances or in wilderness areas often 'foreground the male body' (Edensor 2000:94) and 'frequently advocate a set of bodily techniques, forms of physical training and valued equipment' that dominates how walking 'can be accomplished' (Edensor 2000:96; see also Urry and Larsen 2011:197, Olafsdottir 2013). Due to this, wilderness walking fit into a broad 'ideology of movement' (Urry 2016:18) where certain kinds of bodies are seen to 'fit' into wilderness areas more so than other bodies. As Gunthora Olafsdottir importantly points out, 'the body is the primary technological "tool" to get the job done' when walking (2013:221). While understanding the capacities of tourist bodies is important, these discussions often fit into an anthropocentric frame that positions the tourist body as central to the action, where the surrounding landscapes, materials and wildlife (the nonhuman actors) are relegated to passive entities waiting for the tourist to discover and conquer. What I am suggesting is that there is room for further inspection into the complexity of materials and other nonhuman actors that are present and contribute to such visceral experiences.

Attention to the materials that enable tourist experiences in wilderness areas necessitates a broader understanding of how human and nonhuman action are entangled. To do so, I draw on the notion of 'assemblage' to examine how material-bodily assemblages take shape in wilderness walking. An 'assemblage' might be understood as the coming together of diverse actors (human or nonhuman) into a momentary collection or gathering. In Manuel DeLanda's compelling proposition of 'Assemblage Theory', he describes an assemblage as an 'ensemble in which components have been correctly matched together [that] possesses properties that its components do not have. It also has its own tendencies and capacities' (2016:5). Following similar Deleuzian readings, Ben Anderson and Colin McFarlane suggest that an assemblage 'emphasises gathering, coherence and dispersion' (2011:124), in addition to actions that distribute agencies across relational compositions. Critical thinking about assemblages is 'part of a broader "relational turn"' (Anderson et al. 2012:171) that draws together human and nonhuman actors into 'constellations' (Deleuze and Guattari 2004) where designations of subject and object merge into an accumulation of action. Actor-network analysis echoes the attention to how human and nonhuman actors assemble into configurations of action and agency (Latour 2007, Van der Duim et al. 2012) where the situation and site of the research plays an influential role in 'tracking relations through time and space' (Beard et al. 2016:99). In this way, wilderness walking can be thought of as an assemblage, where the momentary composition of diverse elements draws attention to the way that tourists' bodies work with (and at times against) the materials carried with them.

Assembling a hiking bag

In my observations and conversations that I had while walking for four days on the Three Capes Track, most of the discussions and talking points between tourists were not about the 'nature' and landscapes that we were walking through, but instead were focused on human-centred issues: the equipment we had brought, types of food we were eating, previous travel experiences, how heavy the bag was to carry and so on. The materials that tourists bring with them are generative of a particular kind of touristic experience. Neil Walsh and Hazel Tucker suggest that for backpacking tourists the 'bodies and the objects they interact with momentarily fuse' (2009:234), producing new configurations and embodiments that influence what kinds of tourist experiences are possible. This fusion of the tourist body with material objects opens up a space for encounter and experience that, if only momentarily, configures an assemblage of materials, technologies and bodily actions. At this point, the agency of how action will unfold is not separated from the tourist body or the material objects (Barry 2017).

A brief description of the Three Capes Track helps to set the scene for the types and amount of materials and equipment that tourist bring with them. The Three Capes Track is a highly managed experience of wilderness walking, taking four days to complete the forty-six-kilometre walk on an 'easy to moderate' graded track (Tasmania Parks and Wildlife Service 2017). Although tourists are required to self-cater and carry their own gear in a hiking bag, there are ample facilities provided en route. Each night is spent in huts with bunk beds and mattresses, there are composting toilets and wash basins, kitchen area complete with gas stoves, cooking equipment, interior lighting, fireplace, tank water and a small solar system that includes USB wall sockets for charging small electronic devices (see Figures 13.1 and 13.2).

Figure 13.1 Scenic coastal views along the Three Capes Track (source K. Barry).

Figure 13.2 View of 'Surveyors Hut' on the first night of the walk (source K. Barry).

Due to the extensive facilities provided, tourists walking the track have significantly lighter bags to carry than on most other multi-day walks in Australia. While there are also commercial versions of many multi-day walks available in Australia (where porters or tour guides carry the equipment and food, and 'luxury' cabins are provided), the Three Capes Track is marketed as a walk that 'cater[s] for a broad range of ages and abilities. For many, this will mark their first multi-day walk' (Tasmania Parks and Wildlife Service 2017). After paying the Three Capes Track registration fee, tourists are provided with a 'packing list' that details essentials required for the walk. Examples of items listed are 'walking trousers (quick-dry fabric)', 'warm jacket (e.g. down, fleece or woollen/merino)' and 'sleeping bag (rated to 0 degrees Celsius)' (Tasmania National Parks and Wildlife Service 2017). To be clear, my intention is not to challenge the marketing of walking equipment, or to analyse the planning and strategies of the way national parks suggest the materials that are essential for visitors (I do not want to undermine the safety and practicality of having such materials). However, the way that materials are considered, planned and packed for a multi-day walk signals an immense attention to the materiality of walking that can make or break the overall tourism experience.

While walking the Three Capes Track in April 2017, I interviewed nineteen tourists, asking questions about how they had prepared and packed (see Figure 13.3). The way that people arranged and packed equipment into their bags was a key talking point (both during the interviews and in informal conversations), and how people travelling together (couples, families or groups of friends) shared communal items such as food, first aid kits and other supplies. Many of the tourists I spoke with were new to overnight or multi-day walking, and several explained to me how nervous they were about the weight of their bags and the amount of materials they had to carry. One person described to me that this was her first multi-day walk, confessing that, 'carrying the backpack is hard!' Another tourist recounted her previous experience carrying a twenty-kilogramme bag on a week-long walk. It was the first multi-day walk she had done where she had to carry everything herself. 'It was a killer', she said, explaining that as a result, for the Three Capes Track 'we were really conscious of the weight'. The concerns about

Figure 13.3 Hiking bags on the side of the track (source K. Barry).

carrying heavy bags were echoed in most of the interviews I did. Most people cited fear of walking with a heavy bag due to back problems, lack of fitness or the general concern of bringing too many 'things' that were not necessary. 'I brought too much food ... why did I think I could eat all this?', one person explained to me, laughing.

The 'right' order of packing things into a hiking bag was a common discussion that I overheard in the huts and had people describe in interviews. A 'strategy' or approach to arranging objects within a bag is critical to fit everything in (Barry 2017), and particularly for walking with a large backpack, the placement of objects according to weight is integral to securing the bag close to the torso and upper body. A younger female tourist showed me her bag, which was bought previously for a backpacking trip around Europe. Despite it being a 65-litre bag (which was significantly larger than most other people's on the walk), she told me that she was having trouble packing and arranging items inside it. She described,

> on the first day I had the sleeping bag on the outside, and on the second day I had it on the inside and my jacket tied on the outside. And today I managed to fit everything inside, I just packed it tightly.

One of the friends she was walking with explained further: 'we were speaking to someone on the second day and we learned that we should pack all our heavy stuff at the bottom'. Both said that it made a difference to how the bag 'sat as we walked. Especially because we weren't used to walking with the pack. Just having a bit more balance and stability'. The distribution of objects was 'top-heavy', so as they walked the shoulder straps were pressing down onto their shoulders and upper-back, making the bag sway slightly with each footstep. 'I don't know that I would have got through', she described after re-packing. 'I'd worn it around a bit, so I knew how it *should* sit ... I just obviously didn't know how to put stuff into it'.

The arrangement of objects within the bags obviously made a big impact on the ease of walking, and the pain that the walking body endured. After the first day, even the inexperienced walkers became aware of the position of each item within the bag and in relation to how it would sit when strapped and affixed to their bodies. In line with Tim Edensor's description, these are 'hybrid forms combining bodies and things' that form into 'human-object networks' of the walking tourist (2000:99). The attention to the relationship between the objects, the body and the bag reveals the complexity of assembling and preparing materials before and during walking activity.

Flexive assemblages of tourist bodies and materials

Most hiking bags have several adjustable straps and harnesses to fit the body carrying it: straps around the waste and hips to secure it close to the hip area, cords to pull the shoulder straps tighter or loser, and usually an

Figure 13.4 Photograph of the author's hiking bag. It has a sixty litres capacity, weighed sixteen kg on this walk and is designed specifically for women with wider hip straps (source K. Barry).

internal harness system that can shift the entire harness (including sternum, hip and shoulder straps) up and down in relation to the body (see Figure 13.4). When using a hiking bag for the first time, significant adjustment is needed to 'fit' the bag to your body's size, shape and the weight of the contents. Hiking bags are generally taller and slimmer than a day backpack, designed to fit snugly vertically along one's back and to use the hips to bear the weight. Most hiking bags are designed to be sex specific, labelled as either 'mens' and 'womens', reflecting the 'normal' proportion and sizes of the torso and hips. From my own experience, small adjustments are needed before each walk, as the weight of the bag, the volume of it and the position of it on your body change significantly in how it 'feels' when carrying it for long periods of time.

Before each group of tourists set out for the second day of walking, the Hut Ranger offered advice for how to position the bags on their bodies to make their task of carrying the weight a little easier. The Hut Ranger spent time discussing how their packs 'felt', inquiring about how the bag was moving *with* their bodies. She asked questions such as, 'How is it sitting on your shoulders? Is it cutting in?' Or, 'Does it swing much when you walk fast?' She grabbed and shook the bags while people were standing there wearing them so that their torso and legs would wobble considerably. Several people nearly toppled over as the weight of their bag was thrown into a swinging motion, and their body (which was obviously not closely tethered to the bag) would flounder and sway trying to re-stabilise.

The Hut Ranger described to me that there was a specific process for adjusting a hiking bag, which she had been taught when first starting the posting on the Three Capes Track:

> I start with getting them to put the bag on, and then make sure they've done up their hip strap and the collar bone strap to what they think is good and feels comfortable. And I look at it and try to firstly align the hip straps to their hips. ... Then I have a look where the straps on the bag are sitting against their back. And if I can see lots of holes, and a big gap between the top of the shoulders and the hip strap and the bag ... then something's really not right. I usually then try tightening the straps here [points to her shoulders] ... so it brings the bag closer.

She explained that the harness system of the hiking bag (a metal or plastic internal frame) provides support and distributes the weight of the bag's contents across the large surface adjacent to the back of the person carrying it. One tourist who had her bag adjusted that morning said to me that they had not realised how much their bag 'flopped around' separate to their body while walking.

Watching this process of adjusting a hiking bag in relation to tourist bodies reveals the extent that walking equipment is created to fit to a certain type of tourist body. While most bags can be adjusted extensively, they still maintain a universalised shape of the tourist body: one that is athletic, of a common height and weight, and has symmetrical limbs and torso (see Edensor 2000, Olafsdottir 2013). Importantly, this assemblage of the bag and the tourist body privileges able bodies that are capable of bearing significant weight on the back (ten to sixteen kilogrammes, in the case of this walk) and able to negotiate lifting this large weight up onto the back and lowering it down again. There is a lot of trust and expectation that tourists know how to operate and manoeuvre their bags (for instance, to adjust their straps and bags accordingly) and that their movements *with* the bag will fit seamlessly to their body's capabilities. The fear of carrying too much stuff, or hurting one's back, or not knowing the best way to pack it in the bag, resonated through the interviews. The materials of walking – the hiking bag and contents – have a considerable agency and the potential to determine the outcomes and experience of the walk.

In the literature on backpacking tourists, several authors have found that bags are considered as a symbol of a tourist's identity and sub-cultural category of the backpacker (Jack and Phipps 2005, Hyde and Olesen 2011). In a notable study, Neil Walsh and Hazel Tucker (2009) explored how the bodily performances of backpacker tourists were influenced by the hiking bag as an emblem of their identity and at times a restriction for how they moved. They suggest that 'these material objects construct a fine line ... between travel freedom and corporeal constraint' (2009:233). Following these insights from Walsh and Tucker, in my own experiences walking with a large and heavy bag, I know first-hand that walking does not always go to plan, and is never a seamless or easy experience. The body in motion propels unexpected and at times haphazard interactions with the materials it is carrying. For instance, the transition from walking on a flat surface to climbing up an incline or stairs causes one's steps to sway side to side, instigating shifts and re-positioning of the bag (see Figure 13.5). While the bag should cling to the body, the tourist needs to be able to re-act to these changes in weight and distribution by shifting their balance and pace to suit. In such moments, the tourist body and the materials of the bag assemble together, interacting and negotiating with each movement. These are movements where both the body and the materials need to shift, adjust and flex as they re-act to the co-produced movements.

The ability to be re-active and flexible to such unexpected movements requires an awareness of the potential movements that may occur. It is an understanding that comes from practice and experience as tourists negotiate their relationships with other tourists, objects and movements. This is to acknowledge that tourist practices are part of a 'collective' mode of action (Latour 2007, Van der Duim et al. 2012, Beard et al. 2016) where the individual tourist is entangled within an array of other actors (both human and nonhuman). While an assemblage is a momentary coming together of diverse elements, which 'can only ever be a provisional process' as relations shift (Anderson and McFarlane 2011:126, DeLanda 2016), what I am describing is the awareness one might have to such potentials for collective action to take hold of a situation. To describe this awareness, I use the word 'flexive', which encompasses both the act of assembling together and the

Figure 13.5 Walking up a set of stone stairs (source K. Barry).

inter-active capacity of tourist bodies and materials. Being flexive is to be able to bend and adapt, but not in a *re*-flexive way – it is to sense movement one step ahead, anticipating the movements and unexpected encounters due to the situation one is in. Flexivity might describe the feeling or awareness of assemblages as a 'continuous process of movement and transformation as relations and terms change' (Anderson et al. 2012:177). That is, there is an emphasis on 'assemblage as a verb' (2012:174), which indicates a process and a practice that arises through experience. In the above examples from the interviews with tourists and the Hut Ranger, the awareness of their own bodily capacities and the constantly shifting relations between themselves and the material object of the bag (as well as its contents and the gravitational pull) are brought to the foreground. In this way, to be flexive is to consider movement as a relational force, where each actor in the assemblage is adaptive and malleable in terms of their actions and movements that are executed in conjunction with other actors in the assemblage.

With each step, the tourist body recalibrates and adjusts as the assemblage of objects – hiking boots, backpack, food, first aid kits, water and so on – is bounced around, shifting the distribution of weight, and therefore forcing the walking tourist body to re-act and redistribute their actions in accordance with these co-produced movements. Flexivity can be thought of as a potential for movement and adjustment that is not necessarily executed on the conscious level. It might be the slightest adjustment of one's force of a footstep, or the body's recalibration as weight in the bag shifts from side to side. These are instances where the assemblage of human bodies and nonhuman materials come together in a coordinated deployment of co-produced movements. John Wylie's eloquent description of his walking experiences, of hearing the 'sound of breathing and the rustle of the rucksack shifting about awkwardly' indicates how the situation and atmosphere is assembled, where 'the pre-established boundary between self and landscape, subject and object, could become soluble, osmotic, in the engaged, involved practice of walking' (2005:239). Wylie's reflections, and the recounts from tourists that I interviewed, reveal how these tourist experiences of walking are much more reliant upon the assemblages of human and nonhuman action that we might initially think.

As I found in the interviews and observations during the four days walking the Three Capes Track, the majority of conversations revolved around the material 'stuff' we had brought, the quality of equipment, the technologies and gadgets that made the walking process easier for the body. It is arguable that all of these material items played a significant role in the experience of our traversing the stunning landscapes of the Tasman National Park. Perhaps the interactions that tourists' bodies have with materials, in these strenuous battles, the rubbing of the bag straps, the rustle of objects moving with each swaying footstep, are far more integral to the tourist experience, fostering an unexpected yet embodied connection to the journey through wilderness areas.

Conclusion: rethinking the assemblages of bodies and materials in tourism

In any tourism situation, the tourist's body is central to the sensations, actions and experiences that unfold. Although visiting wilderness areas is imbued with the expectation of immersive experiences and soaking up the natural surrounds, the materials that enable one to move through these areas play a significant role in how the experiences forms. Moments where tourists become aware of their bodies in relation to materials, such as in the strain of carrying a heavy hiking bag or the rubbing of a strap, draw attention to ways that tourism experiences are co-produced by a myriad of actors. Thinking about situations where materials 'structure, define, and configure interaction' (Van der Duim 2007:968) involves acknowledging that human capabilities are extended by 'various objects and mundane technologies' that extend 'this kinaesthetic sense' (Urry 2016:48) of how one moves through the world.

In the example I have focused on here – the interactions of tourists with their hiking bags and equipment – an assemblage emerges where human action is entangled with nonhuman materials that enables, supports, disrupts and at times re-routes the walking experience. This might be through the material characteristics and properties that determine how tourists interact with their bags: the weight of the bag (picking it up, carrying it up a steep incline), the mass and shape of the bag (whether it aligns to your back and fits to the shape of your hip bones) or the volume of the bag (think of when you can't 'fit' everything into a bag). These material traits and capacities (such as waterproof, windproof, light-weight, absorbent, reflective) play a significant role in the planning and preparation for a walk, but are also tied to the imaginations and expectations of what tourists will feel and do in the walk. The division between human action and the nonhuman material as a passive intermediary is overcome, if only momentarily, in favour of a delicate negotiation of bodily sensations and material capacities.

In this chapter, I have analysed the ethnographic observations and interviews that draw attention to the relationships of tourist bodies, materiality and the co-production of tourism experiences. These insights attend to the state of constant readjustment and repositioning of tourist bodies in relation to material actors, flexing and moving with a variety of influences. It is a way of describing assemblage with a more specified application for concerns in tourism – where social influences and ideals, and environmental concerns congeal. For activities in wilderness areas, where emphasis is often placed on the ability of the tourist body, the sustainability of the activities or the ideals of feeling in sync with 'nature', an increase in attention to how tourists consume and produce their encounters *with* anthropocentric materials can only enhance conservation and sustainable practices. The interviews and observations on the Three Capes Track bring to focus the interactions that tourists have with material items when they adjust, shift, reposition and flex. These haphazard relationships draw the body into a flexive state, where the body is negotiated as part of the assemblage of material-bodily action. Being adaptive to situations where things do not go according to plan, or having to re-adjust and re-purpose materials to move easier can be seen not as defeat or an impediment to tourism experiences, but rather as an alternative and opportunity for new kinds of experiences. These moments are encounters where tourists become aware of how their bodies are entangled with the complexity of materials, environments and their own ideals, actions and expectations.

Attention to such moments of negotiation and interaction with materials is one way of re-thinking how tourists' bodies perform and co-produce certain kinds of tourism experiences. It brings into questions the manner in which tourists' bodies are expected to fit to a certain body shape, size and ability, reflecting socio-cultural ideals of human versus the natural world. The materials that have become essential for experiencing wilderness areas reinforce these ideals of how tourist bodies should perform and what they should feel. Material properties and capacities inevitably determine how the tourist body can move alongside these materials, how these material capacities work with and compliment the movements of the body, and what kind of feelings and affects the body might experience as it moves through the world.

References

Anderson, B. and McFarlane, C. (2011) Assemblage and geography. *Area*, 43(2): 124–127. doi:10.111/j.1475-4762.2011.01004x

Anderson, B., Kearnes, M., McFarlane, C. and Swanton, D. (2012) On assemblage and geography. *Dialogues in Human Geography*, 2(2): 171–189. doi:10.1177/2043820612449261

Bain, D., Brown, L., Connellan, I., Daly, J., Daly, L., Dixon, G. and van der Knifjj, G. (Eds.) (2006) *Walking in Australia*. Footscray, VIC: Lonely Planet Publications Pty Ltd.

Barry, K. (2017) *Everyday Practices of Tourism Mobilities: Packing a Bag*. Oxon and New York: Routledge.

Beard, L., Scarles, C. and Tribe, J. (2016) Mess and method: Using ANT in tourism research. *Annals of Tourism Research*, 60: 97–110. doi:10.1016/j.annals.2016.06.005

Benediktsson, K. and Lund, K. A. (Eds.) (2010) *Conversations with Landscape*. Farnham: Ashgate.

DeLanda, M. (2016) *Assemblage Theory*. Edinburgh: Edinburgh University Press.

Deleuze, G. and Guattari, F. (2004). *A Thousand Plateaus: Capitalism and Schizophrenia*, B. Massumi (trans.). London: Continuum.

Dorwart, C. E., Moore, R. L. and Leung, Y. (2009) Visitors' perceptions of a trail environment and effects on experiences: A model for nature-based recreational experiences. *Leisure Sciences*, 32(1): 33–54. doi:10.1080/0490400903430863

Edensor, T. (2000) Walking in the British countryside: Reflexivity, embodied practices and ways to escape. *Body & Society*, 6(3–4): 81–106.

Edensor, T. (2017) Seeing with light and landscape: A walk around Stanton Moor. *Landscape Research*, 4(6): 616–633. doi:10.1080/01426397.2017.1316368

Franklin, A. (2006) The humanity of wilderness photography? *Australian Humanities Review*, (38): 1–16. Available at: www.australianhumanitiesreview. org/archive/Issue-April-2006/EcoFranklin.html [Accessed 8 September 2017].

Franklin, A. (2014) On why we dig the beach: Tracing the subjects and objects of the bucket and spade for a relational materialist theory of the beach. *Tourist Studies*, 14(3): 261–285. doi:10.177/1468797614536331

Gren, M. and Huijbens, E. H. (Eds.) (2016) *Tourism and the Anthropocene*. Abingdon, Oxon: Routledge.

Gyimóthy, S. and Mykletun, R. J. (2004) Play in adventure tourism: The case of Arctic trekking. *Annals of Tourism Research*, 31(4): 855–878. doi:10.1016/j.annals.2004.03.005

Hannam, K. and Ateljevic, I. (Eds.) (2007) *Backpacker Tourism: Concepts and Profiles*. Clevedon: Channel View Publications.

Hillery, M., Nancarrow, B., Griffin, G. and Syme, G. (2001) Tourist perception of environmental impact. *Annals of Tourism Research*, 28(4): 853–862.

Hyde, K. F. and Olesen, K. (2011) Packing for touristic performances. *Annals of Tourism Research*, 38(3): 900–919.

Ingold, T. (Ed.) (2011) *Redrawing Anthropology: Materials, Movements, Lines*. Farnham: Ashgate.

Ingold, T. (2012) Introduction, in M. Janowski and T. Ingold (eds.) *Imagining Landscape: Past, Present & Future*. Farnham, Surrey and Burlington: Farnham: Ashgate, pp. 1–18.

Jack, G. and Phipps, A. (2005) *Tourism and Intercultural Exchange: Why Tourism Matters*. Clevedon, Buffalo and Toronto: Channel View Publications.

Latour, B. (2007) *Reassembling the Social*. New York: Oxford University Press.

Lund, K. A. (2013) Experiencing nature in nature-based tourism. *Tourist Studies*, 13(2): 156–171. doi:10.1177/1468797613490373

Lury, C. (1997) The objects of travel, in C. Rojek and U. John (eds.) *Touring Cultures: Transformations of Travel and Theory*. London and New York: Routledge, pp. 75–95.

Merriman, P., Revill, G., Cresswell, T., Lorimer, H., Matless, D., Rose, G. and Wylie, J. (2008) Landscape, mobility, practice. *Social & Cultural Geography*, 9(2): 191–212.

Michael, M. (2000) These boots are made for walking…: Mundane technology, the body and human-environment relations. *Body & Society*, 6(3–4): 107–126.

Olafsdottir, G. (2013) '…sometimes you've just got to get away': On trekking holidays and their therapeutic effect. *Tourist Studies*, 13(2): 209–231. doi:10.1177/1468797613490379

Palsson, G. (2013) Ensembles of biosocial relations, in T. Ingold and G. Palsson (eds.) *Biosocial Becomings: Integrating Social and Biological Anthropology*. New York: Cambridge University Press, pp. 22–41.

Pietilä M. and Fagerholm N. (2016) Visitors' place-based evaluations of unacceptable tourism impacts in Oulanka National Park, Finland. *Tourism Geographies*, 18(3): 258–279.

Richards, G. and Wilson, J. (eds.) (2004) *The Global Nomad: Backpacker Travel in Theory and Practice*. Clevedon: Channel View Publications.

Scarles, C. (2010) Where words fail, visual ignite: Opportunities for visual authoethnography in tourism research. *Annals of Tourism Research*, 37(4): 905–926. doi:10.1016/j.annals.2010.02.001

Tasmania Parks and Wildlife Services. (2017) *Three Capes Track*. Available at: www. threecapestrack.com.au/ [accessed 4 August 2017].

Urry, J. (2016) *Mobilities*. Cambridge: Polity Press.

Urry, J. and Larsen, J. (2011) *The Tourist Gaze 3.0*. London: SAGE Publication Ltd.

Van der Duim, R., Ren, C. and Johannesson, G. T. (Eds.) (2012) *Actor-Network Theory and Tourism: Ordering, Materiality and Multiplicity*. Oxon: Routledge.

Van der Duim, R. (2007). Tourismscapes: an actor-network perspective. *Annals of Tourism Research*, 34(4): 961–976.

Walsh, N. and Tucker, H. (2009) Tourism "things": The travelling performance of the backpack. *Tourist Studies*, 9(3): 223–239. doi:10.1177/1468797610382706

Wearing, S. and Whenman, A. (2009) Tourism as an interpretive and mediating influence: A review of the authority of guidebooks in protected areas. *Tourism Analysis*, 14(5): 701–716.

Wylie, J. (2005) A single day's walking: Narrating self and landscape on the South West Coast Path. *Transactions of the Institute of British Geographers New Series*, 30(2): 234–247.

14 Phenomenological anthropology of interactive travel

Mediated responsivity and inter-placed mobilities

Christopher A. Howard and Wendelin Küpers

Introduction

This chapter explores the convergence of embodiment, tourism and mobile technologies in a globally networked context. The proliferation of media in the twenty-first century corresponds to a qualitative and quantitative increase in virtual, imaginary and corporeal mobilities (Urry 2007, Howard 2012, Germann Molz and Paris 2013, Hannam et al. 2014). In a world of accelerated and overlapping mobilities, possibilities for moving and dwelling in multiple realities have expanded and intensified, facilitating what Germann Molz (2012) calls 'interactive travel'. Living in a world that is increasingly 'on the move' points to a situation in which mobile devices, social media and networking technologies facilitate a 'coordinated togetherness' on a planetary scale. By reconfiguring spatial and social relations, interactive travel problematises long-standing tourism concepts such as home and away, the ritual process and the tourist gaze. It also opens new lines of inquiry for a less developed but central aspect of tourism: embodiment. We aim to address this gap here, taking a particular methodological focus on the phenomenological concept of responsivity in the context of interactive travel.

As will be discussed, responsivity is a basic feature of our embodied human condition while media is an extension and augmentation of embodied cognition. Phenomenological analysis of how these play out in tourist experience, we aim to show, opens new and fruitful ground for tourism anthropology. Situating embodied tourists in the immediate environments in which they travel *and* the digital worlds that accompany them via networked technologies allows for a deeper understanding of contemporary tourist mobilities. Responsivity becomes an especially relevant concept for approaching the relational coupling of bodies, places and technologies. Correspondingly, we develop the concept of 'interplace' or process of 'interplacing'. This neologism shall refer to a place, action and condition in which multiple places and mobile subjects are relationally configured and mutually constituting across different spatiotemporal scales. The chapter especially highlights the role that mobile technologies play in mediating and reconfiguring perceptions of place and space. Specifically, we consider how the situated technological practices of global travellers reveal a tendency to respond and to drift in and out of their immediate emplacements via digitally mediated extensions of embodied presence.

Following Heidegger, this contemporary moment and its configured movements and affects can be interpreted as the age of 'digital *Ge-stell*' (en-framement). By this we refer to a specific historical situation in which digital technologies augment the inherent spatial tendencies of human beings, what Heidegger calls 'de-distancing' and 'bringing near' (Heidegger 1996, Sloterdijk 2012). Travelling with(in) networked technologies extends the experiential field of embodied tourists by de-distancing the physical boundaries between here and elsewhere. In the age of digital *Ge-stell*, tourism is no longer a matter of 'getting away from it all' and 'being there', but rather being here and there; that is, being inter-placed. Mobile technologies allow for social, work and other relations to continue at a distance, enabling tourists to be responsive in what comes to appear as a 'planetary landscape' (Augé 2008). After outlining responsivity and its connection to the body, place in and digital media, we discuss some ethnographic findings and offer some implications and conclusions.

Embodied responsivity in tourism

For a long time, the body and embodied dimensions of tourism, at least in a rigorous, enlivened sense, have been largely neglected (or framed dualistically or in gendered ways) in tourism studies (Veijola and Jokinen 1994). Despite having a close connection between tourism encounters and bodily senses, the corporeality of the travelling experience remains underexplored (Small 2007). A few astute observers, however, have called for a moving beyond the passive gaze of consuming tourists into the embodiment of acts; that is, into the actual, sensual 'doing' of tourism (Edensor 2000, Franklin and Crang 2001, Crouch 2002, Pons 2003). As Edensor (2001:61) argues, tourism is replete with unconsidered embodied practices, especially common sense and habitual performance that are all part of the fleshiness of journeys (Crouch 2007) and sensuousness of 'tourist bodies' (Pritchard and Morgan 2011) and tourist encounters (Crouch and Desforges 2003).

Based on an extensive literature review about the use of the body in research over the past two decades, Longhurst and Johnston stated, 'undoubtedly, the body, bodies, embodiment, corporeality and other related terms are currently being used within a wider variety of frameworks than in the past' (2014:273) and they confirm that today, embodiment tends to carry with it a greater sense of acceptability. However, they conclude by expressing ambivalence about scholarship on embodiment, as it has not destabilised masculinism in the disciplines asking, 'has 'the body' become little more than a ubiquitous marker of identity and difference, emptied of its power to unsettle the masculinist epistemology...' (ibid. 273). Critically, they problematise that many of the power relations (patriarchal, heterosexist, racist, neoliberal) that structure bodily daily lives have not improved dramatically for the better since the mid-1990s (ibid. 274).

Correspondingly, a phenomenology of the body and embodiment offers an approach for considering these concepts in relation to experiences of travelling. The body, as Merleau-Ponty (2013) observed, is not only our ontological starting point but also the constitutive medium for making sense of lived experience that ultimately outruns and overwhelms linguistic expression. We are always catching up to the sensations, affections and moods that are already experienced as meaningful on the level of the lived body. As such, the body figures principally in tourism in the very basic sense that there is no world to experience without a body. This is not an isolated body or monad; tourists encounter manifold others as they move through shared worlds. Whether fleeting or sustained, these sensuous encounters point not only to the inter-subjective nature of experience, but even more fundamentally to what Merleau-Ponty calls inter-corporeality. Being corporeally intertwined with Others means we live in a world that demands we respond to it.

Demand and response are keys concepts in the phenomenology of alterity and Otherness of Bernhard Waldenfels, whose work has recently been shown to hold great potential for anthropology (Lysemose 2013, Leistle 2015, 2016, Cahill et al. 2017), including tourism anthropology (Picard and Giovine 2014, Howard 2015). Waldenfels' major contribution to phenomenology is his focus on responsivity, which he argues takes place *before* intentionality (Waldenfels 1990, 2007, 2011). Taking responsivity as a primary feature of human existence requires turning from intentional agents to the demands, claims and affects that come from elsewhere. For Waldenfels (2007), our movements, initiatives and intentions are preceded by things that happen to or befall us by virtue of living in a shared world. Being situated in a responsive nexus, we are called or even condemned to respond to the Others we encounter. Responding to the *alien* is by no means limited to verbal expressions or even to human relations. Rather it is a basic feature of all sensing, saying and doing, of all embodied and motor sensory behaviour and experience. As responsive beings, subjects or collectives are always already 'haunted' by foreignness, and they emerge creatively out of affecting happenings that are lived out in relation to Others. Importantly, responsivity extends to the digital worlds and virtual Others that have become coextensive with our physical worlds and actual Others (Miller 2013). Indeed, in his ethnography of Facebook Miller concludes, there are no clear lines separating the so-called 'real' and virtual worlds; rather, the online worlds of Facebook and the practical worlds of everyday life are dynamically intertwined and mutually constituting.

The logic of response and the phenomenology of the alien have radical consequences for other problematic, long-standing (Western) dualisms, such as mind/body, self/other and subject/object. Following Waldenfels, these dualisms break down as we come to see that the alien is already part of us, '...my own body could be described as a half-alien body, charged by alien intentions, but also desires, projections, habits, affections, and violations, coming from others' (2011:56). Foreignness or alienness announces itself and solicits us on the level of the lived body in terms of pathos or affect, as a kind of pre-reflexive suffering or irritation, 'we are touched by others before being able to ask who they are and what their expressions mean. The alienness of the Other overcomes and surprises us, disturbing our intentions before being understood in this or that sense' (Waldenfels 2011:53). Radically, the experience of the alien points to a becoming-alien of experience itself (Waldenfels 1990:23). This type of self-estrangement – being confronted by one's own otherness – is a common lesson gleaned from ethnographic fieldwork and is central to the reflexive epistemology that guides the anthropological and sociological projects more generally (Bourdieu and Wacquant 1992, Bourdieu 2003, Hage 2012). Responding to and negotiating otherness first and foremost on the level of the lived body is also central to the tourist experience, as only a few authors to date have explored (Fullagar 2001, Howard 2016, Picard and Robinson 2016).

The crossing of boundaries or thresholds between self and other opens new and important perspectives on ethical and political aspects of our relational co-existence and notions of selfhood. A responsive phenomenology can also help us better understand the meanings and implications of mobile technologies in tourism contexts. For instance, digitally connected tourists are called to respond to the communicative demands of the multiple realities they inhabit and take with them 'on the road'. At the same time, they must respond to the situated sensations, affects and demands of the places they travel through. This complex situation – being here and there – affords a multiplying and augmenting of our basic responsive capacity.

'Being-in' and responding-to place

The outlined significance of embodied responsivity can be shown in relation to its connection to a relational understanding of place and movement. In and through temporalised places is where the world (including tourist sites) manifests itself to human beings. Contrary to dualistic and de-temporalised approaches, a phenomenological understanding considers these as the interdependent elements of lived experience and the existential grounds for all events and movements. Equipped with a spatial framework, body subjects mediate and navigate within and towards places via primordial and socio-culturally specific environing practices (Merleau-Ponty 2013). Movements, rhythms and interactions between bodies and places facilitate the co-creation of what Casey calls *'place-scapes'*, in which bodies and environments form 'congruent counterparts' (Casey 1993:25). Body-world coupling forms a dynamic spatio-temporal connection that is always perceived, mediated and oriented through emplaced bodies (Varela et al. 1991, Dreyfus 2009).

Emplacement refers to an immediate and concrete placement in which the interplay between a living body and place is situated (Casey 2001). Emplaced being thus entails sensing, feeling, moving, orienting, thinking and acting through a body that is co-constituted by the places within which it is practically engaged. Place, as Malpas notes, is thus 'a structure comprising spatiality *and* temporality, subjectivity *and* objectivity, self *and* other' (Malpas 1999:163 original emphasis). Relationally, a particular place is neither bounded nor static; places are open, multi-layered, and emerging milieu within a dispersed and inherently indeterminate process of responsive and continual reconfiguration (Casey 1993, Massey 2005, Ingold 2008, Küpers 2010). Furthermore, travelling is made possible by and mobilised through embodied flows of information and capital, people, objects, organisations, institutions, information and communication systems, machines, buildings, signs, transportation and other infrastructures (Urry and Larsen 2012). While all places undergo continuous change, global cities and tourist zones are particularly subject to reordering processes (Sheller and Urry 2004). Related back to the concept of responsivity, inter-placed mobilities mean tourists must respond in their immediate material environments and the digital worlds they carry and access via mobile media.

Moving does not simply mean leaving one place behind and encountering another. On the contrary, places accompany travellers in embodied forms, such as the cultural habits, dispositions and memories (Howard 2015). Traces of home also travel in cosmopolitan bodies by way of vaccinations and medications (Germann Molz 2006). The artefacts travellers carry and wear – such as clothing, backpacks, books, gifts and other objects – similarly mean that places come into contact with other places. This phenomenon also manifests in social interactions with other travellers and through global commodity chains; bodily subjects leaving traces of themselves in the spaces and places they move through (Thrift 2006). A phenomenological conception of 'inter-place' suggests that it is not so much that boundaries do not exist; rather, they are embodied, materialised, and socially constituted and/or constructed in ways that are 'more real' for some people than others. Globally mobile subjects with their 'inter-placed' lives transcend boundaries enabled by their privileged social positions manifesting an uneven distribution of (im-)mobilities (Cresswell 2010). Having understood places as relational and in motion, we are now in a position to consider empirically how mobile technologies facilitate a responsive 'inter-placedness'.

Phenomenological anthropology of interactive travel

Research background and context

The empirical material presented below is based on a mobile ethnography and autoethnography carried out by the first author in the Himalayan region of Nepal and India in 2011. The research as a whole aimed to explore the intersections of tourism, pilgrimage and lifestyle mobilities in the context of the Himalayan region. Focusing primarily on travellers from Western societies, semi- and unstructured interviews and participant observation was conducted in and between a number of sites, in Nepal and Sikkim in Northeast India. Interviews and conversations often took place in guesthouses, cafés and restaurants, and along hiking trails. The author, as a fellow traveller, also accompanied participants on shorter hikes and on bus, train and jeep rides, a mobile method that can be called 'moving with'.

For many, these trips were multidimensional, driven by specific aims and ideals within a single journey that was also interpreted as an open 'adventure'. The three central motives identified by the travellers I encountered were (1) coming to the source or origin of spiritual traditions and 'power places', (2) exotic and authentic cultural experiences and (3) nature-based challenges in the form of mountain treks. There was almost always overlap between these, and typically these contemporary *journeys to the East* were incorporated into larger, around the world trip trips. Beyond the perceived power and 'spiritual magnetism' of the Himalayan region, the relatively low cost of travelling there was another motivating factor. The majority of travellers claimed that films, literature and online media played the largest role in informing their images, expectations and perceptions. The overlapping of virtual, imaginary and corporeal mobilities thus became a major focus of the research and meant that the ethnographic field extended beyond local contexts.

Technologically configured place ballets

For the first author, one of the first ethnographic observations during fieldwork in Nepal and India was the ubiquitous use of mobile technologies by contemporary travellers. The fact that many travelled with smart phones, tablets and/or laptops demonstrated that information and communication technologies ICTs have become an intrinsic aspect of contemporary tourism. The diffusion or 'spillover' of internet and mobile technologies is now crossing multiple life domains, including tourism and leisure contexts (Elliott and Urry 2010, MacKay and Vogt 2012, Germann Molz and Paris 2013, Wang et al. 2014, Wang et al. 2016). Elliott and Urry (2010) coin the term 'miniaturized mobilities' to describe the proliferation and impact of ever more compact and sophisticated digital devices such as mobile phones, laptops, tablets and smartphones. As they observe, mobile, networked technologies are a salient feature permeating the social fabric of contemporary mobile lives. While they increasingly open possibilities for and reinforce mobility, it is important to consider how these networked technologies alter social contexts and experiences of place. By allowing for the continuity of everyday life while being 'on the move', new technologies can displace travellers from the physical and embodied travel experience (Paris et al. 2015, Tanti and Buhalis 2017).

Mobile technologies were thoroughly interwoven into the travellers' experience of place. Smartphones, tablets or laptops and Wi-Fi access points were embedded in the daily rhythms and routines of what Seamon calls 'place ballets' (Seamon 1979). A place ballet follows from the corporeal schemes that serve to orient or choreograph the rhythmic movements and practices that constitute everyday place experiences. Free Wi-Fi was a key factor in deciding where to stay and seeking out places to get online was an integral part of the daily routes and routines of tourists. Mobile media usage was most prevalent during interludes in urban and tourist centres like Kathmandu and Pokhara and hill stations such as Darjeeling and Dharamsala. In these places, internet access is more widely available compared to the more remote towns, villages and mountainous areas that were also visited. Technological practices were thus relative to both location and the specific phases of people's trips; the notion of total 'global connectivity' is an illusion of the developed world.

Travellers used mobile devices for communicating via e-mail, instant messaging, Skype, Facebook, Twitter and other social media sites. They also wrote and read blogs, checked news, viewed travel and job sites, managed bank accounts and credit cards, and watched videos of all kinds. Those on longer trips more typically spent exorbitant amounts of time arranging their travel (e.g. accommodation, flights, where to eat). Some worked online, writing reports or on online university courses or theses. Having internet access and a laptop allowed people to maintain continuity with work and life at 'home' from a distance. For example, Jason, an environmental planner on a three-month break from work in Cambodia, travelled to various countries with a laptop that allowed him to work on a report for the Cambodian government while applying for jobs worldwide. During our stay in Pokhara, some days he did not leave the guesthouse, explaining that he had too much work to do. Like Jason, many travellers were between jobs and/or life phases. Despite the centrality of mobile technologies in the lifeworlds of contemporary travellers, they also create tensions and contradictions, especially when internet connectivity is weak or unavailable.

Technological unconscious and the 'will to respond'

In excess, the tendency towards a 'coordinated togetherness' in mobility reflects the growing trend in internet/technology addiction. In places with limited or no coverage – technological dead zones – travellers increasingly experience technology-induced tensions (Pearce and Gretzel 2012, Paris et al. 2015). Pearce and Gretzel (2012) found that travellers reported some positive aspects of being disconnected, such as being free and 'in the moment', they also found such a 'world disruption' caused fear and anxiety. Travelling with 'miniaturized mobilities' in a digitally enframed world means that one is contactable and thus response-able for staying in touch, even in 'technological dead zones'. Hjorth captures the paradoxes of travelling with an 'electronic leash' when she observes how 'the mobile phone sets us 'free' to roam geographically, but its 'always-on' function means that we are seemingly always available' (2012:141). Yet such availability is more complicated when travelling in remote areas, such as the Himalayan region. Even in tourist enclaves such as Kathmandu or Dharamsala, internet connections were often extremely slow or would suddenly become unavailable with the rolling power outages. At other times, travellers are on the move, riding buses or trains for days on end, and may find themselves in 'technological dead zones', places with little or no internet network whatsoever, as was the case in Sikkim.

Or travellers were simply too sick to do anything, including seeking out a sketchy internet connection. Knowing that significant others – especially romantic partners – expect to hear from us, these periods of virtual unavailability may give rise to anxiety and even guilt. As Marisa, an American traveller in her early twenties I interviewed in Darjeeling reflected:

> If I don't get online for more than a week, in the back of my mind I start to worry about all the people and messages I'm neglecting and about how my inbox must be filling up. It's strange 'cause in a way it's great to have a break from all the communication, to be free from it for a little while, but even so I know it's there, waiting for me.

This tendency was especially marked after intervals of relatively prolonged disconnectivity, such as after a multi-day trek, yoga or meditation retreats, or being in remote areas with limited or no Internet access. In such positions, travellers often embraced the sense of freedom that came with temporary disconnectivity, but like Marisa, this was accompanied by anxiety. This is revealing on two levels. First, it shows simply how engrained, habituated and pervasive internet technologies are today. Second, it demonstrates that even when mobile media are not available or in use, they may remain present. Elliott and Urry (2010:10) refer to this phenomenon as the 'technological unconscious'. This concept refers to a background realm in which digitally mediated social relations involving high degrees of absence and distance are processed.

This implies that in our digitalised age in which networked technologies are ever more interwoven into embodied subjectivities, the possibility of dwelling outside of media is shrinking. Maybe there is no longer any place that is really and truly 'out there', away from it all, even deep in the Himalayas. At the centre of the new media revolution is what Hansen describes as a 'massive increase in the capacity for passive sensing' (2012:53). This goes beyond the active uses of media, such as making calls, sending messages or taking photos, to include the sensors that 'passively register massive amounts of behavioural and environmental data without any active involvement, decision to initiate, or even awareness on our part' (ibid.). The challenge and key to addressing today's media involves a radically environmental approach in which human beings cannot be separated from the socio-technical systems and material environments they inhabit.

Responsive mobilities in the age of 'Digital *Ge-stell*'

As described above, using ICTs and mobile technologies were incorporated into the daily rhythms and practices of travellers, who despite being physically distant, remained in close virtual proximity and responsive to their lives and projects at 'home' (Germann Molz 2008). This ability and propensity for staying connected and responding can be related both to the human need for maintaining social bonds and the spatial orientation of human being, characterised by what Heidegger (1996:98–100) calls de-distancing and directionality. The directional and 'bringing near' orientation of what Heidegger refers to as *Dasein* (literally meaning 'being there') is intensified and expanded by the tools of the information age, and with increasing tempo and technological lead to a time-space compression impacting immediate experiences of place.

Paradoxically, the de-distancing or bringing near of distant horizons facilitated by digitally networked communication simultaneously appears to distance us from immediate emplacements. The apparent paradox deepens when we consider the 'adventures' most Himalayan travellers claimed to be having and seeking. As Simmel observes, the deeper meaning of an adventure is given by its occurring 'outside the usual continuity of this life' and standing in contrast to the everyday (1997:224). And yet, by accessing the internet, keeping in touch, and making future travel and life plans, while on the move, the responsive demands of the home-world continue for travellers as they move around the world. Contrasted with previous times, travelling in the twenty-first century becomes an event that no longer takes place really and truly 'out there', but in and across a relationscape of 'heres', 'theres' and 'in-betweens'. This is because mobile media serve the function of bridging, connecting and de-distancing the space and time between places, augmenting what is already a spatial orientation common to the human mode of Being-in-the-world. They also tap into and intensify the responsive imperative.

What do mobile technologies mean for embodied human beings? Casey (2012) argues that fundamental features of our existence suffer neglect in the information society. His first critique is on account of what he describes as the 'irreplaceable value' of being with others in a face-to-face manner by virtue of being in the same place:

> There is simply no substitute for the nuanced reading of the other's face and indeed, his or her whole body … expressions and dialogues made possible by being in the presence of a person are of an intricacy and scope that simply cannot be experienced otherwise.
>
> (Casey 2012:175)

Casey also critiques the 'illusion' of omnipresent availability characterising the wireless world, or the notion that Others are available to me merely because I carry a mobile phone or laptop. As the emplaced corporeal self cannot be everywhere at once, for Casey the wireless world causes human beings to lose touch with the primary requirement for existence: body and place.

Far from being a purely mental or cognitive event, our experiences with ICTs are significantly expanded when understood on the level of the lived body. Embodiment, as Merleau-Ponty (2013) observed, is always already functioning in an 'equipmental' way. As such, there is a reciprocal relationship between bodies and technologies (Ihde 2001). Inasmuch as the lived responsive body is the ground or medium for all experiences, including tourism and being online, the use of technologies is never disembodied. Neither is it neutral; technologies profoundly condition and transform our relation to others, our experiences of places and our environmental perceptions. As Elliott and Urry note, individual selves do not just 'use' or activate digital technologies in everyday life (2010:27). Rather, under conditions of intensive mobilities, the self becomes deeply layered within and reshaped by the influence of enframing technological networks with their regimes to respond.

Yet, this does not necessarily mean that technology must be seen as alienating humans from a supposed original or essential nature. If technology is an 'extension of man', prosthetically equipped, *Homo Faber* is a 'technological animal', encompassing a larger radius of action and optimisation of artificial organs. The philosophical anthropologist Helmuth Plessner had already articulated this in the 1920s when he suggested that being 'ex-centrically positioned' in relation to the natural world, human beings have evolved to become 'artificial by nature' (De Mul 2014). As an underdetermined animal or *Homo absconditus*, humans coevolve with technologies in changing environments and adaptive sociotechnical systems (Plessner 1969).

While mobile technologies alter and reconfigure relations between and experiences of place, self and others in the context of travel, this is part of a broader historical trend in the technologisation of life. Phenomenologically, this development can be seen as enacting, what Heidegger calls Ge-stell or 'enframing', updated here as 'digital Ge-stell' (Howard and Küpers 2017). Global and local mobilities, with their mobilised bodies, devices, transport systems and infrastructures, stand within this technologically enframed order. A hyper-mediated, hyper-mobile world, as McLuhan predicted, turns the world into a global village in which everywhere and everything appears close and accessible (McLuhan 2008). Accessing the *Lonely Planet* website, for example, reveals the world as a storehouse of places to play, experiences to appropriate and collect. Critically interpreted, this could be read as manifesting a pervasive and simultaneous 'will to connect' (Simmel), 'consume' (Baudrillard) and 'control' (Foucault and Deleuze) in late modernity.

For many travellers, Nepal and India were perceived as having unique qualities, such as authenticity, spirituality and sublime landscapes. Observation of mobile practices, however, revealed that in many instances these places appeared as ephemeral backdrops to mobile performances of embodied cosmopolitanism (Germann Molz 2006, Howard 2016). This ephemeral and consumptive orientation seems to be a key feature of the contemporary technological attitudes prevalent in our digitally enframed world. Mobile technologies and networked connectivities afford a life in motion, not allowing people to genuinely dwell in the here and now. Rather, they are on the move constantly in a global interplacement and displacement that seems to be somewhere between everywhere and *now*here (Howard and Küpers 2015).

Conclusion

This chapter has tried to contribute to a processual understanding of embodied mobility as responsive practice and interplacing in the age of 'digital *Ge-stell*'. Findings from ethnographic fieldwork confirmed that embodied technological practices and dynamics facilitate forms of 'dwelling in mobility' (Clifford 1997). As described, contemporary mobile life, with its overlapping virtual, imaginary and corporeal mobilities, is pervasively digitally enframed. While mediated flights from the emplaced present may seem antithetical to visceral, liminal experiences, travel appears to be increasingly technologically configured. Understanding responsiveness and places relationally allows us to see how mobile media are incorporated into specific emplacements.

A relational and processual approach to embodied interplacing recognises that wayfaring, as storied travelling, is lived along open(ing) lines that are part of a responsive meshwork (Ingold 2011:69–70). This mesh is a living contexture of interwoven technologically mediated threads that constitute a geographically dispersed web of moving relationships that is responsive and generating. As this chapter has tried to show, the responsive practices of being and becoming mobile 'take (inter)place' in relation to technologies that are unfolding increasingly connected forms of life.

It would be interesting to further explore how mobile technologies are incorporated into the body schema of travellers (and hosts). What does it mean that technologies become incorporated and thus integral components of travellers repertoires of perceptual and motor capabilities processed and expressed through visual, aural or tactile functions? Correspondingly, it would be revealing to explore how mobile and mobilising technologies are influencing inter-sensorial relationships to 'inter-places'. In the sense of an '*interseriality*' (Kärrholm et al. 2017), it would be enriching to investigate how different sorts of sensing and moving mediated by technology and places do relate to one another and how the 'relation of relations' are handled.

An arts and humanities approach to embodiment, mobility and place, including 'kin-aesthetics' (Merriman and Pearce 2017), can help to examine how inter-placed senses and movements are desired, perceived, felt, enacted, responded to and expressed.

We hope that the presented findings, ideas and discussions invite further explorations into the realities, possibilities and limitations of techno-mediated forms of travel while moving towards alternative understandings and practices of mobile life.

Reflecting on mobile technologies requires thinking about the ways in which embodied actors respond, inter-act and navigate their material-digital worlds. In an era of intensifying global techno-cultural developments, tourism anthropology is called upon to keep abreast with current and future technologies and (post)human 'technicity'. New media and technologies, including Big Data, AI and augmented reality point to travellers increasingly becoming embodied 'cyborgs' (Clark 2004) who move through networked inter-places. What kinds of bodily affordances and subjectivities will such technologies create for tourists? How can tourism anthropology connect to digital ethnography and approaches of virtual and posthuman anthropology (Whitehead and Wesch 2012, Thweatt-Bates 2016, Howard 2017)?

As we have tried to demonstrate in this chapter, Waldenfels' responsive phenomenology marks a significant opening for thinking through how digital media affects embodied experience, mediation and inter-relational Being-in-the-world (Kim 2001, Howard 2015, Hui 2016). Without being technophobic, social scientists are called to critically engage with how technical individuations in an 'automatic society' (Stiegler 2017) are increasingly being organised by a form of 'algorithmic governmentality' (Rouvroy and Stiegler 2016). The danger is vicious circles of stupification via a calculated mobilisation of global, real-time digital mediations for commercial ends.

Embodied responsivity, we hope to have shown, is especially relevant to tourism anthropology and is ripe for ethnographic investigation. Considering the foreseeable increase and intensification of digital culture, with its pressures of expected answers, the need for adequate forms of responding will become more important. As we have shown, the dynamics of technological mobility in relation to places are transforming the embodied involvement and responsiveness of emplaced travellers. Because they shape and are shaped by mediated influences in place, there might be potentials activated for more sustainable and mindful movements. Such an orientation may include cultivating more place-responsive (Cameron et al. 2004) and sustainable mobility practices (Küpers 2015, McCool 2015, Espiner et al. 2017). Integrating corporeal qualities and new technologies can expand how mobile (media) narratives take inter-place. Thereby, there are revealing possibilities and limitations of responsive 'bodied' travelling into and through planetary landscapes of the present and future to come.

References

Augé, M. (2008) Planetary landscapes, in R. Depardon and P. Virilio (eds.) *Native Land: Stop Eject*. Paris: Foundation Cartier Pour L'art Contemporain, pp. 168–175.

Bourdieu, P. (2003) Participant objectivation. *Journal of the Royal Anthropological Institute*, 9 (2): 281–294.

Bourdieu, P. and Wacquant, L. J. D. (1992) *An Invitation to Reflexive Sociology.* Chicago, IL: University of Chicago Press.

Cahill, K. M., Gustafsson, M. and Wentzer, T. S. (2017) *Finite but Unbounded: New Approaches in Philosophical Anthropology.* Berlin: De Gruyter.

Cameron, J., Mulligan, M. and Wheatley, V. (2004) Building a place: Responsive society through inclusive local projects and networks. *Local Environment*, 9: 147–161.

Casey, E. S. (1993) *Getting Back into Place: Toward a Renewed Understanding of the Place-World.* Bloomington: Indiana University Press.

Casey, E. S. (2001) Between geography and philosophy: What does it mean to be in the place-world? *Annals of the Association of American Geographers*, 91: 683–693.

Casey, E. S. (2012) Going wireless: Disengaging the ethical life, in R. Wilken and G. Goggin (eds.) *Mobile Technology and Place.* New York: Routledge, pp. 175–180.

Clark, A. (2004). *Natural-born Cyborgs: Minds, Technologies, and the Future of Human Intelligence.* Oxford: Oxford University Press.

Clifford, J. (1997). *Routes: Travel and Translation in the Late Twentieth Century.* Cambridge, MA: Harvard University Press.

Cresswell, T. (2010) Towards a politics of (Im)mobility. *Environment and Planning. D, Society and Space*, 28: 17–31.

Crouch, D. (2002) Surrounded by place: Embodied encounters, in S. Coleman and M. Crang (eds.) *Tourism: Between Place and Performance.* Oxford: Berghahn, pp. 207–218.

Crouch, D. (2007) The fleshiness of journeys, encounters, creativity and their landscapes. Paper presented at the Critical Tourism Studies Conference: *The Critical Turn in Tourism Studies: Promoting an Academy of Hope?* Split, Croatia, June 20–23.

Crouch, D. and Desforges, L. (2003) The sensuous in the tourist encounter: Introduction: The power of the body in tourist studies. *Tourist Studies*, 3: 5–22.

De Mul, J. (2014) *Plessner's Philosophical Anthropology: Perspectives and Prospects.* Amsterdam: Amsterdam University Press.

Dreyfus, H. L. (2009) How representational cognitivism failed and is being replaced by body/world coupling, in K. Leidlmair (ed.) *After Cognitivism.* The Hague: Springer Science & Business Media, pp. 39–74.

Edensor, T. (2000) Staging tourism: Tourists as performers. *Annals of Tourism Research*, 27: 322–344.

Edensor, T. (2001) Performing tourism, staging tourism: (Re) producing tourist space and practice. *Tourist Studies*, 1: 59–81.

Elliott, A. and Urry, J. (2010) *Mobile Lives.* New York: Routledge.

Espiner, S., Orchiston, C. and Higham, J. (2017) Resilience and sustainability: A complementary relationship? Towards a practical conceptual model for the sustainability–resilience nexus in tourism. *Journal of Sustainable Tourism*, 25(10): 1385–1400.

Franklin, A. and Crang, M. (2001) The trouble with tourism and travel theory? *Tourist Studies*, 1: 5–22.

Fullagar, S. (2001) Encountering otherness: Embodied affect in Alphonso Lingis' travel writing. *Tourist Studies*, 1: 171–183.

Germann Molz, J. (2006) Cosmopolitan bodies: Fit to travel and travelling to fit. *Body and Society*, 12: 1–21.

Germann Molz, J. (2008) Global abode: Home and mobility in narratives of round-the-world travel. *Space and Culture*, 11: 325–342.

Germann Molz, J. (2012) *Travel Connections: Tourism, Technology, and Togetherness in a Mobile World.* New York: Routledge.

Germann Molz, J. and Paris, C. M. (2013) The social affordances of flashpacking: Exploring the mobility nexus of travel and communication. *Mobilities*, 10(2): 173–192.

Hage, G. (2012) Critical anthropological thought and the radical political imaginary today. *Critique of Anthropology*, 32: 285–308.

Hannam, K., Butler, G. and Paris, C. M. (2014) Developments and key issues in tourism mobilities. *Annals of Tourism Research*, 44: 171–185.

Hansen, M. B. N. (2012) Ubiquitous sensibility, in J. Packer, J. and S. B. C. Wiley (eds.) *Communication Matters: Materialist Approaches to Media, Mobility and Networks.* New York: Routledge, pp. 53–65.

Heidegger, M. (1996) *Being and Time.* New York: University of New York Press.

Hjorth, L. (2012) Still mobile: A case study on mobility, home and being away in Shanghai, in R. Wilken and G. Goggin (eds.) *Mobile Technology and Place.* New York: Routledge, pp. 140–156.

Howard, C. (2012) Speeding up and slowing down: Slow travel and pilgrimage in late modernity, in S. Fullagar, S., K. Markwell and E. Wilson (eds.) *Slow Tourism: Experiences and Mobilities.* Bristol: Channel View, pp. 11–24.

Howard, C. (2015) Being-online-in-the-world: A response to the special issue, 'Being Online'. *Phenomenology & Practice*, 9: 83–88.

Howard, C. A. (2015) Out of practice: Foreign travel as the productive disruption of embodied knowledge schemes. *Indo-Pacific Journal of Phenomenology*, 15: 1–12.

Howard, C. A. (2016) Touring the consumption of the other: Imaginaries of authenticity in the Himalayas and beyond. *Journal of Consumer Culture*, 16: 354–373.

Howard, C. A. (2017) Posthuman anthropology? Facing up to planetary conviviality in the anthropocene. IMPACT: Interdisciplinary Journal of Teaching and Learning. Available at: http://search.bu.edu/?q=posthuman&site=http%3A%2F%2Fsites.bu.edu%2Fimpact

Howard, C. A. and Küpers, W. (2015) En algún lugar entre todas partes y ninguna parte: el viaje en la era de la Gestell o encuadre digital. *Scripta Nova. Revista Electrónica de Geografía y Ciencias Sociales*, 19. Available at: http://revistes.ub.edu/index.php/ScriptaNova/article/view/15090

Howard, C. A. and Küpers, W. (2017) Interplaced mobility in the age of "Digital Gestell". *Transfers*, 7: 4–25.

Hui, Y. (2016). *On the Existence of Digital Objects.* Minneapolis: University of Minnesota Press.

Ihde, D. (2001) *Bodies in Technology.* Minneapolis: University of Minnesota Press.

Ingold, T. (2008) Bindings against boundaries: Entanglements of life in an open world. *Environment and Planning D: Society and Space*, 40: 1796–1810.

Ingold, T. (2011) *Being Alive: Essays on Movement, Knowledge and Description.* New York: Routledge.

Kärrholm, M., Johansson, M., Lindelöw, D. and Ferreira, I. A. (2017) Interseriality and different sorts of walking: Suggestions for a relational approach to urban walking. *Mobilities*, 12: 20–35.

Kim, J. (2001) Phenomenology of digital-being. *Human Studies*, 24(1–2): 87–11.

Küpers, W. (2010) Inter-places - Embodied spaces & places of and for leader-/followership - Phenomenological perspectives on relational localities & tele-presences of leading and following. *Environment, Space, Place*, 2: 79–121.

Küpers, W. (2015) Emplaced and embodied mobility in organizations. *Ephemera*, 15(4): 797–823.

Leistle, B. (2015) Otherness as a paradigm in anthropology. *Semiotica*, 204: 291–313.

Leistle, B. (2016) *Anthropology and Alterity: Responding to the Other*. New York: Taylor & Francis.

Longhurst, R. and Johnston, L. (2014) Bodies, gender, place and culture: 21 years on. *Gender, Place & Culture*, 21(3): 267–278.

Lysemose, K. (2013) Responsive self-preservation: Towards an anthropological concept of responsiveness. *META: Research in Hermeneutics, Phenomenology, and Practical Philosophy*, 5(2): 375–396.

Mackay, K. and Vogt, C. (2012) Information technology in everyday and vacation contexts. *Annals of Tourism Research*, 39: 1380–1401.

Malpas, J. (1999) *Place and Experience: A Philosophical Topography*. Cambridge: Cambridge University Press.

Massey, D. B. (2005) *For Space*. London: Sage Publishers.

Mccool, S. (2015) Sustainable tourism: Guiding fiction, social trap or path to resilience? in T. V. Singh (ed.) *Challenges in Tourism Research*. Bristol: Channel View Publications, pp. 224–234.

Mcluhan, M. (2008) *Understanding Media: The Extensions of Man*. New York: Routledge.

Merleau-Ponty, M. (2013) *Phenomenology of Perception*. London: Routledge.

Merriman, P. and Pearce, L. (2017) Mobility and the humanities. *Mobilities*, 12: 493–508.

Miller, D. (2013) *Tales from Facebook*. Cambridge: Wiley/Polity Press.

Paris, C. M., Berger, E. A., Rubin, S. and Casson, M. (2015) Disconnected and unplugged: Experiences of technology induced anxieties and tensions while traveling, in I. Tussyadiah and A. Inversini (eds.) *Information and Communication Technologies in Tourism* (Proceedings of the international Conference in Lugano, Switzerland, 3–6 February, 2015). New York: Springer, pp. 803–816.

Pearce, P. L. and Gretzel, U. (2012) Tourism in technology dead zones: Documenting experiential dimensions. *International Journal of Tourism Sciences*, 12: 1–20.

Picard, D. and Giovine, M. A. D. (eds.) (2014) *Tourism and the Power of Otherness: Seductions of Difference*. Bristol: Channel View.

Picard, D. and Robinson, M. (eds.) (2016) *Emotion in Motion: Tourism, Affect and Transformation*. Abingdon and Oxon: Taylor & Francis.

Plessner, H. (1969) De homine abscondito. *Social Research*, 36(4): 497–509.

Pons, P. O. (2003) Being-on-holiday: Tourist dwelling, bodies and place. *Tourist Studies*, 3: 47–66.

Pritchard, A. and Morgan, N. (2011) Tourist bodies, transformation and sensuality, in P. Bramham and S. Wagg (eds.) *The New Politics of Leisure and Pleasure*. Basingstoke: Palgrave Macmillan, pp. 153–168.

Rouvroy, A. and Stiegler, B. (2016). The digital regime of truth: From algorithmic governmentality to a new rule of law. *La Deleuziana*, 3: 6–29.

Seamon, D. (1979) *A Geography of the Lifeworld: Movement, Rest, and Encounter*. London: Groom Helm.

Sheller, M. and Urry, J. (eds.) (2004) *Tourism Mobilities: Places to Play, Places in Play*. London: Routledge.

Simmel, G. (1997), Leisure Culture, in D. Frisby and M. Featherstone (Eds.) *Simmel on Culture: Selected Writings*. London: Sage, pp. 219–232.

Sloterdijk, P. (2012) Nearness and Da-sein: The spatiality of being and time. *Theory, Culture & Society*, 29: 36–42.

Small, J. (2007) The emergence of the body in the holiday accounts of women and girls, in A. Pritchard (ed.) *Tourism and Gender: Embodiment, Sensuality and Experience*. Wallingford, Oxon: CABI, pp. 73–91.

Stiegler, B. (2017) *Automatic Society*. Cambridge: Polity.

Tanti, A. and Buhalis, D. (2017) The influences and consequences of being digitally connected and/or disconnected to travellers. *Information Technology & Tourism*, 17: 121–141.

Thrift, N. (2006) Space. *Theory, Culture & Society*, 23: 139–146.

Thweatt-Bates, J. (2016) *Cyborg Selves: A Theological Anthropology of the Posthuman*. New York: Routledge.

Urry, J. (2007) *Mobilities*. Cambridge: Polity Press.

Urry, J. and Larsen, J. (2012) *The Tourist Gaze 3.0*. London: Sage Publications.

Varela, F. J., Thompson, E. and Rosch, E. (1991) *The Embodied Mind: Cognitive Science and Human Experience*. Cambridge, MA: MIT Press.

Veijola, S. and Jokinen, E. (1994) The body in tourism. *Theory, Culture & Society*, 11: 125–151.

Waldenfels, B. (1990) Experience of the Alien in Husserl's phenomenology. *Research in Phenomenology*, 20: 19–33.

Waldenfels, B. (2007) *The Question of the Other*. Hong Kong: Chinese University Press.

Waldenfels, B. (2011) *Phenomenology of the Alien: Basic Concepts*. Evanston, IL: Northwestern University Press.

Wang, D., Xiang, Z. and Fesenmaier, D. R. (2014) Adapting to the mobile world: A model of smartphone use. *Annals of Tourism Research*, 48: 11–26.

Wang, D., Xiang, Z. and Fesenmaier, D. R. (2016) Smartphone use in everyday life and travel. *Journal of Travel Research*, 55: 52–63.

Whitehead, N. L. and Wesch, M. (2012) *Human no More: Digital Subjectivities, Unhuman Subjects, and the End of Anthropology*. Boulder: University Press of Colorado.

15 Afterword

Soile Veijola

Introduction

Old teachers never die, they just lose their class, read the rubber sticker that our relatives in North America sent us in a generous box of Christmas gifts back in the withered, discoloured 1970s. My mum, a teacher, laughed and glued it on the dashboard of her dark-blue, ball-shaped Beetle.

Since the late 1990s, keeping this cruelly optimistic vision clear in my mind, I have tried to raise, renew and blow new life into the theoretical notion of *the body*, the research topic of my youthful academic years, across several generations of students in tourism research at the University of Lapland, in Rovaniemi, Finland. A mixed group, half-and-half, of students and exchange students from all around the world representing a variety of disciplines, attend the rather unimaginatively named course *Cultural and Social Studies of Tourism*. During the course, I 'walk my talks' through the rich scholarship of critical tourism academia.

My original belief, which I continue to share with all the contributors to this book, *Tourism and Embodiment*, is that embodiment is, as the editors' note in the introduction, 'a way of understanding culture and the self in relation to practices of movement, thinking and sensing' (p. 3). As tourists, when we travel to places, we bring along the habits, values and desires of our own cultures and societies through our embodied performances and our corporeal materialities. In many cases, the influence of these socially constructed, embodied, encounters is magnified by the sheer number of tourists visiting a particular destination at any one time.

In class, I have chosen to approach embodiment particularly from the following three angles: sports-related hobbies, tourism work and ethical knowing.

Sport is a good place to start. Looking back at one's personal sporting biography allows one to reflect on the body culture enacted and reproduced by the chosen activity – and to see how it reflects or challenges, among other things, the social order we call *class*. Here, the classic works of Norbert Elias and Pierre Bourdieu are particularly inspiring. But, fortunately, Antoine Hennion's (2001) readings of what love of music, or of any hobby, as I would argue, are made of, point out at least some 'lines of flight' (as Gilles Deleuze might have put it) from predestined symbolic hierarchies of social class. In other words, a hobby can enable us to escape a predetermined place in the social hierarchy by, for example, allowing us to improve ourselves in some way. Thereby providing an opportunity to develop as people in any number of ways and in so doing our place in the predetermined social hierarchy fades into the distance.

Looking back at the attachments, passions and skills associated with a particular activity or sport, and the physical, aesthetic and social body it requires (see also Young 1980, Veijola 1994), we can reflect on our ways of becoming our unique selves.

A focus on tourism work, moves the debate away from a preoccupation with the tourist gaze – or the tourist's body – towards a focus on people whose role in tourism goes beyond being a qualified or non-qualified labour force to be managed efficiently. Employees, the self-employed and those who are part of the informal tourism economy are easily forgotten when focusing on hosts and guests, the classic relational opposition introduced into the anthropology of tourism by Smith (1977). Yet, as research has shown, tourism workers might actually *know* more about tourists than anyone else (see Valtonen 2009). This is important because turning our gaze from the tourist to the perspective of the tourism worker helps me initiate an analytical, rather than uninformed discussion among the students on *gender.*

Through the notion of *hospitality as work*, or a Hostessing Society as myself and Eeva Jokinen have suggested (Veijola and Jokinen 2008), I allow gender to *resurge*, to generate new insights and ideas that build a connection between the students' personal and shared experience of precarious jobs in various tourism businesses – and social theory. Hospitality work valorises gendered realities and symbolic orders.

I present my students with an argument such as 'Gender has no role whatsoever in today's working life', and ask them to prepare to defend or oppose the statement, regardless of their personal views on the matter, using course readings (and other research literature they might choose). With only five minutes for each side to present their arguments, there is no time to make jokes or simplistic claims. Either side must 'win' the debate based on intellectual scholarship.

Listening to and participating in a debate between peers seems to create a joint intellectual agenda among the students. It might also help recognising and dealing with the embodied power relations they encounter in the future, whether as a someone working in tourism or as a tourist (see Veijola and Valtonen 2007). Through body and gender – along with other key concepts in cultural and social theories – it is possible to understand one's own moral participation in the multi-layered, sometimes also unbalanced or 'violent' realities of tourism worlds.

Speaking of violence, ethical knowing is the third aspect that I emphasise as a teacher destined to lose her class one day. To explore it meticulously,

I have designed the course *Ethical Epistemologies of Tourism* for master and doctoral students. Its basic idea is to examine when and whether the stories we tell about tourism in academia and elsewhere are violent narratives – or caring and resourceful ones.

'Who tells what about tourism in which forum and for whose benefit and at whose cost?' is the fundamental question for a teacher in tourism research, and, by and large, the starting point of my co-authored works with Eeva Jokinen since the mid-1980s. What kinds of power relations, moral theories and ontologies are embedded in the narratives, discourses and measurements deemed as knowledge about tourism (see Veijola and Jokinen 2018)?

Thus, a book such as the one at hand, with a generous selection of insightful accounts of embodied experiences in different scenes and settings of tourism, helps its readers to continue investigating various contemporary arrangements of hospitalities and mobilities that we call tourism.

Women on bikes on a rainy night. Too many wheelchairs turning a spa into something else in a visitor's mind. Encounters between bears and humans on trekking paths. Scars on old battlefields. Slow food made in a rush for tourists. Maps of othered leisure spaces. Rowing collectives on water.... Teachers learning through a lifetime together with students.... Tourism is an embodied hosting and guesting of ourselves, others, and of everything we ever experience when we travel.

References

Hennion, A. (2001) Music lovers: Taste as performance. *Theory, Culture & Society*, 18(5): 1–22.

Smith, V. L. (Ed.) (1977) *Hosts and Guests. The Anthropology of Tourism.* Philadelphia: University of Pennsylvania Press.

Valtonen, A. (2009) Small tourism firms as agents of critical knowledge. *Tourist Studies* (Special Issue on Tourism as Work), 9(2): 127–143.

Veijola, S. (1994) Metaphors of mixed team play. *International Review for the Sociology of Sport*, 29(1): 32–49. [Note: Surname misprinted on first page as Viejola].

Veijola, S. and Jokinen, E. (2008) Towards a hostessing society? Mobile arrangements of gender and labour. *NORA – Nordic Journal of Feminist and Gender Research*, 16(3): 166–181.

Veijola, S. and Jokinen, E. (2018) Coding gender in academic capitalism. *Ephemera. Theory & Politics in Organization*, 18(3): 527–549. Available at: www.ephemerajournal.org/contribution/coding-gender-academic-capitalism

Veijola, S. and Valtonen, A. (2007) The body in tourism industry, in A. Pritchard, N. Morgan and I. Ateljevic (eds.) *Tourism and Gender: Embodiment, Sensuality and Experience.* Oxford: CABI Publishing, pp. 13–31.

Young, I. M. (1980) Throwing like a girl: A phenomenology of feminine body comportment, motility and spatiality. *Human Studies*, 3: 137–156.

Index